Judicial Activism in an Age of Populism

This book explores the range of meanings attributed to the terms 'judicial activism' and 'populism' in contemporary times and examines the potential interplay between these two phenomena. Drawing upon various political examples, it discusses the implication of populist movements for democratic institutions, policies, and processes.

The chapters in this volume examine the impact of populism on judicial decision-making in various socio-cultural contexts. The contributing authors explore the implications of populist beliefs, including those which promote anti-democratic perspectives, on the integrity, independence, and the role of the judiciary in a democratic society. This volume offers unique international perspectives on the concern that certain populist initiatives may be and continue to be a threat to democratic foundational values and principles.

Judicial Activism in an Age of Populism will be a beneficial read for students of Politics, Sociology, Public Administration and Management, and Law and Society. It was originally published as a special issue of *The International Journal of Human Rights*.

Sonja Grover is Full Professor at the Faculty of Education at Lakehead University, Canada. She graduated with a PhD from the University of Toronto, Canada. She has devoted more than 20 years to law research, publishing numerous law books and articles in peer-reviewed international law journals. She is Associate Editor of *The International Journal of Human Rights*.

Judicial Activism in an Age of Populism

Edited by
Sonja Grover

LONDON AND NEW YORK

First published 2023
by Routledge
4 Park Square, Milton Park, Abingdon, Oxon, OX14 4RN

and by Routledge
605 Third Avenue, New York, NY 10158

Routledge is an imprint of the Taylor & Francis Group, an informa business

Introduction, Chapters 1, 3, 4 and 6–8 © 2023 Taylor & Francis
Chapter 2 © 2022 Michal Kovalčík. Originally published as Open Access.
Chapter 5 © 2021 Hubert Smekal, Jaroslav Benák and Ladislav Vyhnánek. Originally published as Open Access.

With the exception of Chapters 2 and 5, no part of this book may be reprinted or reproduced or utilised in any form or by any electronic, mechanical, or other means, now known or hereafter invented, including photocopying and recording, or in any information storage or retrieval system, without permission in writing from the publishers. For details on the rights for Chapters 2 and 5, please see the chapters' Open Access footnotes.

Trademark notice: Product or corporate names may be trademarks or registered trademarks, and are used only for identification and explanation without intent to infringe.

British Library Cataloguing-in-Publication Data
A catalogue record for this book is available from the British Library

ISBN13: 978-1-032-44335-5 (hbk)
ISBN13: 978-1-032-44336-2 (pbk)
ISBN13: 978-1-003-37165-6 (ebk)

DOI: 10.4324/9781003371656

Typeset in Minion Pro
by codeMantra

Publisher's Note
The publisher accepts responsibility for any inconsistencies that may have arisen during the conversion of this book from journal articles to book chapters, namely the inclusion of journal terminology.

Disclaimer
Every effort has been made to contact copyright holders for their permission to reprint material in this book. The publishers would be grateful to hear from any copyright holder who is not here acknowledged and will undertake to rectify any errors or omissions in future editions of this book.

Contents

Citation Information		vii
Notes on Contributors		ix
	Introduction *Sonja Grover*	1
1	The impact of populism on constitutional interpretation in the EU Member States *Zoltán Szente and Fruzsina Gárdos-Orosz*	3
2	The instrumental abuse of constitutional courts: how populists can use constitutional courts against the opposition *Michal Kovalčík*	22
3	(De-)judicialization of politics in the era of populism: lessons from Central and Eastern Europe *Jan Petrov*	43
4	Authoritarian populism, conceptions of democracy, and the Hungarian Constitutional Court: the case of political participation *Max Steuer*	69
5	Through selective activism towards greater resilience: the Czech Constitutional Court's interventions into high politics in the age of populism *Hubert Smekal, Jaroslav Benák and Ladislav Vyhnánek*	92
6	Judicial activism, populism and counterterrorism legislation in Kenya: coalition for Reform and democracy (CORD) & 2 others v Republic of Kenya & 10; others [2015] *Oscar Gakuo Mwangi*	114
7	Pandemic and community's sense of justice through *suo motu* in India *Tarun Arora*	134

8 Abortion, same-sex marriage, and gender identity during the Pink Tide: Venezuela compared to Latin American trends 155
Victor Molina

Index 175

Citation Information

The chapters in this book were originally published in *The International Journal of Human Rights*, volume 26, issue 7 (2022). When citing this material, please use the original page numbering for each article, as follows:

Introduction
Sonja Grover
The International Journal of Human Rights, volume 26, issue 7 (2022) pp. 1139–1140

Chapter 1
The impact of populism on constitutional interpretation in the EU Member States
Zoltán Szente and Fruzsina Gárdos-Orosz
The International Journal of Human Rights, volume 26, issue 7 (2022) pp. 1141–1159

Chapter 2
The instrumental abuse of constitutional courts: how populists can use constitutional courts against the opposition
Michal Kovalčík
The International Journal of Human Rights, volume 26, issue 7 (2022) pp. 1160–1180

Chapter 3
(De-)judicialization of politics in the era of populism: lessons from Central and Eastern Europe
Jan Petrov
The International Journal of Human Rights, volume 26, issue 7 (2022) pp. 1181–1206

Chapter 4
Authoritarian populism, conceptions of democracy, and the Hungarian Constitutional Court: the case of political participation
Max Steuer
The International Journal of Human Rights, volume 26, issue 7 (2022) pp. 1207–1229

Chapter 5
Through selective activism towards greater resilience: the Czech Constitutional Court's interventions into high politics in the age of populism
Hubert Smekal, Jaroslav Benák and Ladislav Vyhnánek
The International Journal of Human Rights, volume 26, issue 7 (2022) pp. 1230–1251

viii CITATION INFORMATION

Chapter 6
Judicial activism, populism and counterterrorism legislation in Kenya: coalition for Reform and democracy (CORD) & 2 others v Republic of Kenya & 10; others [2015]
Oscar Gakuo Mwangi
The International Journal of Human Rights, volume 26, issue 7 (2022) pp. 1252–1271

Chapter 7
Pandemic and community's sense of justice through suo motu *in India*
Tarun Arora
The International Journal of Human Rights, volume 26, issue 7 (2022) pp. 1272–1292

Chapter 8
Abortion, same-sex marriage, and gender identity during the Pink Tide: Venezuela compared to Latin American trends
Victor Molina
The International Journal of Human Rights, volume 26, issue 7 (2022) pp. 1293–1312

For any permission-related enquiries please visit:
http://www.tandfonline.com/page/help/permissions

Notes on Contributors

Tarun Arora is Professor and Dean of School of Legal Studies at the Central University of Punjab, India. He is associated with the United Nations Development Programme as Expert on International Biodiversity Law and Life Member at Indian Institute of Public Administration, New Delhi, India. His areas of expertise are environmental law, constitutional law, jurisprudence, and human rights.

Jaroslav Benák is Assistant Professor of Constitutional Law at Masaryk University, Brno, Czech Republic. He clerked for a judge of the Czech Constitutional Court and worked as Researcher in the Center for Non-profit sector research. He has published texts dealing with Czech constitutional law in the international and domestic context. His research interests cover mainly judicial behaviour, law and religion, and access to justice.

Fruzsina Gárdos-Orosz is Director and Senior Research Fellow of the Institute for Legal Studies at the Centre for Social Sciences of the Hungarian Academy of Sciences and Associate Professor of Constitutional Law at the ELTE Law School, Budapest, Hungary. She has published extensively on the development of the Hungarian constitutional system, the constitutional complaint procedure, and the competence of the constitutional court in comparative perspective.

Sonja Grover is Full Professor at the Faculty of Education at Lakehead University, Canada. She graduated with a PhD from the University of Toronto, Canada. She has devoted more than 20 years to law research, publishing numerous law books and articles in peer-reviewed international law journals. She is Associate Editor of *The International Journal of Human Rights*.

Michal Kovalčík is a master's student in the Faculty of Law at Masaryk University, Brno, Czech Republic. He works as student Research Assistant at the Department of the Constitutional Law and Political Science and Judicial Studies Institute at Masaryk University, Brno, Czech Republic. In his initial works, he has focused on the role of courts at the domestic as well as European level.

Victor Molina is Venezuelan Human Rights Defender with over 14 years of experience working for Amnesty International in Latin America. He has a bachelor's degree in Social Communication and advanced law studies in Constitutional Rights and Human Rights and a master's joint degree with the University of Minnesota's Humphrey School of Public Affairs and the College of Liberal Arts, USA.

Oscar Gakuo Mwangi (PhD) is Associate Professor of Political Science at the Department of Political and Administrative Studies at the National University of Lesotho, Lesotho.

His research interests are in in the areas of governance, conflict, and security in the Horn of Africa, east and southern Africa. His teaching areas are in the fields of comparative politics, international relations, and political theory.

Jan Petrov is Junior Research Fellow in Law at the Queen's College at the University of Oxford, UK, and Early Career Fellow at the Bonavero Institute of Human Rights, Oxford. His research interests are in comparative constitutional law, constitutional theory, international law, and human rights.

Hubert Smekal is Senior Researcher at the Judicial Studies Institute at Masaryk University, Brno, Czech Republic, and Lecturer at Maynooth University, Ireland. He cofounded the Czech Centre for Human Rights and Democratization and served as Member of the Human Rights Council of the Czech Government. His academic interests take in the issues of human rights, the political role of the CJEU and ECtHR, and the judicialization of (international) politics. Smekal has published articles, e.g., in *European Constitutional Law Review*, *German Law Journal*, *Netherlands Quarterly of Human Rights*, *Europe-Asia Studies*, *European Political Science*, and *Journal of Mixed Methods Research*.

Max Steuer is Assistant Professor at the O.P. Jindal Global University at Jindal Global Law School, India. An interdisciplinary social scientist with a particular focus on democracy research, his research interests encompass, among others, constitutional adjudication in a comparative perspective (with an emphasis on constitutional courts), freedom of expression, militant democracy, and constitutionalism in the European Union. He has published in peer-reviewed journals and edited volumes in law, political science, sociology, and European studies.

Zoltán Szente is Professor of Law at the National University of Public Service at the Department of Constitutional Law and Comparative Public Law and Research Professor at the Institute for Legal Studies of the Centre for Social Sciences, Budapest, Hungary. He is Co-Founder of the Research Group on Constitutional Interpretation of the International Association of Constitutional Law. He has published widely on Hungarian and comparative constitutional law; constitutional theory; parliamentary law; local government; and European constitutional history in Hungarian, English, German, Russian, and Croatian.

Ladislav Vyhnánek is Assistant Professor of Constitutional Law at Masaryk University, Brno, Czech Republic, teaching courses in constitutional law, human rights, and judicial studies. He has published numerous articles (most recently in *Vienna Journal on International Constitutional Law*, *European Constitutional Law Review*, and *Heidelberg Journal of International Law*) and co-authored several books and book chapters on constitutional studies, most recently on the Czech Constitutional Court, constitutional identity, and judicial treatment of the European Court of Human Rights case law.

Introduction

Sonja Grover

This special issue explores the range of meanings attributed to the terms 'judicial activism' and 'populism', and, in the context of contemporary case law and political examples, examines the potential interplay between these two phenomena. The central questions asked in this special issue are (a) To what extent and how populism – whether of the left or the right-impacts judicial decision-making; (b) what are the implications of populist movements for existing or possible democratic institutions, policies and processes and (c) what are the implications of populism for the integrity, independence and role of the judiciary in a democratic society where the particular brand of prevalent populism promotes anti-democratic perspectives. The papers included in this special issue consider the above issues in various socio-cultural contexts bringing a unique international perspective to the ultimate issue as to whether and in what ways certain populist initiatives may be and continue to be a threat to democratic foundational values and principles.

Here follows a very brief introduction to each of the papers included in the special issue in the order in which the papers appear:

The impact of populism on constitutional interpretation in the EU Member States by Zoltán Szente and Fruzsina Gardos-Orosz explores how populist politics may impact purported constitutional interpretations serving or even counteracting the political objectives of populists.

The Instrumental Abuse of Constitutional Courts: How Populists Can Use Constitutional Courts against the Opposition by Michal Kovalcik explores so-called 'constitutional populism' and the various strategies that have at times been employed by particular segments of the populist activist contingent to undermine the opposition and the independence of the constitutional courts.

De-Judicialization of Politics in the Era of Populism: Lessons from Central and Eastern Europe by Jan Petrov examines what the author characterises as the politicisation of the constitutional courts relying on examples from Central and Eastern Europe of what the author terms 'authoritarian populism'

Authoritarian Populism, Conceptions of Democracy and the Hungarian Constitutional Court: the case of political participation by Max Steuer examines the Hungarian Constitutional Court's decisions at pivotal periods in responding to populist petitions to the court that advocated an illiberal interpretation of democracy as grounded on unrestrained majoritarian positions.

Through selective activism towards greater resilience: The Czech Constitutional Court's interventions into high politics in the age of populism by Hubert Smekal, Jaroslav Benák and Ladislav Vyhnánek argues that sound institutional design and selective activism in judging on political process and separation of powers may boost the resilience of constitutional courts faced with a populist challenge.

Judicial activism, populism and counterterrorism legislation in Kenya: Coalition for Reform and Democracy (CORD) & 2 others v Republic of Kenya & 10 others [2015] by Oscar G. Mwangi examines the relationship between populism and judicial activism in a key 2015 Kenyan High Court decision concerning Kenya's omnibus Security Laws (Amendment) Act, No 19 and the implications of the case for the independence of the Kenyan courts.

Pandemic and the Community's Sense of Justice through suo motu in India by Tarun Arora explores the Supreme Court of India's judicial response to issues arising in connection with the COVID-19 Pandemic and examines the Court's role through *suo motu* proceedings.

Abortion, same-sex marriage, and gender identity during the Pink Tide: Venezuela compared to Latin American trends by Victor Molina examines the contrasts between Venezuela and certain other Latin American countries in terms of the impact of certain forms of populism on the left leaning Executive's willingness to advance reproductive rights and the basic human rights of women and the LGBT community.

Disclosure statement

No potential conflict of interest was reported by the author(s).

The impact of populism on constitutional interpretation in the EU Member States

Zoltán Szente and Fruzsina Gárdos-Orosz

ABSTRACT
The birth and spread of the term 'populist constitutionalism' shows that one of the distinctive features of modern populism is that it has specific constitutional ambitions insofar as it seeks to achieve its political goals through constitutional means. The constitutional ambitions of populist politicians, which are considered by many scholars as a feature of modern populism, often make it inevitable for courts to respond, in the course of constitutional review, to challenges to traditional constitutional values and institutions. Courts can respond to these claims in different ways. For example, they can engage in an activist stance, resisting the attempts that endanger the established constitutional order, they can defer to the changing constitutional policy of the political branches, or, possibly, they can try to keep their distance from political struggles. The study, based on the results of our comparative international research, examines how populism influences the methods of interpretation in the jurisprudence of constitutional courts and other relevant high courts,whether they have developed new interpretative instruments, or have used the classical ways of constitutional interpretation when facing populist aspirations. The article contributes to the present-day scholarly discourse on the effects of populism on constitutional justice in Europe.

1. Introduction

Today, populism is a worldwide trend in politics. Although there is no consensus on the definition of populism, and it is often seen as a political ideology, or simply a style or a special method of communication, most scholars agree that its modern form challenges the traditional structures and even values of constitutional democracies. Populism is an essentially political concept. However, it is beyond any doubt that populist politics has important constitutional implications. The emergence and spread of the concept of 'populist constitutionalism' clearly indicates that one of the distinguishing features of modern populism is that it has wide-ranging constitutional aspirations, insofar as it seeks to achieve its political goals by constitutional means.[1] The intended transformation of the idea of constitutionalism does not leave the methods and practice of constitutional interpretation untouched, because the constitutional meaning is formed by the interpretation of the usually abstract constitutional provisions.

Because of this ambition on the part of modern populism, the topic has also attracted the interest of constitutional scholarship, and an academic debate has developed on the question of whether populism has a specific theory of constitutionalism or not.[2] As populist constitutionalism is itself a contested concept, a significant part of the constitutional law discourse deals with the conceptualisation of this phenomenon. In addition, there is a growing literature on populist constitutional politics, describing the various techniques they use to transform the institutions of liberal democracies usually in an authoritarian direction. These works are a major contribution to our understanding of the relationship between populism and constitutionalism, but little attention has been paid to the narrower issue of how populist politics affects constitutional interpretation. It can be assumed that if today's populists see the constitution and constitutional change as a truly effective instrument of power, this is also true for constitutional interpretation. Experience shows that where authoritarian or nationalist populism – which seems to be the dominant form of contemporary populism – comes to power, it will use independent institutions such as constitutional courts or other high courts which adjudicate constitutional cases in the interests of the Executive, or at least to influence constitutional interpretation which determines the meaning of the constitution. Indeed, if populists control constitutional interpretation in one way or another, they can use this to remove constitutional obstacles to political decision-making, i.e. to legitimise the decisions they make which might otherwise be considered unconstitutional.

In fact, such political ambitions not only neutralise the counterweight role of constitutional courts and equivalent judicial bodies in the system of separation of powers, but also expect them to perform new (mainly legitimating) functions. The constitutional review is therefore not removed from the system of the exercise of power; however, the 'executive control of the constitutional court indirectly gives the government an important say in how the constitution should be interpreted'.[3] In this way, it can also be a powerful weapon in political struggles.

All this justifies a special examination of how the methods of constitutional interpretation are used and changed in populist regimes. Our article therefore explores how populist politics affects established methods of constitutional interpretation. Do populists prefer particular methods of interpretation (such as originalism or textualism) or do they support a reinterpretation of certain substantive constitutional values and concepts?[4] It seems reasonable to assume that certain interpretative methods serve populist goals better than others. If, for example, populists dominate the legislature, they are likely to favour the plain meaning rule (textualism), or interpretation based on original intent, because, in principle, these methods may provide most deference to the lawmakers, whereas a moral or contextual reading of the constitution allows for broader judicial discretion and thus may impose more severe constraints on the legislature. Nevertheless, historical examples justify caution. While, for example, legal positivism had a strong tradition in the Weimar Republic, the Nazi regime, which may be an extreme example of authoritarian populism, was distrustful of this method (because of their disrespect towards the surviving laws of the Weimar era), and preferred a conception of natural law that could in a sense unscrupulously enforce the ideology of National Socialism, based on dubious and uncertain ('contradiction-transcending') legal concepts.[5]

It is therefore reasonable to assume that populists prefer different methods of interpretation depending on the political context and legal culture of their country. If, in the majority of cases, none of the 'technical' methods of interpretation lead to the desired result or influence the judges' behaviour in the expected direction, the outcome of constitutional interpretation may be most influenced by a reinterpretation of the substantive legal concepts used.

In this study, we will focus on the interpretative practice of constitutional courts and other high courts that decide constitutional disputes, being aware that constitutional interpretation may also be carried out by other public authorities. Indeed, in some cases, the latter may take precedence. In Poland, for example 'the populist revolution relied greatly on constitutional arguments and interpretations put forward by the political branches of government and by their committed supporters'.[6]

Therefore, it is also worth paying attention to the involvement of actors who have an influence on the interpretation of the meaning of the constitution, even where the protection of the constitution is ensured through judicial review. Our work is based on survey data reported by national experts from the 27 EU Member States and the United Kingdom (which was still a member country of the EU when the survey started). We have included in our analysis those European countries in which populism has emerged as a significant political force in recent years: where populist parties have come to power either as the dominant governing force or as minority coalition partners, or where they have formed a strong opposition to traditional parties and have been able to influence constitutional politics.

Based on this, our research covered constitutional changes between 2010 and 2020 in the following countries: Austria; the Czech Republic; Croatia; Greece; Hungary; Italy; Poland; Romania; Spain; and the United Kingdom. In all of these countries populism has appeared in one form or another. During this period, populists came to power in Austria, the Czech Republic, Hungary, Poland, Italy and the United Kingdom, while they took up significant positions in opposition in Croatia, Greece, Romania and Spain. The different political positions and influences of the populist parties provide a broad framework for comparison, as did the different approaches adopted as constitutional courts reacted to the constitutional aspirations of these governments and parties. It is also worth noting that in Hungary, since 2010, the populist governing parties have had a constitution-making majority in Parliament, which makes this country an optimal testing ground for the constitutional effects of populism, since the government's supermajority makes it capable of achieving any constitutional change, as has been demonstrated by past practice.

Although populism is an essentially contested concept, for the sake of comparability, we have taken as a basis one of the most widely used concepts of this political phenomenon, according to which it is 'a thin-centered ideology that considers society to be ultimately separated into two homogeneous and antagonistic camps, 'the pure people' versus the 'corrupt elite', and which argues that politics should be an expression of the *volonté générale* (general will) of the people.'[7]

The discussion we present here has the following structure and methodological considerations. The first part briefly discusses the different national varieties of populism, based on the place of populist parties in the political system during the period under study and the constitutional changes they sought to bring about, whether in government or in opposition. Of course, it is only possible to describe the most fundamental intentions, but it is important to see the challenges faced by the courts in each country in deciding constitutional disputes. Although there may be controversy regarding whether to classify the various parties and movements as 'populists', we have relied on the opinion of the experts who prepared the national reports in each country, asking them to justify their classification and to formulate it in accordance with the widely accepted perception in the national polities.

Then, we look at the interpretation strategies of the high courts concerned. In order to assess and compare possible judicial behaviours, we divide countries into three categories, as follows: countries in which.

(a) no significant changes in the applied methods of constitutional interpretation have taken place or, if they have, they were clearly not inspired by a populist political agenda;
(b) there have been significant changes in the use of either procedural or substantive constitutional interpretation, the effect of which was supportive of populist aspirations; or
(c) there have been significant changes in the use of either procedural or substantive constitutional interpretation, but their application was used by the court to resist populist claims.

With respect to this grouping, it is of course questionable what constitutes a 'significant' change in the application of constitutional interpretation methods, since in practice courts in the course of constitutional adjudication usually use several different interpretative methods. However, this does not mean that the static or dynamic nature of interpretative practice cannot be assessed. A significant change was considered to have occurred when a court tended to use new approaches in relation to the relatively standard interpretative methods previously applied to similar types of cases. To assess this, we have used a distinction between 'procedural' and 'substantive' methods of constitutional interpretation.[8] By 'procedural' methods we meant a classification distinguishing between different interpretive principles and theories,[9] such as textualism, originalism, purposivism or natural law. In contrast, 'substantive' interpretation focuses on certain constitutional values, such as the notion of human dignity or 'general freedom of action' in the jurisprudence of the German Federal Constitutional Court;[10] the interpretative practices that define the protection of the basic structure of the constitution as a main function of judicial review can also be included in this category.[11] However, while the formal modalities of constitutional interpretation are primarily aimed at standardising the process of interpretation, and constitutional changes in this way can be achieved mainly by alternating between different methods, in this form of interpretation the same results can be reached only by reinterpreting the content of substantive constitutional values.

Finally, the last part of this article gives an explanation for the different judicial strategies, emphasising the relevance of the political context in which courts operate, as well as a summary of our main findings and the implications of the research that might be further elaborated in the future.

2. Populism and constitutionalism

2.1. National varieties of populism

Like any political ideology or practice, populism takes many forms in different countries and political systems. This is important because the different political positions provide different opportunities for such political forces to influence constitutional politics and to bring about changes in the practice of constitutional interpretation that suit their interests. As we have already pointed out, one extreme case in this respect is Hungary, where populists had a constitution-making majority throughout the period under study, which allowed them to implement all the constitutional changes they wanted in their own interest. In some European countries, although populists gained a parliamentary majority after 2010 and became a dominant force in the governing coalition, they were not able to achieve formal constitutional changes on their own. In other countries, they have entered government but, because of their minority position, have not been able to fulfil their constitutional ambitions. Nonetheless, in some cases, they have been able to exert considerable influence on the legislative agenda or, as in Poland, they have even achieved constitutional change through alternative means, through parliamentary legislation or changes to the prevailing interpretation of the constitution.

Finally, there were also examples of populists only being able to use their position in opposition to put pressure on those in government to make the changes to the constitutional framework or practices that they desired. Even in these countries, however, there may have been legal reforms that pursued or achieved populist goals. In addition, despite the different national contexts and political aspirations, some changes in public law were likely to have been motivated by widespread dissatisfaction with the existing political elite and its vested interests. Such discontent may have manifested itself, for example, in the Brexit campaign and referendum in the UK, while in Spain Catalan separatism was also motivated in some ways by a revolt against the existing constitutional and political order. But whatever the cause of social discontent, populism offered new solutions and methods of decision-making compared to traditional policy-making mechanisms.

Therefore, the impact of populism is not to be underestimated, even when it is in opposition. It would therefore be a mistake to ignore the effects of the constitutional aspirations of populists, even if only in opposition, while self-evidently, the stronger position in the government they had and the greater their social support, the more opportunities they had to achieve their aspirations through constitutional means.

However, for the purpose of our topic, what is important is not only the legislative and executive positions that populist parties occupied during the period under review, and, consequently, how they were able to inspire, initiate or implement constitutional reforms, but also the situation of the constitutional courts and other higher courts adjudicating constitutional disputes, i.e. the political and public law context in which they had to react to the challenges of populism.

Among the countries involved in our study, populist forces became governmental actors in five countries: in Hungary, Poland, the Czech Republic, Italy and Austria. Nevertheless, as indicated before, there are significant differences within this group in terms of the impact on constitutional matters.

In the post-communist Central European countries, populists took the lead in government in Hungary, Poland and the Czech Republic after 2010. It is particularly surprising that these three countries were previously generally considered to be the most advanced and western-oriented states in the region.

Among countries with more significant democratic traditions, populists have gained strong government positions in Italy and Austria after 2010, even if they have not yet proved to be as durable or dominant as in the Central European countries mentioned above.

Although populists can obviously have a greater impact on constitutional politics when they are involved in government, experience shows that they are often able to push for certain constitutional changes even when they play an opposition role. The main reason for this over the last decade has been that global crises such as the global economic depression, the 2015 refugee crisis or the health crisis caused by the coronavirus have favoured the kind of crisis management – in a sense the unorthodox politics – that otherwise populist movements tend to encourage. Our survey shows that populist parties exerted some kind of influence outside of the government in five of the countries examined: in Croatia, Greece, Romania, Spain, and the United Kingdom.

2.2. Populist constitutionalism

A characteristic feature of the contemporary worldwide decline of liberal democracy, the constitutional effects of populism, is often referred to as populist constitutionalism. This term, and the theories behind it, suggest that modern populism has created a new form of constitutionalism with specific characteristics that distinguish it from other, more traditional forms of constitutionalism. In other words, populists in power achieve similar constitutional changes determined by their populist attitudes and aspirations.

Although the notion of populist constitutionalism is as much a contested concept as populism itself, there is a broad consensus among scholars on its most important features.[12] In particular, modern nationalist or authoritarian populists who challenge constitutional democracies seem to take great care to formally preserve democratic institutions and procedures, while at the same time introducing significant constitutional reforms when they can, in order to stabilise their power. This ambition includes the adoption of new constitutions, as in Peru in 1995, Venezuela in 1999, Ecuador in 2008, Bolivia in 2009, and Hungary in 2011, or wide-ranging constitutional changes such as in Turkey in 2017, or in Poland after 2015.

Some authors claim that populist constitutionalism is a coherent political theory[13] which offers an alternative to liberal constitutionalism, based on the direct legitimacy of power and the greater involvement of the people.[14] Others think that it is an aspirational idea, and a normative concept, but simply one that operates in the opposite direction to liberal constitutionalism,[15] or a procedural vision of democracy'.[16] According to the most ambitious approach, populism has a *sui generis* constitutionalism, a counterpart of the liberal one, which can be characterised by government-run, institutionalised reforms, such as in Venezuela, Bolivia, or Hungary.[17] Populists create a radically different constitutional polity compared to the liberal legal-constitutional system, so it can be seen as a kind of response to constitutional orthodoxy.[18]

However, most scholars define populist constitutionalism not only as the antithesis of liberal constitutionalism, but also on the basis of one or more of its characteristics. While some simply adapt the main features of populism (as a political phenomenon) to populist constitutionalism, others attribute special importance to one or more characteristics, such as the preference for popular sovereignty and direct democracy vis-à-vis representative democracy, claiming that the will of the people is the only real source of the legitimacy of public power.[19] Anti-elitism and anti-institutionalism are also often emphasised as hallmarks of populist constitutionalism, referring in particular to the non-elected or anti-majoritarian institutions, such as constitutional courts, supreme and ordinary courts, and other politically neutral bodies such as election commissions or ombudsmen.[20] EU institutions, international courts and human rights organisations – as foreign actors – are also frequently classified in the same group as structures or organisations which hinder the realisation of the will of the people. There is also a broad consensus among scholars that populists are against pluralism, considering themselves the only exclusive representatives of the real interests of the people.[21] Populist constitutionalism can be characterised by extreme majoritarianism, which regards electoral empowerment as an expression of the will of the people and, on that basis, rejects the constitutional restriction of power.[22] Others point to the concentration of power in the hands of a charismatic, strong leader as a usual trait of populist constitutionalism.[23] Beyond these, some other criteria are attributed to this sort of constitutionalism, such as the instrumentalisation of law,[24] the preference for constitutional identity (frequently tying it to nationalistic or religious values),[25] abusive legal borrowing,[26] clientelism,[27] and state capture, i.e. the 'colonization' of the state.[28]

It should be added that some scholars claim that populist (or illiberal) constitutionalism is an oxymoron because constitutionalism as such can only be liberal.[29]

But whatever the definition of populist constitutionalism, if populists really want to create a specific, autonomous form of constitutionalism, in all cases they have to want to influence or change the way in which the constitution is interpreted.

3. New interpretative doctrines or methods?

In order to investigate how the courts performing constitutional adjudication responded to the challenges posed by the populist political agenda, we first examined the way in which constitutional interpretation had changed in the course of judicial reviews of populist aspirations. One theoretical possibility was that the interpretive practice remained unchanged, i.e. the constitutionality of the legal reforms concerned was judged by the courts in the traditional way or, alternatively, practice changed from the previously dominant or customary methods, for example, establishing new judicial constructions or applying different standards compared to the previous jurisprudence.

In the next stage of our analysis, we investigated if there were changes in the methods of constitutional interpretation, and if so, what they were exactly, i.e. whether they extended to the principles of interpretation applied, or aimed at the reinterpretation of certain substantive constitutional concepts, including the use of new (possibly created or borrowed) categories. Constitutional courts could, of course, react to populist reforms in a variety of ways, i.e. they could change the interpretative principles they were applying (which is also common in other cases), or they could reinterpret some substantive constitutional concepts, while referring to others in the traditional way. In addition, the attitudes towards activism and deference represent another dimension of possible judicial strategies, as the same methods can be applied extensively, or moderately.

Finally, as the third step, we summarised how the continuity or the changes in constitutional interpretation have had repercussions on populist claims; i.e. whether the courts, by way of constitutional interpretation, have resisted or supported populist aspirations, or, possibly, have had a neutral effect on them.

3.1. Interpretative practice without significant changes – the business-as-usual model

Some of the courts examined in this study did not change their previous interpretative practice in cases that could be considered to be populist in nature. However, this does not necessarily mean no change, as different judicial strategies or patterns of behaviour may underlie the use of similar methods of interpretation to those used in the past, as will be shown below.

In the period under review, Austria was one of the best examples of the business-as-usual-model. Nevertheless, while no significant changes in the interpretative practice of the Austrian Constitutional Court can be detected, the Court has shown an increasingly self-restrained stance in the past decade, especially in the field of fundamental rights protection. In the period from the 1970s until the second half of the 2000s, the Court pursued an activist practice for promoting basic rights, boldly using teleological reasoning and interpreting substantive concepts such as equality, from which the Court 'derived a whole set of principles and rights'.[30] This judicial activism enabled the Court to provide an effective guarantee against the first wave of recent Austrian populism in the early 2000s. This can be illustrated by the Slovenian Minority Case (2001), in which the Court struck down legislation that would have increased the percentage threshold of a minority population necessary for the introduction of bilingual signs. The decision provoked a strong reaction and an attack on the Court from the populist Freedom Party led by its charismatic leader, Jörg Haider, but the Court ultimately won, and retained its authority.[31] However, after 2008, the Court showed a more deferential approach which illustrates our presumption that even when there is no change in the applied methods of constitutional interpretation, there can be different outcomes, depending on whether the courts pursue an activist or self-restraining practice.

The Italian Constitutional Court can be classified in the same group, as this Court responded to populist initiatives in a similar way. According to our research, although this Court had various opportunities to curb populist initiatives, it eventually refrained from taking decisions likely to be controversial, on procedural bases.[32] Such cases include the so-called *decreti sicurezza* (security decrees) adopted in 2018 and 2019 respectively.[33] The first decree 'substantially eliminated the residence permit for humanitarian reasons', whereas the second decree reinforced the first one, and both decrees were 'characterised in particular by a xenophobic and foreigner-hostile inspiration, and aimed at suppressing dissent and minorities' right to expression'.[34] Nonetheless, while the appeals brought by eight regions against these decrees were rejected by the Court on formal grounds, so they proved to be inadmissible,[35] in a rather questionable decision,[36] some ordinary courts acted against populist attempts and annulled individual decisions using the doctrine of 'constitutionally conforming interpretation' which used to be applied otherwise by the Constitutional Court. This doctrine was originally elaborated by the Constitutional Court in order to save otherwise constitutionally questionable legislation by specifying its content in such a way that it conforms to the constitution.

The interpretive practice of the Romanian Constitutional Court also remained unchanged in cases that can be considered populist. However, this jurisprudential continuity is not welcome inasmuch as it means the conservation of certain old weaknesses of constitutional argumentation, such as the argumentative fallacies of 'non sequiturs, tautologies, contradictions and selective treatment of case law'.[37] This shows that there is no close correlation between the quality of constitutional interpretative practice and the nature of responses to populist demands. The decision no. 358/2018 of the Romanian Constitutional Court can be considered an example of this phenomenon. In this ruling, the Court decided on the constitutionality of removing the leader of the National Anti-Corruption Office (at that time, Laura-Codruța Kövesi). This case was rooted in a conflict between the Ministry of Justice and the President in which the question at issue was whether the Head of State may refuse the initiative of the Government to remove a high official. In this instance, the Court decided in favour of the Minister of Justice. It is instructive that, as a commentator noted, 'while the result itself is clearly formalist […], not all the language of the Court is formalist. In fact, the Court uses extensive and creative interpretation to reach the otherwise formalist result'.[38]

In the Czech Republic, the Constitutional Court, in the first two decades of its existence, developed its case law, and expanded its powers. From 2013 on, however, a more deferential practice began.[39] All the signs indicate that the Court perceived the emergence of populism in politics, and at the same time it ceased its previous activism (i.e. the extension of its jurisdiction) and some of its decisions were not even 'in line with the earlier case law'.[40] At the peak of this course of judicial self-restraint, the Constitutional Court refused the justiciability of the declaration of the state of emergency in 2020. However, the interpretive toolkit and the self-understanding of the Court have remained unchanged.

As opposed to the cases discussed so far, the continuity of constitutional jurisprudence has effectively checked populist ambitions in Spain. In this country, at least according to some scholars, neither Catalan separatism, nor the national populist parties 'managed to generate a jurisprudential line of interpretation of the constitution that can be defined as populist', because the Spanish Constitutional Court resolutely resisted such aspirations.[41]

This was made possible by the fact that the previous interpretative practice of the Constitutional Court provided appropriate tools, so the Court did not have to resort to new, previously unemployed instruments to counter certain populist initiatives. In the case of Catalan separatist aspirations, it has acted in defence of the Constitution against unilateral legislative acts which were backed by significant popular support in Catalonia.[42]

The business-as-usual model can be applied to the United Kingdom, where during the protracted Brexit controversies, the Supreme Court's decisions were consistent with the well-established judicial practice reviewing the prerogative powers of the Executive, giving priority to the principle of parliamentary sovereignty, and rejecting the special legal status and judicial enforceability of constitutional conventions.[43] The Court delivered two highly relevant decisions in the post-Brexit era. In Miller 1,[44] the Court decided on 'the use of the prerogative and the necessity of parliamentary approval' in 2017, while in Miller 2,[45] in 2019, it decided on 'the application by the government of the royal prerogative enabling the prorogation of Parliament.'[46] It is argued that although in both cases the Court stepped up firmly, no new methods were used.[47]

3.2. Changing interpretive practice to promote populist aspirations

In those countries where populist-inspired cases led to changes in interpretive practice, these effects occurred in different ways. The results of our research show that most often certain substantive concepts have come into the mainstream of constitutional interpretation, in some cases bringing real innovations into jurisprudence.

Changes of this nature occurred in Greece, where the Council of State (endowed with the power of constitutional review of laws) stood up for the putative interests of the people, relying heavily on the concept of constitutional identity. Previously, when dealing with the debt crisis, the Council had raised sovereignty issues rather than this substantive value. In 2008, however, in a case concerning religious education in schools, the Council revived and gave normative force to the Constitution's 'prevailing religion' clause, which had previously been considered a mere declaratory provision. In doing so, the Council said that the Greek Orthodox religion is a centrepiece of Greek constitutional identity. In addition to this, the Council also referred to the preamble of the Constitution, which includes religious references.[48] This conception treated national identity as a pre-constitutional phenomenon that could be invoked against external threats to the country. It is also to be noted that on this occasion, the Council preferred the contextual interpretation of the Constitution. However, neither constitutional identity as a newly discovered substantive concept nor the contextual method have become general or pervasive modes of constitutional interpretation. However, these interpretive tools are now available and can be revived at any time in the future, and not just in cases in which they have been used so far (i.e. judgments on nationality, Sunday laws and religious education).

New interpretive techniques with the purpose of promoting the populist agenda were also present in the new case law of the Hungarian Constitutional Court.[49] First of all, similarly to its Greek counterpart, the invention of new substantive concepts and the reinterpretation of older ones have been observed in its jurisprudence in recent years. In this country, the so-called 'historical constitution' i.e. an unwritten constitution having effect before the end of the Second World War and the 'constitutional identity' became the crucial categories of the newly established case law, while the concepts of 'human dignity' and the 'rule of law', which had, for a long time, played a similar, central role in the Court's jurisprudence, became increasingly obscured, or at least, reinterpreted. Notably, the concept of constitutional identity was introduced by the Court in a case related to migration,[50] because at the time of this ruling, the constitutional text did not include any reference to constitutional identity (the relevant clause was inserted into the text only in 2018, when the government parties regained their constitution-making majority in the Parliament), and it had previously been an unknown concept in Hungarian constitutional law. In that event, the Court helped the Government, which had previously unsuccessfully tried to introduce this concept into the constitutional text, and organised an invalid national referendum to oppose the European Union's migration policy. So, this decision is a clear example of a situation in which courts might actively promote a populist agenda. It is also worth noting that the populist government, which had a constitution-making majority between 2010 and 2015 and after 2018, exploited this power when it laid down the preferred interpretive methods in the text of the 2011 Fundamental Law.[51] It is surprising however, that the Constitutional Court, which was packed by the governing parties in the 2010s, did not resorted to these theoretically binding modalities of constitutional interpretation, or at least, these methods have not played a prominent role in the recent jurisprudence of the Court. The deference specific to this Court was based on a mixture of interpretative modalities in the same way as had been the case in its activist era in the past, but this time used to support the governmental power rather than to counterbalance it.

Populism has also had a very significant effect on constitutional interpretation in Poland. Populist tendencies have probably had the greatest influence on constitutional interpretation in this country. The reason for this was, as we saw, that the populists who came to power in 2015 did not have a constitution-making majority in Parliament. However, as they, like their Hungarian counterparts, had strong ambitions to transform the constitutional framework, they sought a different solution, which they found first and foremost in a significant reinterpretation of the unchanged constitutional text. As a commentator claims, 'the populist revolution relied greatly on constitutional arguments and interpretations put forward by the political branches of government and by their committed supporters – interpretations which were proposed and enforced precisely against the judges and the courts'.[52] In this process, however, the Constitutional Tribunal, which was quickly packed by the populist government, used traditional interpretive techniques for these new purposes. While, for example, the Court has preserved its earlier practice of providing guidelines to ordinary courts on how the various constitutional provisions should be interpreted, it started to use this tool in a narrowly tailored way, namely, to defend the controversial measures of the populist majority. Interestingly, the functioning of the Polish Constitutional Tribunal can provide a strong argument for sceptics of constitutional interpretation, as this body tends to produce radically differing results, despite using the same interpretative techniques used previously by a differently composed Court. This new interpretive practice can be characterised as a 'cherry-picking model', as the use of textual interpretation illustrates. On the one hand, in several cases this modality produced the desired outcome: for example, the Constitution stipulates that an age limit for judges can be set by ordinary statue, and it was argued on a textual basis that as no other conditions are laid down, the Parliament enjoys a wide margin of appreciation in this respect. As a result, the legislature may effectively 'sack all the sitting judges [...] by lowering the age of retirement'.[53] However, textual interpretation in other cases did not provide the desired end at all. This occurred, for example, when the fixed six-year-term of the President of the Supreme Court was questioned; consequently, the populists started 'speculating that maybe a six-year term is not really a term but a time limit and that it means a 'maximum of six years', so in fact it can be cut short by parliament if necessary'.[54] All in all, the example of the Polish Constitutional Tribunal demonstrates the power of interpretation, which of course can also be used to support nationalist populism.

3.3. Changing interpretive practice to counteract populist initiatives

As we have seen, the Greek Council of State and the Hungarian Constitutional Court, despite discovering some new substantive constitutional concepts or reviving certain categories that had been entrenched in the constitutional text but not used before, did not used them to prevent populist constitutional or legislative reforms, but rather to promote or defend them. The concepts of resuscitated 'historical constitution' or 'prevailing religion', or the newly discovered 'constitutional identity' were effectively conceptions applied to underpin certain populist-inspired legislative acts. On the contrary, the Croatian Constitutional Court used this kind of interpretation in connection with the constitutional review of popular constitutional initiatives, based on the assumption that some of these initiatives pursued populist goals such as anti-elitism, the restriction of minority rights and backing of identity politics.[55] In this context, the instrument of a 'popular initiative' was available to support certain populist aspirations, most notably the initiative aimed at curtailing minority rights.[56] However, in resisting this temptation, the Court had recourse to contextual interpretation to develop certain substantive concepts, bestowing upon them high constitutional values, such as constitutional identity or unconstitutional constitutional amendments. Likewise, it reserved some unenumerated powers for itself, such as the constitutional review of popular constitutional initiatives, even though they can be seen as a manifestation of the constituent power (since successful referendums result in an immediate amendment of the constitutional text). It is worth noting that by elaborating such substantive concepts, the Court extracted constitutional values from the Constitution which were not explicitly in the text, i.e. judicial activism was used here to counter populism. As far as the applied techniques of constitutional interpretation are concerned, the Constitutional Court used several different methods inconsistently, and these modalities 'varied significantly from case to case'.[57] Eventually, the Court rejected the popular constitutional initiatives aimed at restricting minority rights by the proportionality test, refused the initiative to change the electoral system on the basis of a grammatical interpretation, and then, referring to the systematic interpretation, also declared the referendum to prevent the outsourcing of certain public services unconstitutional.

4. Conclusions

Just as in another comparative study, where we concluded that European constitutional courts and other high courts conducting constitutional review responded in different ways to the challenges posed by global crises affecting constitutional systems,[58] the current comparative research also led to the outcome that the national courts adjudicating constitutional disputes reacted in different ways to the problems raised by the recent wave of European populism. In this case the various judicial strategies may be manifested not only in the substantive outcome of the constitutional interpretation but also in the methods applied. If the assumptions often made in the academic literature that nationalist populism – which seems to be the dominant version of this political movement today – poses serious challenges to the constitutional systems of liberal democracies, undermines the functioning of traditional institutions and seeks to establish an alternative constitutional design, it is plausible to assume that populist ambitions also affect the traditional and well-established forms and methods of constitutional interpretation. Presumably, the power of interpretation is therefore greatly appreciated in the eyes of populists. And if this is the case, it can also be presumed that they seek to develop specific and/or new interpretive methods that will most effectively help them to achieve their goals. Nevertheless, the results of our comparative research do not support this presumption. There is no indication that populists would prefer a particular method of constitutional interpretation because they expect it to support their aspirations more effectively. In fact, various interpretive modalities might be beneficial for them in certain cases, whereas the very same methods might be burdensome in others. This was especially shown in Hungary and Poland, where courts use a cherry-picking model in order to support populist aspirations. The same is true for substantive concepts, such as constitutional identity; in Hungary and Greece the introduction of the concept served arguably populist purposes, while in Croatia it was applied to strengthen the Constitutional Court's powers in combating populist aspirations. This conclusion might be generalised; as a wide-ranging comparative analysis shows, there is no evidence that populists would favour any particular method of constitutional interpretation.[59] It can be said at most that although some new constitutions (like the Hungarian 2011 Fundamental Law) prescribe mandatory interpretive methods more often than old ones – presumably in order to influence the future constitutional interpretation –, when this occurs, populism is not the main explanatory variable. The populists' approach appears to be much more a result-oriented one, which shows that they only care about achieving their goals, no matter how they do so, or which method of interpretation is used. A relevant analysis has come to the conclusion that when constitutions contain binding guidelines for interpretation, they are mostly intended to establish and promote liberal democracy.[60] Yet 'established liberal democracies rarely entrench such rules in their constitutions, because they rather consider constitutional interpretation to be the domain of independent courts'. In fact, it is more a characteristic of the populist conception of constitutionalism that it calls into question the very idea that the ultimate interpreter of the constitution should be a body, such as a constitutional court, whose members are not directly elected by the people or which is not politically accountable to the people.[61]

Among the countries we studied, Hungary was the only one where populists had a majority large enough to fully achieve their constitutional goals. They have made ample use of this opportunity, for example by unilaterally adopting a new constitution that includes their preferred methods of constitutional interpretation. In principle, therefore, we have strong evidence for which interpretative methods are preferred by populists. But in reality, modern populism covers political movements of very different character. And indeed, as we have shown above, there are many varieties and forms of modern populism, which do not follow a single political ideology and, in particular, do not pursue similar constitutional politics. The Hungarian example is therefore instructive, but it does not provide a compelling argument as to the influence that populists, if they can, have on the method of constitutional interpretation. In other countries, such as Poland, the result of interpretation proved – as we have seen – to be more important, but no favoured interpretative principle or method emerged to legitimise the change of practice in order to achieve populist ends. All things considered, whether we found that the judicial body performing constitutional adjudication resisted populist challenges or supported them, the judicial conduct and strategy applied depended primarily not on legal philosophy or theory but on the political context surrounding the courts. In those countries where populists were strong enough to pack the constitutional courts or the equivalent judicial body, such as in Hungary and Poland, they attempted to exploit this opportunity to replace judges with their own adherents. But even in these cases, the new judges, or the biased courts as a whole did not develop new interpretative principles or technical methods to legitimize the majority will. Instead, they invented some new substantive concepts or revived several 'dormant' clauses of the constitutional text. Another technique was to shift the emphasis of certain abstract provisions such as the right to human dignity or the rule of law. But the most frequent interpretative process was the selective or mixed use of traditional interpretative principles and tools depending on the desired outcome. It is also our finding that the political subordination of a constitutional court has not necessary resulted in judicial deference. If the preferred political claims did not have the necessary political support, the packed court's active involvement was required. In Hungary, for example, where the government majority could shape the constitution as they want, the Constitutional Court has pursued a self-restraining stance in recent years, while in Poland, where the governing parties did not have a sufficient majority to amend the Constitution, populists urged judicial 'passivism' only in opposition, while the Constitutional Tribunal's activism was no longer criticised when in government, because certain legislative reforms, mainly in the sphere of the judiciary, required an activist court to reinterpret the unchanged constitution.

Then, in a number of countries where the mainstream parties were able to retain their voters' support, or the fragmentation of the party structure prevented populist movements from coming to power or reaching a position in which they could influence the composition of the high courts, these courts could more easily maintain their positions in the system of the separation of powers and were not forced to substantially change their previous interpretative practice. Yet, as the Austrian, Czech and Italian examples illustrate, sometimes even under such circumstances, some constitutional courts started a more self-restraining practice, showing deference to the decisions of political branches, even if they remained otherwise intact. This leads us to conclude that if such a constitutional court relinquishes its earlier activism in the hard cases generated by a populist agenda, this can be better explained by its own institutional interest or the pressure of public opinion, rather than by the national legal culture or the influence of populist parties.

It is also worth noting that, although in principle the traditional principles and techniques of constitutional interpretation provided most constitutional courts with effective tools to confront and reject populist legislative reforms that seek to destroy or significantly transform the constitutional framework, only some constitutional and supreme courts used the available interpretive toolbox for this purpose. Where this did happen (as in Spain or Croatia), the domestic political stakes (such as the unity of the state against Catalan separatism, or the impending EU accession) were surely too high to be jeopardised by populist endeavours.

Overall, where populists are in opposition, and where the constitutional or supreme court is in a strong position, the business-as-usual model is most likely; and vice versa, where populists rule and have been able to change the competence or composition of the court(s) reviewing the constitutionality of legislation, there has been a change in constitutional jurisprudence in favour of populist objectives.

Finally, as regards interpretive activities, our research outcomes show that where populism has influenced the interpretive practice of the courts, no new theory of interpretation has evolved, and no close connection can be established between populist constitutionalism and the specific methods of constitutional interpretation. In other words, populists do not have any favourite interpretive method or theory even where they should have been able to do so. Experience shows that this is not necessary; even a constitutional court serving populist demands does not need to resort to new methods of interpretation; it is enough to invoke methods or refer to substantive concepts that had not been used, or were applied in different ways before, or it may find the most appropriate ways to be deferential to the political will of the government. In practice, the proper modalities of interpretation are chosen on a pragmatic basis, from case to case, depending on the desired outcome, and there is no consistent interpretive theory or practice behind this approach. Consequently, if populists are able to achieve informal constitutional changes by influencing constitutional jurisprudence, the methods of constitutional interpretation play a merely instrumental role. So even the most sophisticated argumentations can be used to justify blatantly unconstitutional laws and initiatives.

In sum, we have not found any evidence that the constitutional ambitions under discussion would have elaborated any specific theory or methods of constitutional interpretation. Our findings indicate that present-day European populism considers constitutional interpretation only in a purely instrumental way, handling constitutional interpretation as a tool to achieve their political objectives and goals.

Notes

*. This article is based on international research conducted in the framework of the project "*Democratic Efficacy and the Varieties of Populism in Europe*" (DEMOS) funded by the European Union's Horizon 2020 research and innovation programme under grant agreement No. 822590. The findings of our research were published in Fruzsina Gárdos-Orosz and Zoltán Szente (eds.), Populist Challenges to Constitutional Interpretation in Europe and Beyond, Routledge, 2021. We thank János Mécs junior research fellow for his assistance.

1. See for example: Paul Blokker, 'Populism as a Constitutional Project', *International Journal of Constitutional Law* 17, no. 2 (2019): 535-553. It should be noted, however, that some opinions, as far as authoritarian populism is concerned, do not attach particular importance to formal rules because they believe that these regimes use primarily informal means. See. Steven Levitsky and Lucan A. Way, *Competitive Authoritarianism: Hybrid Regimes After the Cold War* (Cambridge: Cambridge University Press 2010), 78–81.

2. Some argue that constitutionalism also makes sense without a liberal character. See Mark Tushnet, 'The Possibility of Illiberal Constitutionalism?', *Florida Law Review* 69, (2017): 1367–1384; Tom Ginsburg and Aziz Z. Huq, *How to Save a Constitutional Democracy* (Chicago: The University of Chicago Press, 2018). Under some views populist constitutionalism can even be understood as a coherent political theory. See Oran Doyle, 'Populist Constitutionalism and Constituent Power', *German Law Journal* 20, no.2-3. (2019): 164. Another strand of the literature claims that illiberal constitutionalism is an oxymoron. See for example Gábor Attila Tóth, 'Constitutional Markers of Authoritarianism', *Hague Journal on the Rule of Law* 11, (2019): 37–61; Gábor Halmai, 'Populism, Authoritarianism and Constitutionalism' *German Law Journal* 20, special issue no.3 (2019): 296–313.

3. Pablo Castillo-Ortiz, 'The Illiberal Abuse of Constitutional Courts in Europe', *European Constitutional Law Review* 15, no.1. (2019): 70.

4. Formal modalities of constitutional interpretation are primarily aimed at standardising the process of interpretation, and constitutional changes in this way can be achieved mainly by alternating different methods; in this form of interpretation the same results can be reached only by reinterpreting the content of substantive constitutional values. Fruzsina Gárdos-Orosz and Zoltán Szente, 'The art of constitutional interpretation', in *Populist Challenges to Constitutional Interpretation in Europe and Beyond*, eds. Fruzsina Gárdos-Orosz and Zoltán Szente (New York: Routledge, 2021), 40.

5. Oliver Lepsius, 'The Problem of Perceptions of National Socialist Law or: Was there a Constitutional Theory of National Socialism?' in *Darker Legacies of Law in Europe. The Shadow of National Socialism and Fascism over Europe and its Legal Traditions*, eds., Christian Joerges and Navraj Singh Ghaleigh, (Oxford: Hart Publishing, 2003) 38–39.

6. Wojciech Brzozowski, 'Whatever works: constitutional interpretation in Poland in times of populism', in *Populist Challenges to Constitutional Interpretation in Europe and Beyond*, eds. Fruzsina Gárdos-Orosz and Zoltán Szente (New York: Routledge, 2021), 176.

7. Cas Mudde and Rovira Kaltwasser, *Populism: A Very Short Introduction*, 2nd ed. (Oxford: Oxford University Press, 2017), 5.

8. Gárdos-Orosz and Szente, 'The art of constitutional interpretation', 37-40.

9. On the major explanatory factors of the differences in constitutional interpretation in the various constitutional polities, see Jeffrey Goldsworthy, 'Constitutional Interpretation' in *The Oxford Handbook of Comparative Constitutional Law*, eds., Michael Rosenfeld and András Sajó (Oxford: Oxford University Press, 2013), 706–717.

10. Donald P. Kommers, 'Germany: Balancing Rights and Duties', in *Interpreting Constitutions: A Comparative Study*, ed., Jeffrey Goldsworthy (Oxford: Oxford University Press 2007), 323.

11. See, for example, this doctrine in Indian constitutional law. Sudhir Krishnaswamy, *Democracy and Constitutionalism in India: a Study of the Basic Structure Doctrine* (Oxford: Oxford University Press 2009).

12. For an overview of the concept of populist constitutionalism, see: Zoltán Szente, Populism and populist constitutionalism', in *Populist Challenges to Constitutional Interpretation in Europe and Beyond*, eds. Fruzsina Gárdos-Orosz and Zoltán Szente (New York: Routledge, 2021), 3-28. and Mark Tushnet and Bojan Bugarič, *Power to the People. Constitutionalism in the age of Populism.* (Oxford: Oxford University Press, 2022.) 56-77.

13. Oran Doyle, 'Populist constitutionalism and constituent power', 165.

14. David Landau, 'Abusive Constitutionalism', *UC Davis Law Review* 47, no. 189 (2013): 541.

15. Mark Tushnet, 'The Possibility of Illiberal Constitutionalism?', *Florida Law Review* 69, (2017): 1367, 1368, 1371.

16. Théo Fournier, 'From rhetoric to action, a constitutional analysis of populism', *German Law Journal* 20, special issue 3, (2019): 362-381.

17. Manuel Anselmi, *Populism: An Introduction* (New York: Routledge, 2018), 87.

18. Neil Walker, 'Populism and constitutional tension', *International Journal of Constitutional Law* 17, no.2. (2019): 529.

19. Valerio Fabbrizi, 'Constitutional Democracy in the Age of Populisms: A Commentary to Mark Tushnet's Populist Constitutional Law', *Res Publica* 26, no.3. (2019): 433, 438.;

Bojan Bugarič, 'Central Europe's descent into autocracy: A constitutional analysis of authoritarian populism', International Journal of Constitutional Law 17, no.2. (2019): 599.; Kolja Möller, 'Populismus und Verfassung. Der autoritäre Populismus als Herausforderung für die liberale Demokratie', *Zeitschrift Für Politik* 66, no.4 (2019): 433–435; Paul Blokker, 'Populist Counter-Constitutionalism, Conservatism, and Legal Fundamentalism', *European Constitutional Law Review* 15, no.3. (2019): 536–537.

20. Bojan Bugaric and Alenka Kuhelj, 'Varieties of Populism in Europe: Is the Rule of Law in Danger?', *Hague Journal on the Rule of Law* 10, no.1. (2018): 27, 69.

21. Jan-Werner Müller, 'Populism and constitutionalism', in *The Oxford Handbook of Populism*, eds. Cristóbal Rovira Kaltwasser and others, (Oxford: Oxford University Press, 2017); Bugaric and Kuhelj, 'Varieties of populism in Europe', 20, 26.

22. Landau, 'Abusive Constitutionalism' 533.; Kim Lane Scheppele, 'Autocratic Legalism', *The University of Chicago Law Review* 85, no.2. (2018) 562.

23. Bugaric and Kuhelj, 'Varieties of populism in Europe', 27; Landau, 'Abusive Constitutionalism', 539; Takis S. Pappas, 'Populists in Power', *Journal of Democracy* 30, no. 2. (2019): 70, 71–72.

24. Blokker, 'Populist Counter-Constitutionalism', 545; Landau,'Abusive Constitutionalism' 532.

25. Halmai, 'Populism, authoritarianism and constitutionalism', 310; Cesare Pinelli, 'The Rise of Populism and the Malaise of Democracy', in, *Critical Reflections on Constitutional Democracy in the European Union* eds., Sacha Garben, Inge Govaere and Paul Nemitz, (Oxford: Hart Publishing, 2019), 42.

26. Kim Lane Scheppele, 'The Rule of Law and the Frankenstate: Why Governance Checklists Do Not Work', *Governance* 26, no. 4. (2016): 560; Rosalind Dixon and David Landau, '1989-2019: From democratic to abusive constitutional borrowing', *International Journal of Constitutional Law* 17, no.2. (2019):490.

27. Pappas, 'Populists in Power', 72, 74.

28. Pappas, 'Populists in Power', 73; Landau, 'Abusive Constitutionalism', 200.

29. See, for example, Gábor Attila Tóth, 'Constitutional Markers of Authoritarianism'; Gábor Halmai, 'Making of 'Illiberal Constitutionalism' With or Without a New Constitution: The Case of Hungary and Poland', in *Comparative Constitution Making*, eds., David Landau and Hanna Lerner (Northampton: Edward Elgar Publishing, 2019) 302-303.

30. Konrad Lachmayer, 'Formalism and judicial self-restraint as tools against populism? – Considerations regarding recent developments of the Austrian Constitutional Court', in *Populist Challenges to Constitutional Interpretation in Europe and Beyond*, eds. Fruzsina Gárdos-Orosz and Zoltán Szente (New York: Routledge, 2021), 88.

31. Ibid. 90-91.

32. Gianmaro Demuro and Riccardo Montaldo: 'The populist reforms in Italy and the instrument of the constitutionally conforming interpretation', in *Populist Challenges to Constitutional Interpretation in Europe and Beyond*, eds. Fruzsina Gárdos-Orosz and Zoltán Szente (New York: Routledge, 2021).

33. Law Decree no. 113 of 2018; Law Decree no. 53 of 2019.

34. Demuro and Montaldo, 'The Populist Reforms in Italy', 166.

35. Judgment No. 194 of 2019 of the Italian Constitutional Court.

36. Demuro and Montaldo, 'The Populist Reforms in Italy',170.

37. Alexandra Mercescu, 'Non sequiturs in constitutional adjudication. Populism or epistemic deficit?', in *Populist Challenges to Constitutional Interpretation in Europe and Beyond*, eds. Fruzsina Gárdos-Orosz and Zoltán Szente (New York: Routledge, 2021) 208.

38. Ibid. 206.

39. Ibid. 99-105.

40. Zdeněk Kühn, 'The Czech Constitutional Court in times of populism – From judicial activism to judicial self-restraint', in *Populist Challenges to Constitutional Interpretation in Europe and Beyond*, eds. Fruzsina Gárdos-Orosz and Zoltán Szente (New York: Routledge, 2021) 102.

41. Francisco Balaguer Callejón, 'Constitutional interpretation and populism in contemporary Spain', in *Populist Challenges to Constitutional Interpretation in Europe and Beyond*, eds. Fruzsina Gárdos-Orosz and Zoltán Szente (New York: Routledge, 2021) 222.
42. Ibid. 228-229.
43. See John McEldowney, 'Populism, UK sovereignty, the rule of law and Brexit', in *Populist Challenges to Constitutional Interpretation in Europe and Beyond*, eds. Fruzsina Gárdos-Orosz and Zoltán Szente (New York: Routledge, 2021).
44. R (Miller) v Secretary of State for Exiting the European Union [2016] EWHC 2768 (Admin) and [2017] UKSC 5.
45. R (Miller) v The Prime Minister and others [2019] UKSC 41.
46. McEldowney, 'Populism, UK sovereignty', 233.
47. Ibid. 247-249.
48. Apostolos Vlachogiannis, 'Constitutional identity as a populist notion? The Council of State and the forging of the Greek constitutional identity through the crisis', in *Populist Challenges to Constitutional Interpretation in Europe and Beyond*, eds. Fruzsina Gárdos-Orosz and Zoltán Szente (New York: Routledge, 2021), 135.
49. See Fruzsina Gárdos-Orosz, 'Constitutional interpretation under the new Fundamental Law of Hungary.' in *Populist Challenges to Constitutional Interpretation in Europe and Beyond*, eds. Fruzsina Gárdos-Orosz and Zoltán Szente (New York: Routledge, 2021), 143-159.
50. Decision no. 22/2016. (XII. 5.) of the Hungarian Constitutional Court.
51. See Articles N (1), R (3) and (4) of the Hungarian Fundamental Law.
52. Brzozowski, 'Whatever works',176.
53. Ibid. 184.
54. Ibid. 185.
55. Djordje Gardasevic, 'Popular initiatives, populism and the Croatian Constitutional Court', in *Populist Challenges to Constitutional Interpretation in Europe and Beyond*, eds. Fruzsina Gárdos-Orosz and Zoltán Szente (New York: Routledge, 2021), 112-114.
56. Ibid. 118. The initiative aimed to 'prescribe that in territories of local self-government, state administration and judicial units, the official use of a national minority language and script could be implemented only if members of a national minority made up at least half of the population in such units'.
57. Ibid. 124.
58. Zoltán Szente and Fruzsina Gárdos-Orosz, eds., *New Challenges to Constitutional Adjudication in Europe. A Comparative Perspective.* (New York: Routledge, 2018).
59. Anna Gamper, 'An 'Instrument of Government' or 'Instrument of Courts'? The impact of political systems on constitutional interpretation and the case of populism', in *Populist Challenges to Constitutional Interpretation in Europe and Beyond*, eds. Fruzsina Gárdos-Orosz and Zoltán Szente (New York: Routledge, 2021).
60. Ibid. 60.
61. Ibid. 60-61.

Acknowledgments

We thank János Mécs, junior research fellow, for his assistance.

Disclosure statement

No potential conflict of interest was reported by the author(s).

Funding

This work was supported by the "Populism in policy and law making" project funded by the National Research Development and Innovation Office [grant number 29245] and by the

"Democratic Efficacy and the Varieties of Populism in Europe" (DEMOS) project funded by the European Union's Horizon 2020 research and innovation programme [grant number 822590].

OPEN ACCESS

The instrumental abuse of constitutional courts: how populists can use constitutional courts against the opposition

Michal Kovalčík

ABSTRACT
If populists capture the constitutional court, the system of separation of powers will change. The constitutional court does not act as a counterweight to the ruling majority but rather as a tool for the ruling majority itself to advance its interests. This article unpacks this aspect of populist constitutionalism, which I referred to as the instrumental abuse of constitutional courts. Most importantly, it presents and analyses five different techniques by which populists can abuse the constitutional court as an instrument against opposition. These techniques are the 'governing, do not disturb' technique, consisting in not quashing unconstitutional acts; the legitimation technique, through which populists justify their actions; the delegation technique, through which populists shift responsibility for potentially unpopular actions to the constitutional court; the outright counter-opposition technique, through which populists can achieve the liquidation of their opponents; and the extra-legal technique, involving the use of the authority of judges in the media.

Introduction

When a Polish woman finds out that her foetus is irreversibly damaged, she currently cannot legally undergo an interruption.[1] This is also one of the consequences of how populists use the constitutional courts for their purposes and to fight the opposition. In populist constitutionalism, the constitutional courts do not act as a counterweight to the ruling majority but rather as a tool for the ruling majority itself to advance its interests. The aim of this article is to analyse this manifestation of populist constitutionalism and, based on this analysis, to present different techniques by which populists can abuse the constitutional court.

Populist constitutionalism encompasses many different manifestations such as constitutional amendments, changes in electoral laws and legislation affecting the institutional organisation of states, disregard for existing constitutional practices and attempts to introduce new ones or interpretation of existing constitutional rules against their original purpose. One of these manifestations is what I call the instrumental abuse of

This is an Open Access article distributed under the terms of the Creative Commons Attribution-NonCommercial-NoDerivatives License (http://creativecommons.org/licenses/by-nc-nd/4.0/), which permits non-commercial re-use, distribution, and reproduction in any medium, provided the original work is properly cited, and is not altered, transformed, or built upon in any way.

constitutional courts, encapsulating how populists use constitutional courts for their purposes and against opposition.[2]

This phenomenon was mentioned in some recent studies – both theoretical[3] and empirical.[4] Nevertheless, only Rosalind Dixon and David Landau and Pablo Castillo-Ortiz addressed this argument in more detail on examples of illiberal constitutionalism.[5] In this article, I am building on these studies and unpacking this phenomenon from the perspective of populist constitutionalism and separation of powers. Most importantly, I will grasp the practical dimensions of the instrumental abuse of constitutional courts by populists analytically and provide a theoretical framework describing five possible techniques for how populists can do this.

The instrumental abuse of constitutional courts is observed in the clearest way in Poland and Hungary, which, unfortunately, represent sort of a laboratory of populist constitutionalism. Therefore, these countries poses an inspiration as well as an empirical basis for this analysis. However, as populism is a global phenomenon,[6] populist constitutionalism and its manifestations can occur anywhere, and that is why I do not necessarily link the following conclusions only to a particular state. Thus, the analysis stems from empirical examples mostly from Poland, however, the model of five techniques presented below is intended to be general, applicable to all countries with a similar institutional framework where populists will take power. Moreover, some of the techniques presented bellow are only potential, not so far used in real politics. For these reasons, I will create an imaginary populist in an imaginary country, which will serve as a vehicle for the following analysis. The institutional setting of the imaginary country is based on the setting of countries in Central and Eastern Europe. Its essential aspects are parliamentary democracy and, most notably, a concentrated model of constitutional review. Simply put, to the extent that a given state resembles Popularia, the article's conclusions will be applicable to such a state.

First up, though, I will provide a brief overview of populist constitutionalism and outline its dimensions. The second chapter follows up by unpacking the situation of captured constitutional courts from the perspective of separation of powers and explains why populists can use constitutional courts as a tool to advance their interests. The third chapter unfolds this argument and presents five techniques of the instrumental abuse of constitutional courts. Finally, the fourth chapter deals with the negative and positive consequences.

The article is not intended as a playbook for populists. Instead, it builds a theoretical framework for a more systematic grasp of described phenomena. Moreover, it attempts to point out the dangers of taking control of the Constitutional Court, which may not be obvious at first glance and have not yet been thoroughly addressed in the existing literature. The work could also become a starting point for thinking about how to set up constitutional frameworks in such a way that particular abuses do not occur or are much more difficult to implement.

Populist constitutionalism and its dimensions

If many scholars referred populism to as a contested concept,[7] this is even more true of populist constitutionalism as it represents the interconnection between populism and another ambiguous term, constitutionalism. This part thus aims to clarify this concept for a better understanding of the following sections unpacking one of its manifestations.

For the purpose of this article, I employ the widely-accepted[8] Cas Mudde's definition of the populism as a thin-centred ideology that considers society to be ultimately separated into two homogeneous and antagonistic groups, 'the pure people' against 'the corrupt elite', and which argues that politics should be an expression of the general will of the people.[9] Apart from this antagonistic relationship between two groups and the emphasis on the general will of the people, antipluralism is the third necessary aspect of populism.[10] Only they, the populists claim, represent the people and their will; the others, whether political rivals or just those who do not support the populists are an amoral and reprehensible elite.

Constitutionalism, on the other hand, I perceive from both the negative and positive perspectives as a set of established processes and institutions regulating the exercise of state power; this state power is exercised within and through defined structures.[11] Although some scholars link constitutionalism with various normative ideas such as political liberalism,[12] at least for analytical purposes is more useful to take a thinner, value-neutral approach.[13] The definition of constitutionalism affects the answer to whether or not it can be interconnected with populism. If we fill constitutionalism with the normative ideas of political liberalism, we inevitably conclude that populist constitutionalism is a contradiction in terms, and there is no such thing.[14] Conversely, if we concede that constitutionalism can also be illiberal,[15] the existence of populist constitutionalism must be admittable as well. Populist constitutionalism represents one of the types of illiberal constitutionalism. It (mis)uses the constitutional framework to achieve its ideas of the good state, even though these ideas may not seem appropriate from the perspective of the Western model of liberal democratic states.[16]

However, populist constitutionalism is not another normative critique of legal constitutionalism such as political or democratic constitutionalism.[17] Contrariwise, it is an empirical concept based on the phenomenon of political reality. Its content emerges from how populists use constitutional frameworks in practice, not primarily on ideals predetermined by academics. It is important to note that just as there are dozens types of populism,[18] we can also observe many varieties of populist constitutionalism.[19] Nonetheless, for the purposes of this article, I am using the 'pure' version of populism and populist constitutionalism without connection to a particular 'thin'or 'thick' ideology. I am working with the core features of populism as well as populist constitutionalism, which can be observed in all of their varieties.[20]

One of the key methods of populist constitutionalism is what Rosalind Dixon and David Landau called 'abusive constitutional borrowing'.[21] Populists borrow designs, concepts, and principles inherent in legal (liberal) constitutionalism and use them for their purposes in the selective, acontextual or/and anti-purposive way.[22] A perfect example is their attitude to the judiciary – populists are only opposed to courts as long as they produce outcomes that are unfavourable or 'morally wrong' from their perspective. Once they do not, populists no longer discard the courts' powers but rather use them to their advantage.[23]

Based on the current empirical knowledge, populist constitutionalism manifests itself in three dimensions: (1) populist constitutional-making; (2) populist quasi-constitutional law-making; and (3) populist constitutional interpretation. The first dimension encompasses the creation of a new constitution or amendments to the existing one. In contrast to the following two dimensions, it requires that populists have the political power needed, according to the existing constitution, to change the constitution. This is the case, for instance, of Viktor Orbán and his Fidesz party in Hungary, where, thanks to the constitutional majority obtained in the 2010 elections, Orbán's government was able to adopt a new constitution.[24]

Those populists who do not hold such political power usually combine the second and third dimensions. Quasi-constitutional law-making, the second dimension, comprises changing the existing constitution through ordinary laws, for which populist governments have political power.[25] They enact laws that directly affect and often unconstitutionally alter constitutionally enshrined institutions – electoral laws, laws regulating the judiciary, the prosecution or the regulation of the media are, for example, at stake.

The third dimension involves informal 'changes' to the constitution through its interpretation, whereby original liberal democratic values are replaced by others, exalted by populists. Furthermore, this interpretation is often selective, out of its original purpose and can therefore be described as acontextual formalism.[26] The aforementioned narratives of populism – mainly an idea of virtuous people as a homogeneous entity with the same interests – as well as the particular ideology to which populism is linked are also reflected in the interpretation. For instance, nationalist populism will strongly emphasise national identity in its interpretation.[27] Populists also disregard existing unwritten rules and constitutional conventions and create their own, new ones instead.[28] This dimension manifests itself both in ordinary political action (e.g. the interpretation of constitutional rules in parliamentary debate) and in the application of the constitution in acts of the executive (e.g. questions of the appointment of judges or members of various councils), and can also be accepted directly or indirectly through the arguments of the parties by populist-leaning courts. The third dimension is closely related to the second and often serves as a justification for a particular expression of the quasi-constitutional law-making, which critiques labels anti-constitutional.

In the next sections, I will follow up on these three dimensions and will thoroughly discuss one of these manifestations of populist constitutionalism – the instrumental abuse of constitutional courts.

Take over the constitutional courts and disruption of separation of powers

The second and third dimensions (i. e., populist quasi-constitutional law-making and populist constitutional interpretation) are, in countries with a concentrated model of a constitutional review, inextricably linked to the control of constitutional courts, which would otherwise presumably curb circumvention or outright violation of the constitution. Jarosław Kaczynski, the leader of Poland's populist and co-ruling Law and Justice party, knows well such a situation from his party's first government engagement between 2005 and 2007, when the Polish Constitutional Tribunal, still independent at the time, thwarted several reforms relating to the media, assembly law and lustration.[29] Therefore, in order to implement the above-described dimensions of populist constitutionalism, it is necessary to win over the Constitutional Court, which is supposed to guard the Constitution and possesses the power to annul acts of parliament and government. In other words, populists must 'domesticate' constitutional courts.[30]

The difference between populist regimes and authoritarian or totalitarian regimes, especially those of the twentieth century, is (among other things) that while the latter generally put constitutional courts out of business altogether and entrust politically sensitive matters to other authorities, the current populists in government seek to dominate constitutional courts as soon as possible and then use them to their advantage.[31] Pablo Castillo-Ortiz calls the populist approach to the (constitutional) courts 'opportunistic instrumentalism' – as long as they do not produce the right results from a populist point of view, the populists describe courts as elitist bodies that restrict the will of the pure people; once they have captured them, the enemy becomes a friend.[32]

The ways how to control constitutional courts vary depending (again) on the political power of the populists, the institutional design of the state in question, and possibly the political culture. In any case, to rein the constitutional court as a centralised body made up of a small number of judges is not a very difficult mission. We can distinguish between informal and formal (legal) ways of capturing (constitutional) courts.[33] The informal ones include both 'sticks', i.e. negative tools such as in the long-term not very effective threatening of individual judges with various sanctions ranging from disciplinary sanctions, salary reduction to reassignment to a lower position, and 'carrots', i.e. various benefits for judges who will rule as required.[34] Informal instruments also encompass the threat of budget reductions for a particular court.

Formal tools of capture are so-called court-packing and court-curbing. Court packing means an intentional irregular change in the personal composition of the court that creates a new majority of the *protégés* at the court or restricts the old one.[35] There are many techniques of court-packing, such as lowering the retirement age of judges, increasing their number (and thus altering the majority on the court), or shortening the length of their terms at office.[36] The result should be a court packed with loyalists that is personally subordinate to the populist government.[37] The essence of court-curbing lies in the blocking or at least hindering of the court functions. This may consist, for instance, in the non-publication (and thus ineffectiveness) of court judgments or in the modification of the majority necessary for invalidation of the legislation.[38] Court-curbing, however, does not allow, or only to a very limited extent, to use the court actively for its own purposes. The last and very different formal way is the creation of a completely new court while abolishing or marginalising the existing one. Given that this is a very radical step, it is not a very common and potentially likely method.

If courts are taken over, the balance of power is dramatically disrupted.[39] The system of separation of powers, as one of the principles of legal constitutionalism, will change. A crucial aspect of it – the system of checks and balances – means that each branch of government has swords against the other, by which one branch keeps the other within proper limits and shields by which one branch defends itself from undue interference by the other.[40] Swords can then be identified, in the classical sense, with checks and shields with balances.[41] Constitutional courts, as the fundamental institutions of the judiciary, have, within this system, swords in particular in the form of the ability to review (and strike down) legislative and executive acts. Yet, if populists take control of both the legislative (thanks to electoral victories) and the executive (derived from the legislative) powers, and if they also capture the constitutional court (let us leave aside ordinary courts for now), they will have swords in their hands, with which they will not stab themselves, but – naturally – their enemies. Checks and balances will therefore no longer operate so much between the branches of state power but will be used against those who would threaten the populist unity of power – opposition. It is worth repeating at this point that by 'opposition' I mean, in a broad sense, all critics of populist government – from political opponents to civil society and the media to academics.

Thus, after the capture, the function of constitutional courts is turned completely upside down. Rather than acting as a watchdog for political actors, they function as a partner in helping to eliminate most of those watchdogs.[42] Hence, constitutional courts perform a different function in populist constitutionalism than in legal one.[43] Once the ruling populists succeed in packing them with their own people, they may be instrumental not in protecting democracy and the rule of law but rather in the decline of these values.[44]

To conclude this section, let me illustrate the above theoretical discussion with the example of Poland. When the populist Law and Justice party took power in October 2015, Jaroslaw Kaczynski declared that he wanted to 'build a Budapest on the Vistula'[45], in comparison to his declared role model, Viktor Orbán, he was in a different situation. Kaczynski could not employ the first dimension of populist constitutionalism because PiS did not win a constitutional majority in the elections. Moreover, in the 2019 elections, it also lost the Senate, whose approval is needed to pass a constitutional amendment. Thus, in Poland, we can observe a combination of the second and third dimensions of populist constitutionalism – both bypassing and amending the constitution through ordinary laws and informal changes through constitutional interpretation. An example of the second dimension, quasi-constitutional law-making, is the lowering of the retirement age for Supreme Court judges from the original 70–65. There would be nothing very controversial about this in itself unless this change also affected all existing judges, whose constitutionally mandated length of tenure was thus reduced.[46] Under the second dimension of populist constitutionalism belongs, for instance, the fundamental change in the prosecution system in 2016, when the position of the previously independent Prosecutor General was merged with the position of the Minister of Justice. From then on, the Minister of Justice can interfere in the criminal proceedings and reverse the decision of any of the subordinate prosecutors.[47] The example of Poland also shows that especially the second dimension of populist constitutionalism is the most problematic from the perspective of the rule of law, as the outright violation of the statutes is easily visible. This is also why Poland faces more activity by the European Commission and many proceedings before the Court of Justice for breaches of the rule of law than Hungary, where we can observe rather the first dimension.[48]

An example of the third dimension, populist constitutional interpretation, can be seen in the interpretation of how the National Judicial Council, which is responsible for the appointment of judges, is to be elected. The Polish Constitution, specifically Article 187, only explicitly lays down how many members of the Council are appointed by the President, the Sejm, and the Senate. The rest of the Council is to consist of judges. Although the meaning and purpose of the norm imply that the 'non-political' part of the members is not only to be formed but also elected by the judges themselves, the ruling party interprets this to mean that they are selected by the Sejm, which PiS controls.[49]

Hand in hand with both dimensions went the endeavour to control the Constitutional Tribunal. To do this, PiS initially grasped a strategy of court-curbing to paralyse the

Constitutional Tribunal. They, for instance, increased the majority required to quash a statute, restricted its jurisdiction or refused to publish some undesirable decisions in the official gazette.[50] Concurrently, PiS sought to control the court through court-packing. Already in the autumn of 2015, shortly after the parliamentary elections, President Andrzej Duda refused to appoint all five new constitutional judges elected by the 'old Sejm', in which the now opposition Civic Platform had a majority. With three of them, it was blatantly unconstitutional.[51] Despite this, all five judges were re-elected by the PiS-dominated 'new Sejm'.[52] Other court-packing techniques appeared within the court. In spring 2017, one of the unconstitutionally appointed judges and soon to be vice-president, Julia Przyłębska, sent her opponent and the current president, Stanislaw Biernat, on forced leave, where he remained until the end of his mandate.[53] Przyłębska, who subsequently became President of the Constitutional Tribunal in Biernat's place, also altered the composition of the individual senates in the way that pro-government judges would always have a majority and, in this vein, changed the judge rapporteur – including ongoing cases.[54] Due to a combination of the court-packing and natural turnover, pro-government judges gradually prevailed. Therefore, the Constitutional Tribunal has become an instrument of the pro-government majority.[55] As Wojciech Sadurski points out, 'the ruling party uses it (the Constitutional Tribunal) as a vehicle for its own political plans, and in particular as an ally in the confrontation with other bodies, such as the SC.'[56]

How a ruling party could use the constitutional court as a vehicle for its own plans, I will elaborate on in the following section.

Five techniques of how constitutional courts could be abused against opposition

Let us imagine a country in Europe that is a member of the European Union and the Council of Europe. Let us call it Popularia. This fictional state – with an constitutional and geopolitical setting akin to that of countries in Central and Eastern Europe – will serve as a vehicle for the ensuing presentation of five techniques of the instrumental constitutional court's abuse by populists in a particular country. Thanks to the imaginary state, the analysis is able to go beyond the so far empirical knowledge (see the fourth technique), and, further, it is emphasised that the subsequent techniques are not necessarily linked to the one, specific state.

Popularia is a standard parliamentary republic with a bicameral parliament and is considered by international reports to be a free country with a competitive party system. The institutional design enshrined in the constitution was designed along the lines of legal constitutionalism. We find here separation of powers as we know it in most European Union countries, and also the Constitutional Court, as a judicial body for the protection of constitutionality, with the power to abstract as well concrete constitutional review. Its powers do not differ from those of other constitutional courts in Central and Eastern European countries.

Two years ago, parliamentary elections were held in Popularia. A populist party, led by a charismatic leader called Populus, won a solid majority of seats in both chambers. Populus's party thus possesses a majority to pass ordinary laws, lacking the mandates to reach the qualified majority needed for constitutional laws. In any case, as Prime

Minister, Populus has formed a government whose actions over the last two years have been indicative of the second and third dimensions of populist constitutionalism (i.e. quasi-constitutional law-making and constitutional interpretation). In less than two years of government, Populus has managed to take control of the Constitutional Court, aided both by the fact that the presidential office responsible for appointments is held by a politician favours Populus and by the fact that the mandate of a third of the judges expired during this year. The necessary majority of judges loyal to the ruling party was then obtained by Populus using court-packing techniques. The Constitutional Court of Popularia is thus personally subordinate to the ruling party.

Populists do not usually substantially alter the powers of constitutional courts; they use them as they were designed by legal constitutionalism. For example, the Polish Constitutional Tribunal Act of 2016, when the court was already under the control of the ruling Law and Justice party, made only cosmetic changes, even though the government had the majority to draft the law as it wished.[57] Similarly in Popularia, the ruling party did not make any formal changes to the Constitutional Court's powers.

Nevertheless, as described above, the real role of constitutional courts changed crucially. Although they were originally intended to protect the minority from the oppression of the majority, in populist constitutionalism they are more likely to protect the majority. They are used in various ways by the ruling majority as a tool against opposition.[58] It is worth repeating at this point that by opposition I mean, in a broad sense, critics of the populist government – from political opponents to civil society and the media to academics.

Let us now use the example of our imaginary populist Populus to explain how the constitutional court can be used against opposition in this institutional framework. In the following paragraphs, I will present five techniques of such an instrumental abuse of constitutional courts which are: (**1**) the 'governing, do not disturb'[59] technique; (**2**) the legitimisation technique; (**3**) the delegation technique; (**4**) the outright counter-opposition technique; and (**5**) the extra-legal technique. These techniques emanate predominantly from the empirical knowledge of populist constitutionalism in Poland (that is not the case of the fourth technique though) and analysis of the existing literature on this topic.

(**1**) **The 'governing, do not disturb' technique.** The first technique can be referred to as passive. The Constitutional Court simply does not interfere negatively with Populus' government, not throwing a spanner in its works. Quasi-constitutional law-making very often circumvents the Constitution or directly violates some constitutional norms. Similarly, interpreting constitutional rules selectively, acontextually or against their original purpose will in most cases establish unconstitutionality. In legal constitutionalism or other, in which the constitutional court lives up to its role as the guardian of constitutionality, the constitutional court would have to strike down such acts – whether they are legislation or other derogable acts of the executive. For example, in Poland, the Constitutional Tribunal, before the government managed to capture it, quashed several laws (or amendments)[60] regulating its functioning and directly affecting its independence in December 2015 and early 2016.[61]

Populus no longer has to fear a similar intervention by the highest judicial body. The Constitutional Court, staffed with subordinate judges, will dismiss any petitions for a declaration of unconstitutionality and uphold the acts of the Populus government, not only those restricting the rights of opposition. The same was the case with the aforementioned legislation on the Constitutional Tribunal in Poland, which the Constitutional Tribunal found constitutionally compliant at the end of 2016, although a few months earlier, when it was still independent, on acts with analogical content it had ruled the opposite.[62] The aim of this technique is thus to reshape the constitutional court into a passive bystander who does not interfere with the government's actions anyway. It is able to do so but is unwilling to do so.[63]

(2) **The legitimisation technique**. The second technique is closely related to the previous one, but goes even further. The essential social function of courts lies in their power to authoritatively resolve disputes between parties.[64] Moreover, Populus as a shrewd populist knows that the people of his country, after years of liberal constitutionalism, perceive courts as independent arbiters with a high degree of expertise in legal matters (despite any reservations about them). Therefore, if the opposition challenges the constitutionality of his acts, Populus can either appeal to the Constitutional Court's judgment rejecting opposition claims and declaring the act as in accordance with the constitution (see the previous method), or he can initiate proceedings before the Constitutional Court himself to demonstrate what the (un)constitutionality is all about. The Constitutional Court, thanks to its function of authoritatively settling disputes between the parties, is capable of resolving, at least ostensibly, this dispute between the government and opposition. It is no coincidence that it will decide in favour of the Populus government, otherwise Populus would not even have made such a proposal. This will increase the legitimacy of such an act – it is not only part of the political scene that now thinks that the act is in accordance with the Constitution, but also the highest judiciary body. Overcoming every other institutional obstacle, even if de facto illusory, increases the legitimacy of the act in question.

Accordingly, constitutional courts act as a 'rubber stamp'.[65] All unconstitutional acts receive the stamp of constitutional conformity from the court, which formally has the power to quash them, but does not use it against the government (unless it is desirable), otherwise it would become a snake Ouroboros devouring itself. The constitutional courts have only an ornamental function in this respect – they do not use their swords (checks) against the ruling majority.[66] On the contrary, they serve as a legitimising tool.[67]

As indicated, this technique can be used in two ways: passively and actively. The passive way consists in the fact that the captured constitutional court dismisses the opposition's motions to strike down government acts (i.e. the first technique). This, in addition to the very survival of the act, also increases its legitimacy since the dispute between the government and opposition has been authoritatively decided by someone third, formally impartial and independent, and the act in question has overcome another institutional obstacle. The populists of course rhetorically exploit the court's judgment in this vein. By contrast, the active use of the constitutional court as a legitimising instrument means that the populists themselves initiate proceedings before the Constitutional Court in order to pronounce the issue. Thus, if the Populist government passes a controversial law, members of the government, or the president, or just ordinary members of parliament, can petition for an ex ante or ex post review of the law by the constitutional court (both possibilities are allowed by the Constitution of Popularia). The court will declare it constitutionally compliant and, in its reasoning (or statements for media), ideally even praise the government for passing such legislation.[68]

For a real-life example, we can return to Poland, where a law stipulating a hierarchy of public assemblies prioritises those that are held periodically (i. e. especially assemblies organised by PiS). These regular assemblies are then protected from any counter-assemblies organised by opposition.[69] Following the the government-aligned President Duda's motion, the Constitutional Tribunal found, contrary to the majority opinion of human rights lawyers, that the law is not unconstitutional and does not violate the right to peaceful assembly.[70]

The degree to which the use of constitutional courts as a legitimation tool is effective depends on public perception of them. If there is no public trust in the judiciary, the application of this tool will be limited. Similarly, the effectiveness will be low unless there is at least a minimal degree of autonomy of the court from political power.[71] Yet, we are talking here about a dynamic factor which can be influenced in various ways over time. As far as particular judgments are concerned, their authority, and concurrently their capacity to be used for legitimation, is enhanced by reasoning based on legal rather than political arguments.[72] In the long run, rulings adverse to the government may contribute to the outward autonomy of constitutional courts from the government.[73] Public trust in the courts can be increased by the populists themselves through their media outputs, which may be even more effective through a media sympathetic to them.

Thus, the effectiveness of legitimation techniques is directly proportional to the level of credibility and subsequent authority of a particular court. This factor also affects the following technique as well as the fifth, extra-legal technique.

(3) The delegation technique. Our imaginary Prime Minister Populus, although he and his party possess the majority to pass laws, is reluctant to take some steps which he actually wanted to make. He fears both the disapproval in society, even among his supporters, those whom he considers to be 'virtuous people', and the reaction at the level of the European Union and the Council of Europe. He has therefore thought of shifting the burden to another authority, which will take the planned step while bearing any negative consequences. He will have his cake and eat it too.

I referred to this technique of abuse of the constitutional court as a delegative one. It is based on the principle of outsourcing – the political power passes unpopular decisions, which risk losing political points, to formally independent bodies.[74] The latter will try to justify such a decision with legal arguments. Populists may then criticise the judgment and accept it as a necessary evil, concurrently referring to the principles of separation of powers and judicial independence. Alternatively, if 'their' part of the people reacts positively, they may side with the court.

We can distinguish two subtypes of this technique: internal and external. The internal use is directed inwards – the reason for delegation is the potential loss of political points on the domestic scene and the respective delegated action has primarily domestic implications. Usually, populists will use it in order to repeal certain unwanted legislation, adopted by the previous government, by 'corrupt elites', as the constitutional court will declare such legislation unconstitutional.[75] This either achieves the populists' objective in the matter, or the court judgment at least opens the door to the adoption of new legislation. But then it will no longer be a question of will, but of necessity – there is 'nothing else left' for the populists, they 'really have to' adopt the new, proper legislation if the previous one was unconstitutional.

An example of internal delegation we can observe in the decision of the Polish Constitutional Tribunal, which, on the motion of several PiS and the United Right MPs, struck down as unconstitutional one of the three exceptions allowing women to undergo an abortion – serious irreversible damage to the foetus.[76] The unpopularity of this outcome is evidenced by the fact that hundreds of thousands of people took to the streets of Polish cities in the following weeks to protest for women's rights.[77] The tightening of abortion policy was primarily the wish of PiS President Jarosław Kaczynski, who described the first wave of demonstrators as 'dark forces that want to destroy Poland'.[78] However, the government, headed by Prime Minister Morawiecki, moderated its statements in the face of the growing protests and decided not to publish the judgment in the official gazette, even though the Constitution does not allow such an action.[79] As soon as the massive protests ceased, the government published the judgment, and it came into force in January 2021.[80] The Conservative Party thus succeeded in pushing through a tightening of abortion policy without having to undergo the legislative process.

The external model of delegation includes those actions where the government does not very fear the public reaction, as much as other states or supranational institutions of which it is a part, while the delegated action itself is also directed outwards. It may be an international political act that the government itself does not want to take and prefers to avail itself of the authority of a formally independent constitutional court. Such a move will look much more elegant if it comes from a judicial institution rather than the executive.

An example of external delegation is the judgment of the Polish Constitutional Tribunal, which found Articles 1, 4(3) and 19(1) of the Treaty on the European Union contrary to the Polish Constitution.[81] According to the Constitutional Tribunal, the EU institutions can on the basis of these articles act beyond the competencies delegated to them by Poland, the Constitution has ceased to be Poland's supreme law with a priority of validity and application, and Poland cannot function as a sovereign and democratic state. For these three principal reasons, the Constitutional Tribunal held that EU law (and the judgments of the Court of Justice) will be binding in Poland only within the limits of the Polish Constitution and its interpretation by the Constitutional Tribunal.[82] This review was initiated by Prime Minister Mateusz Morawiecki, whose government has long faced criticism from the EU for violating the rule of law.[83] This criticism was institutionalised in the form of the launch of the procedure under Article 7(1) TEU for the risk of violating the fundamental values of the EU as set out in Article 2 TEU (i.e. democracy, the rule of law or human rights), as well as in several verdicts of the Court of Justice stating the non-fulfilment of obligations under the founding treaties.[84] The ruling party thus needed trump cards to justify its transgressions on the European scene. It itself is reluctant to open conflict with the EU, as Poland grossly benefits from EU membership, both economically and politically, and can therefore be labelled as an 'externally constrained regime'.[85]

Given that the majority of Poles support their country's membership of the EU,[86] Prime Minister Morawiecki, following the release of the judgment on the supranational level, denied the notion that such a ruling constitutes a step towards so-called polexit (i. e. Poland leaving the EU). Nonetheless, he said that he would respect the decision and that 'the national constitution must remain the supreme law in Poland'.[87] Minister of Justice Minister Ziobro, in a much harsher tone aimed at his domestic audience, described the ruling as 'a very important verdict for the whole nation, facing the EU's efforts to treat Poland as a quasi-colonial state'.[88] This judgment, on the other hand, is considered by the vast majority of the expert community to be a factually incorrect ruling issued on political orders.[89]

That said, the internal and external aspects of this technique can be mutually combined. It is possible, for instance, that populists will be afraid of external reaction, but the delegated action will be aimed inwards, and vice versa.

The limits of the delegation technique, like those of legitimation, lie in the public perception of the respective constitutional court and, in the case of external delegation, in its authority at the supranational level. The use of this technique is also limited by the procedural setting in a particular state. The Polish abortion case shows the advantages of the possibility of an abstract ex ante review at the suggestion of an executive, but the technique can also be used by populists in an abstract ex post review, as in the case of the aforementioned EU case law.

(4) **The outright counter-opposition technique**. The fourth technique is the most aggressive presented and often resembles the abuse of the judiciary by authoritarian and totalitarian regimes.[90] Simultaneously, it is also the most diverse technique – it includes several ways of use the constitutional court to directly and negatively impact the personal sphere of opposition representatives. Therefore I mention bellow only a few possible examples of this technique, the list is not intended to be exhaustive. This technique differs from the delegative technique since only the court has this power (and not the government or parliamentary majority), and this exclusive power is abused. Dixon and Landau classify such court's activity as 'strong abusive judicial review' as opposed to the less intense 'weak abusive judicial review' under which would probably fall, for example, the first and second techniques (i.e. 'governing, not to disturb' and legitimisation).[91]

Let's take a look at our Popularia. The Populus' government is facing an economic crisis that is drastically taking political points away from it. Furthermore, some independent media constantly confront Populus with scandals involving himself or his ministers, which also helps the opposition parties. Ahead of the forthcoming elections, the fight against opposition must be stepped up a notch, and the Constitutional Court will again help. In addition to the techniques described above, which of course will also still be very useful, Populus is coming up with ways to marginalise or even completely politically eliminate its opponents directly through the Constitutional Court. In Populus, as in other member states of the Council of Europe,[92] the Constitutional Court can, on the motion of the government or the president, dissolve a political party that violates the constitution and laws or threatens the democratic rule of law, public order or morality. Hence, on Populus' motion, the Constitutional Court can prevent an opposition party from participating in the upcoming elections, for example, because it is a liberal party supporting marriage for all, which, according to the interpretation of right-wing conservative populism, violates morality or other, genuine constitutional values.

The Constitutional Court will also act against opposition directly if it fails to provide protection for their individual rights in the constitutional complaint procedure. Although the state does not have the possibility of filing a constitutional complaint in Popularia to overturn the decisions of the lower courts, in private disputes between individual members of the government and their political opponents or independent journalists, where the opposition's freedom of expression will be at stake, the Constitutional Court can already contribute to the suppression of this freedom in a particular case and, moreover, bring about a chilling effect for all future cases.[93]

If Populus still do not win the election, he can use the Constitutional Court to rule on electoral matters, whether to invalidate a particular vote, a voting procedure or even the election itself. A subsequent re-run of the election may help to reverse the initial unfavourable result for the populists.

Nevertheless, the use of this technique can significantly reduce the effectiveness of the previous techniques, which presuppose at least a certain degree of autonomy and credibility for the respective constitutional court. The use of outright anti-opposition techniques, particularly in relation to elections, also constitutes a direct attack on democracy as such and will usually entail overstepping, temporarily or permanently, the fine line between populist and authoritarian constitutionalism.[94]

(5) **The extra-legal technique**. The last way how to abuse the constitutional court for own, populist purposes is closely linked to the legitimation technique. Unlike it, however, it takes place outside the court. Individual judges can support government action through their public appearances and, by contrast, criticise opposition positions. In doing so, they take advantage of their respected status and aura of independent legal expertise. Although it is not the role of the (constitutional) judges to comment on controversial political issues, the degree of restraint can and does vary even where constitutional courts are not subordinate to the ruling majority.[95]

Therefore, in some controversial issues, Populus may ask one of the judges of the Constitutional Court to support, for instance, a bill criticised by opposition in the media as unconstitutional. In reality, this is also the case in Poland, where Julia Przyłębska, the aforementioned president of the Constitutional Tribunal, stated in a television interview in July 2017 that the bill of the controversial judicial reform does not threaten the separation of powers and meets the expectations of the whole society, while at the same time chastising opposition for presenting unjustified opinions of foreign observers about the violation of the rule of law in Poland.

Even though this technique is rather complementary to others, it can play its role in combating opposition views. The summary of all five techniques provides the following Table 1.

Table 1. Five techniques of the instrumental abuse of constitutional courts.

	The technique of the abuse the CC	The essence of the technique
1.	The 'governing, do not disturb' technique	The CC does not quash unconstitutional acts
2.	The legitimisation technique	Enhancing the legitimacy of acts through constitutional review
	– Passive	Dismissing opposition motions to repeal government acts and declare them constitutionally compliant
	– Active	Populists themselves initiate a constitutional review
3.	The delegation technique	Populists delegate unwanted actions to the CC
	– External	Delegation of domestic issues with an impact within the state
	– Internal	Delegation of actions directed beyond national borders with impact on the international scene
4.	The outright counter-opposition technique	Direct attacks on the opposition – its existence, speeches or electoral results
5.	The extra-legal technique	Use of the authority of judges for support in the media

The instrumental abuse of constitutional courts and its consequences

Although the five techniques of the instrumental abuse of constitutional courts were demonstrated on fictitious Popularia and were mostly supplemented by examples from Poland, this theoretical framework may be fully employed for analysis in all countries meeting the following four requirements. First, such a country must be ruled by populists (i. e. populists must gain a majority in parliament). Second, there must exist a concentrated model of constitutional review (i. e. the existence of one supreme judicial body with power to constitutional review). Third, such a constitutional court must be captured by populists (i. e. personally subordinated to populists), and, finally, such a country must not degenerate into authoritarianism, for which the populist regimes have a strong tendency.[96] If all these four conditions are met, this framework will be fully applicable. This, however, does not exclude cases where it will be applicable only partially, to some extent.

The techniques presented, especially when used together and over a long period of time, do constitute not only an abuse of legal constitutionalism but also a threat to democracy as such, even if we perceive it only in Schumpeter's procedural sense.[97] Indeed, the capture of the Constitutional Court opens the way to the suppression of fundamental 'democratic' rights such as the right to equal and free elections and the related freedom of expression or freedom of assembly – by whichever of these techniques is used.[98] In the techniques described, we find all three aspects that denote that 'democracy dies', as Steven Levitsky and Daniel Ziblatt write about in their popular book: (1) to capture the referees; (2) to sideline the key opposition players (both personnel and institutional); and (3) to rewrote the rules of the political game by tilting the playing field.[99] While the first aspect is a prerequisite of all techniques, the second and third can be done much more easily under the instrumental abuse of the constitutional court.

The instrumental abuse of the constitutional court may not even end when the populists actually lose the elections and governmental power. If the new, non-populist government does not want to employ court-packing methods, there is a threat that the constitutional court, still captured by the populists (currently in opposition), will thwart reforms on the pretext of their unconstitutionality. Then, the constitutional court will no longer serve as a populist tool 'against opposition', but as a populist tool 'in opposition' or 'against the government'. In these circumstances, the constitutional court could also be abused by a minority in parliament.

In this context, it is necessary to distinguish between the instrumental abuse of the constitutional court as an element of populist constitutionalism and so-called 'judicial populism', which Mátyás Bencze describes as a way of court decision-making that seeks to please the majority opinion of the public.[100] However, judicial populism involves judges who are independent of the other branches of government. Their decisions are influenced by certain extra-legal influences, but not by political pressure from the executive.

In the long run, the abuse of the constitutional court as an instrument of the majority may also cause a decline in public trust in the constitutional court and the judiciary as a whole – as was the case in the communist and post-communist countries.[101] And it may also entail a lower level of legislative quality. The constitutionality of laws will be disregarded neither by those who control the court nor by those who know that they will not be protected by it.[102]

These were negative consequences, but what about positive ones? A positive may be a potential reconfiguration of the institutional framework that will be more resistant to populist attacks. As Arato and Cohen argue, the abuse of constitutionalism comes into play where there is 'authoritarian potential' in a liberal constitution.[103] Similarly, Smekal, Benák and Vyhnánek in their article provide reasons why a better institutional design of the Czech Constitutional Court has prevented it from being taken over by populists in the way that has happened in neighbouring countries with similar historical and cultural contexts.[104] The normative critiques of political or democratic constitutionalism and their calls for broader constitutional participation[105] are also worth taking into account when thinking about institutional reforms in new and consolidated democracies. The question is whether we need to let all the dimensions of populist constitutionalism manifest themselves in order to think in this way and to leave complacency with the current legal constitutionalism model.

Conclusion

One of the last phenomena of political reality is populist constitutionalism. It manifests itself in three dimensions: (1) populist constitutional-making; (2) populist quasi-constitutional law-making; and (3) populist constitutional interpretation. If a populist government does not possess a constitutional majority, we find in its actions only the second and third dimensions, which are inextricably linked to its control of the constitutional court. Therefore, the effective implementation of these dimensions requires the constitutional court, which is supposed to guard the constitution and has the power to annul acts of parliament and government.

In this article, I have focused on how populists have abused these institutions for their own purposes I have explained that if populists captured the constitutional court, its function would be turned completely upside down – rather than acting as a watchdog for political actors, they become a partner facilitating to eliminate of most such watchdogs. Constitutional courts thus perform a different role under populist constitutionalism than they do under legal constitutionalism. They serve the ruling power as a tool to fight the opposition.

I have unpacked this principal argument and, based on empirical knowledge and analytical literature on populist constitutionalism, I specifically define five possible techniques for how this tool can be used. I refer to them as techniques of the instrumental abuse of the constitutional courts. These are (1) the 'governing, do not disturb' technique, consisting in not quashing unconstitutional acts; (2) the legitimation technique, through which populists justify their actions; (3) the delegation technique, through which populists shift responsibility for potentially unpopular actions to the constitutional court; (4) the outright counter-opposition technique, through which populists can achieve the liquidation of their opponents; and (5) the extra-legal technique, involving the use of the authority of judges in the media. These techniques not only treat the institutions and narratives of legal constitutionalism selectively, contextually, and against their original purpose but also pose a threat to democracy itself.

The above conclusions represent the main contribution of this text. This theoretical framework thus provides an original systematic grasp of the current and lively topic of the rise of populism and the rule of law decay around the world. It seeks to move

forward with the analytical view on this issue. Although the analysis stems from empirical examples mostly from Poland, the framework may be employed for analysis in all countries with a similar institutional setting where populists will take power.

Nevertheless, the conclusions are primarily theoretical, drawing on existing empirical knowledge and subsequent literature. The subject of further research could therefore be whether the techniques presented are in fact manifested in all countries where populists take power or whether some techniques are used more than others. The limits lie, of course, in the institutional (in)sameness of the systems of each country, which may not allow for some techniques or, on the contrary, create room for entirely new ones. Although in research on the phenomena of political realities, science will usually be a little behind the times, the insights also contained in this paper can become a starting point for thinking about setting up constitutional frameworks in such a way that particular techniques of abuse will not occur, or at least will be much more difficult to implement.

The article is not intended as a playbook for populists. Rather, it attempts to point out the dangers of taking control of the Constitutional Court, which may not be obvious at first glance and have not yet been thoroughly addressed in the existing literature. The work could also become a starting point for thinking about how to set up constitutional frameworks in such a way that particular abuses do not occur or are much more difficult to implement.

Notes

1. Aleksandra Gliszczyńska-Grabias and Wojciech Sadurski, 'The Judgment That Wasn't (But Which Nearly Brought Poland to a Standstill): "Judgment" of the Polish Constitutional Tribunal of 22 October 2020, K1/20', *European Constitutional Law Review* 17, no. 1 (March 2021): 131, https://doi.org/10.1017/S1574019621000067.
2. By opposition I mean, in a broad sense, critics of populist government - from political opponents to civil society and the media to academics.
3. Mirosław Wyrzykowski and Michał Ziółkowski, 'Illiberal Constitutionalism and the Judiciary', in *Routledge Handbook of Illiberalism* (New York: Routledge, 2021); Pablo Castillo-Ortiz, 'The Illiberal Abuse of Constitutional Courts in Europe', *European Constitutional Law Review* 15, no. 1 (March 2019): 48–72, https://doi.org/10.1017/S1574019619000026; Rosalind Dixon and David Landau, *Abusive Constitutional Borrowing: Legal Globalization and the Subversion of Liberal Democracy*, 1st edition (Oxford, United Kingdom: Oxford University Press, 2021); Zdeněk Kühn, 'The Judiciary in Illiberal States', *German Law Journal* 22, no. 7 (October 2021): 1231–46, https://doi.org/10.1017/glj.2021.71; Hubert Smekal, Jaroslav Benák, and Ladislav Vyhnánek, 'Through Selective Activism towards Greater Resilience: The Czech Constitutional Court's Interventions into High Politics in the Age of Populism', *The International Journal of Human Rights* 0, no. 0 (26 November 2021): 1–22, https://doi.org/10.1080/13642987.2021.2003337; András Sajó, *Ruling by Cheating* (Cambridge, United Kingdom ; New York, NY: Cambridge University Press, 2021).
4. Wojciech Sadurski, *Poland's Constitutional Breakdown*, Oxford Comparative Constitutionalism (Oxford, New York: Oxford University Press, 2019).
5. Castillo-Ortiz, 'The Illiberal Abuse of Constitutional Courts in Europe'; Dixon and Landau, *Abusive Constitutional Borrowing*.
6. See e. g. Carlos de la Torre, ed., *Routledge Handbook of Global Populism*, 1st edition (London, New York: Routledge, 2018).
7. E.g. David Landau, 'Personalism and the Trajectories of Populist Constitutions', *Annual Review of Law and Social Science* 16 (2020): 293–309, https://doi.org/10.1146/annurev-

lawsocsci-041420-113519; Sadurski, *Poland's Constitutional Breakdown*, 20; Agnes Akkerman, Cas Mudde, and Andrej Zaslove, 'How Populist Are the People? Measuring Populist Attitudes in Voters', *Comparative Political Studies* 47, no. 9 (1 August 2014): 1326, https://doi.org/10.1177/0010414013512600; Kurt Weyland, 'Clarifying a Contested Concept: Populism in the Study of Latin American Politics', *Comparative Politics* 34, no. 1 (2001): 1–22.

8. See e.g. Cynthia Miller-Idriss, 'The Global Dimensions of Populist Nationalism', *The International Spectator* 54, no. 2 (3 April 2019): 18, https://doi.org/10.1080/03932729.2019.1592870; Vlastimil Havlík, 'Technocratic Populism and Political Illiberalism in Central Europe', *Problems of Post-Communism* 66, no. 6 (2 November 2019): 370, https://doi.org/10.1080/10758216.2019.1580590; David Fontana, 'Unbundling Populism', *UCLA Law Review* 65 (2018): 1487.

9. Cas Mudde, 'The Populist Zeitgeist', *Government and Opposition* 39, no. 4 (2004): 243, https://doi.org/10.1111/j.1477-7053.2004.00135.x.

10. Jan-Werner Müller, *What Is Populism?* (Philadelphia: University of Pennsylvania Press, 2016), 20.

11. See Petra Dobner and Martin Loughlin, eds., *The Twilight of Constitutionalism?* (Oxford: Oxford University Press, 2010), 55; N. W. Barber, *The Principles of Constitutionalism* (Oxford, United Kingdom: Oxford University Press, 2018), 19.

12. Gábor Halmai, 'Populism, Authoritarianism and Constitutionalism', *German Law Journal* 20, no. 3 (April 2019): 311, https://doi.org/10.1017/glj.2019.23; Ronald Dworkin, 'Constitutionalism and Democracy', *European Journal of Philosophy* 3, no. 1 (1995): 2, https://doi.org/10.1111/j.1468-0378.1995.tb00035.x; Keith E. Whittington, R. Daniel Kelemen, and Gregory A. Caldeira, eds., *The Oxford Handbook of Law and Politics*, 1st edition (Oxford: Oxford University Press, 2010), 281.

13. Mark Tushnet, 'Authoritarian Constitutionalism. Some Conceptual Issues.', in *Constitutions in Authoritarian Regimes*, ed. Tom Ginsburg and Alberto Simpser (New York: Cambridge University Press, 2014), 36–49.

14. Gábor Halmai, 'Is There Such Thing as 'Populist Constitutionalism'? The Case of Hungary', *Fudan Journal of the Humanities and Social Sciences* 11, no. 3 (1 September 2018): 329, https://doi.org/10.1007/s40647-018-0211-5.

15. See Tushnet, 'Authoritarian Constitutionalism. Some Conceptual Issues', 36–49; Paul Blokker, 'Varieties of Populist Constitutionalism: The Transnational Dimension', *German Law Journal* 20, no. 3 (April 2019): 334, https://doi.org/10.1017/glj.2019.19.

16. See Bojan Bugarič, 'The Two Faces of Populism: Between Authoritarian and Democratic Populism', *German Law Journal* 20, no. 3 (April 2019): 190, https://doi.org/10.1017/glj.2019.20; Paul Blokker, 'Populist Constitutionalism', in *Routledge Handbook of Global Populism*, ed. Carlos de la Torre, 1st edition (London, New York: Routledge, 2018), 125.

17. See for more detail Richard Bellamy, *Political Constitutionalism: A Republican Defence of the Constitutionality of Democracy* (Cambridge: Cambridge University Press, 2007), https://doi.org/10.1017/CBO9780511490187; Jeremy Waldron, 'Constitutionalism: A Skeptical View', *NYU School of Law, Public Law Research Paper No. 10-87*, 1 May 2012; Paul Blokker, *New Democracies in Crisis?*, 1st edition (Routledge, 2015), 23–30.

18. See Cristobal Rovira Kaltwasser et al., eds., *The Oxford Handbook of Populism*, 1st edition (Oxford, United Kingdom ; New York: Oxford University Press, 2018); Torre, *Routledge Handbook of Global Populism*.

19. See Blokker, 'Varieties of Populist Constitutionalism'.

20. Cf. Jan-Werner Müller, 'Populism and Constitutionalism', in *The Oxford Handbook of Populism*, ed. Cristobal Rovira Kaltwasser et al., 1st edition (Oxford, United Kingdom ; New York: Oxford University Press, 2018).

21. Dixon and Landau, *Abusive Constitutional Borrowing*.

22. Dixon and Landau, 36–7.

23. Sadurski, *Poland's Constitutional Breakdown*, 253.

24. Tímea Drinóczi and Agnieszka Bień-Kacała, 'Illiberal Constitutionalism: The Case of Hungary and Poland', *German Law Journal* 20, no. 8 (December 2019): 1140–66, https://doi.org/10.1017/glj.2019.83.

25. See Maciej Bernatt and Michał Ziółkowski, 'Statutory Anti-Constitutionalism', *Washington International Law Journal* 28, no. 2 (1 April 2019): 487.
26. Dixon and Landau, *Abusive Constitutional Borrowing*, 184.
27. Wyrzykowski and Ziółkowski, 'Illiberal Constitutionalism and the Judiciary', 526.
28. Sadurski, *Poland's Constitutional Breakdown*, 255.
29. Wojciech Sadurski, *Rights Before Courts: A Study of Constitutional Courts in Postcommunist States of Central and Eastern Europe*, 2nd ed. (Springer Netherlands, 2014), 8, https://doi.org/10.1007/978-94-017-8935-6.
30. Wyrzykowski and Ziółkowski, 'Illiberal Constitutionalism and the Judiciary', 518.
31. Cf. Kühn, 'The Judiciary in Illiberal States', 1243.
32. Castillo-Ortiz, 'The Illiberal Abuse of Constitutional Courts in Europe', 68; see also Müller, 'Populism and Constitutionalism'.
33. David Kosař, 'The Least Accountable Branch', *International Journal of Constitutional Law* 11, no. 1 (1 January 2013): 260, https://doi.org/10.1093/icon/mos056.
34. Kosař, 260.
35. David Kosař and Katarína Šipulová, 'How to Fight Court-Packing', *Constitutional Studies* 6, no. 1 (2020): 135.
36. For further details see Kosař and Šipulová, 'How to Fight Court-Packing'.
37. Wyrzykowski and Ziółkowski, 'Illiberal Constitutionalism and the Judiciary', 528.
38. Dixon and Landau, *Abusive Constitutional Borrowing*, 92.
39. Cf. András Sajó and Renáta Uitz, *The Constitution of Freedom: An Introduction to Legal Constitutionalism* (Oxford: Oxford University Press, 2017), 128, https://doi.org/10.1093/oso/9780198732174.001.0001.
40. Barber, *The Principles of Constitutionalism*, 79–82.
41. David Kosař, Jiří Baroš, and Pavel Dufek, 'The Twin Challenges to Separation of Powers in Central Europe: Technocratic Governance and Populism', *European Constitutional Law Review* 15, no. 3 (September 2019): 434, https://doi.org/10.1017/S1574019619000336.
42. Castillo-Ortiz, 'The Illiberal Abuse of Constitutional Courts in Europe', 67.
43. Wyrzykowski and Ziółkowski, 'Illiberal Constitutionalism and the Judiciary', 519.
44. Smekal, Benák, and Vyhnánek, 'Through Selective Activism towards Greater Resilience', 3.
45. Jan Cienski, 'The Duda in Poland', POLITICO, 24 May 2015, https://www.politico.eu/article/upset-in-poland-2/.
46. Sadurski, *Poland's Constitutional Breakdown*, 106–7.
47. Sadurski, 124.
48. See Laurent Pech, Patryk Wachowiec, and Dariusz Mazur, 'Poland's Rule of Law Breakdown: A Five-Year Assessment of EU's (In)Action', *Hague Journal on the Rule of Law* 13, no. 1 (April 2021): 1–43, https://doi.org/10.1007/s40803-021-00151-9.
49. Sadurski, *Poland's Constitutional Breakdown*, 258.
50. Sadurski, 258.
51. Sadurski, 62–5.
52. Sadurski, 62–5.
53. Kosař and Šipulová, 'How to Fight Court-Packing', 142.
54. Sadurski, *Poland's Constitutional Breakdown*, 69.
55. Andrew Arato and Jean L. Cohen, *Populism and Civil Society: The Challenge to Constitutional Democracy* (New York: Oxford University Press, 2022), 72.
56. Sadurski, *Poland's Constitutional Breakdown*, 81.
57. Wyrzykowski and Ziółkowski, 'Illiberal Constitutionalism and the Judiciary', 519.
58. Kühn, 'The Judiciary in Illiberal States', 1244.
59. Inspiration for the name of this technique comes from the Czech documentary film 'Governing, Don't Disturb!' (2007) directed by Tomáš Kudrna.
60. The judgment of the Polish Constitutional Tribunal of 9 December 2015, K 35/15, and the judgment of 9 March 2016, K 47/15.
61. Sadurski, *Poland's Constitutional Breakdown*, 71.
62. Sadurski, 73–4.

63. See Smekal, Benák, and Vyhnánek, 'Through Selective Activism towards Greater Resilience', 3.

64. Martin M. Shapiro, *Courts: A Comparative and Political Analysis*, Paperback ed (Chicago: University of Chicago Press, 1986), 27.

65. Dixon and Landau, *Abusive Constitutional Borrowing*, 82.

66. Castillo-Ortiz, 'The Illiberal Abuse of Constitutional Courts in Europe', 68.

67. Tamir Moustafa, 'Law and Courts in Authoritarian Regimes', *Annual Review of Law and Social Science* 10, no. 1 (3 November 2014): 286, https://doi.org/10.1146/annurev-law-socsci-110413-030532.

68. See e. g. statements of the Chief Justice of the Poland's Constitutional Tribunal, Julia Przyłębska. Sadurski, *Poland's Constitutional Breakdown*, 82.

69. Sadurski, 151.

70. Sadurski, 152–3.

71. Dixon and Landau, *Abusive Constitutional Borrowing*, 85.

72. Dixon and Landau, 85.

73. Dixon and Landau, 92.

74. Wyrzykowski and Ziółkowski, 'Illiberal Constitutionalism and the Judiciary', 517.

75. Cf. Castillo-Ortiz, 'The Illiberal Abuse of Constitutional Courts in Europe', 69.

76. Gliszczyńska-Grabias and Sadurski, 'The Judgment That Wasn't (But Which Nearly Brought Poland to a Standstill)', 131.

77. Jan Cienski, 'Protests Shake Poland as Government Looks for a Retreat on Abortion Ruling', POLITICO, 30 October 2020, https://www.politico.eu/article/poland-abortion-protests-shake-government-retreat/.

78. Magdalena Miecznicka, 'Polish Protesters Are Aghast at Abortion Ban's Moral Hypocrisy', 3 November 2020, https://www.ft.com/content/1fc1b1b1-8b58-4bba-8f98-69317f9b98df.

79. Gliszczyńska-Grabias and Sadurski, 'The Judgment That Wasn't (But Which Nearly Brought Poland to a Standstill)', 135.

80. Gliszczyńska-Grabias and Sadurski, 138.

81. The judgment of the Polish Constitutional Tribunal of 7 October 2021, K 3/21.

82. See Stanislav Biernat and Ewa Letowska, 'This Was Not Just Another Ultra Vires Judgment!', *Verfassungsblog* (blog), 2021, https://verfassungsblog.de/this-was-not-just-another-ultra-vires-judgment/.

83. Jakub Jaraczewski, 'Gazing into the Abyss', *Verfassungsblog* (blog), 2021, https://verfassungsblog.de/gazing-into-the-abyss/.

84. Pech, Wachowiec, and Mazur, 'Poland's Rule of Law Breakdown', 2.

85. See András Bozóki and Dániel Hegedűs, 'An Externally Constrained Hybrid Regime: Hungary in the European Union', *Democratization* 25, no. 7 (3 October 2018): 1182, https://doi.org/10.1080/13510347.2018.1455664.

86. Kublik, 'Kto się boi polexitu. Sondaż Ipsos dla OKO.press i 'Wyborczej'', Gazeta Wyborcza, 1 October 2021, https://wyborcza.pl/7,75398,27647569,ipsos-dla-oko-press-i-wyborczej.html.

87. Maia de la Baume and David M. Herszenhorn, 'Ursula von Der Leyen, Mateusz Morawiecki Clash in European Parliament', POLITICO, 19 October 2021, https://www.politico.eu/article/ursula-von-der-leyen-mateusz-morawiecki-clash-rule-of-law-european-parliament/.

88. PAP, 'Justice Minister Praises Polish Constitution Supremacy Ruling', The First News, 8 October 2021, https://www.thefirstnews.com/article/justice-minister-praises-polish-constitution-supremacy-ruling-25261.

89. Jaraczewski, 'Gazing into the Abyss'; Biernat and Letowska, 'This Was Not Just Another Ultra Vires Judgment!'; Paul Craig, 'Op-Ed: 'The Rule of Law, Breach and Consequence'', EU Law Live, 21 October 2021, https://eulawlive.com/op-ed-the-rule-of-law-breach-and-consequence-by-paul-craig/; Adam Łazowski and Michal Ziółkowski, 'Knocking on Polexit's Door?', *CEPS* (blog), 21 October 2021, https://www.ceps.eu/knocking-on-polexits-door/; Herwig C. H. Hofmann, 'Sealed, Stamped and Delivered', *Verfassungsblog* (blog), 2021, https://verfassungsblog.de/sealed-stamped-and-delivered/; Rule of Law, '25 Retired

Judges of the Constitutional Tribunal Appeal to PM Morawiecki to Withdraw His Motion in K 3/21 Case', Rule of Law, 2021, https://ruleoflaw.pl/25-retired-judges-morawiecki-k-3-21/.

90. See e. g. Zdeněk Kühn, *The Judiciary in Central and Eastern Europe: Mechanical Jurisprudence in Transformation?*, Law in Eastern Europe, v. 61 (Leiden; Boston: Martinus Nijhoff Publishers, 2011), 36–62.

91. Dixon and Landau, *Abusive Constitutional Borrowing*, 94.

92. Venice Commission, 'Guidelines on Prohibition and Dissolution of Political Parties and Analogous Measures' (Venice: European Commission for Democracy through Law, 10 January 2000), 20.

93. See Judith Townend, 'Freedom of Expression and the Chilling Effect', in *The Routledge Companion to Media and Human Rights* (Routledge, 2017).

94. See David Landau, 'The Myth of the Illiberal Democratic Constitution', in *Routledge Handbook of Illiberalism* (New York: Routledge, 2021), 434.

95. See e. g. statements of the Chief Justice of the Czech Constitutional Court about the personal history of the Czech Prime Minister ČTK, 'Rychetský: Nečekal jsem, že můžeme mít premiérem takovou osobu. Uzavření hranic bylo protiústavní', iROZHLAS, 2020, https://www.irozhlas.cz/zpravy-domov/pavel-rychetsky-babis-nouzovy-stav-koronavirus_2011301008_pj.

96. Landau, 'The Myth of the Illiberal Democratic Constitution', 434.

97. Joseph A. Schumpeter, *Capitalism, Socialism, and Democracy*, 3rd edition (New York: Harper Perennial Modern Classics, 1950), 269.

98. See Dixon and Landau, *Abusive Constitutional Borrowing*; Sadurski, *Poland's Constitutional Breakdown*, 262.

99. Steven Levitsky and Daniel Ziblatt, *How Democracies Die* (New York: Crown, 2018), 177.

100. Mátyás Bencze, 'Judicial Populism and the Weberian Judge—The Strength of Judicial Resistance Against Governmental Influence in Hungary', *German Law Journal* 22, no. 7 (October 2021): 1294, https://doi.org/10.1017/glj.2021.67.

101. Kühn, 'The Judiciary in Illiberal States', 1241.

102. Castillo-Ortiz, 'The Illiberal Abuse of Constitutional Courts in Europe', 70.

103. Arato and Cohen, *Populism and Civil Society*, 180.

104. Smekal, Benák, and Vyhnánek, 'Through Selective Activism towards Greater Resilience'.

105. See for more detail Bellamy, *Political Constitutionalism*; Waldron, 'Constitutionalism'; Blokker, *New Democracies in Crisis?*, 23–30.

Disclosure statement

No potential conflict of interest was reported by the author(s).

Funding

This work was supported by Masaryk University (Specific research – support for student projects) [grant number MUNI/A/1439/2021].

ORCID

Michal Kovalčík http://orcid.org/0000-0002-8023-7360

(De-)judicialization of politics in the era of populism: lessons from Central and Eastern Europe

Jan Petrov

ABSTRACT
Law and politics scholarship has been preoccupied with judicialization of politics, often treated as a linear, intensifying trend. This article, however, argues that the rise of populism, particularly East-Central European authoritarian populism, has brought new dialectical dynamics to the judicialization narrative. I examine the relationship between the populist rule and the judicialized structure of governance, and revisit the judicialization theories by providing a conceptual toolkit for analysing the populist backlash against judicialization. The populist ideology suggests that populists should seek de-judicialization. Analysis of Hungarian and Polish cases, however, shows that populists combine different short- and long-term strategies seeking de-judicialization of politics and extreme politicisation of the judiciary, subject to the scope of populists' power and developments in time. Consequently, constitutional courts captured by populists are not always muted. They can be actively exploited for advancing the government's agenda. These measures affect the judicialized triadic structure of governance, normally consisting of the government, the opposition, and an impartial constitutional court. Depending on the techniques employed, the populist court-curbing can lead to a partial return to the dyadic structure, deformation of the triadic structure, and, in the long-term, to the 'charade' triadic structure turning the constitutional court into an inferior actor.

1. Introduction

In the last three decades, law and politics scholars have been preoccupied with the theme of judicialization of politics.[1] They have argued that legislators' zone for political decisions has been significantly curtailed by courts, especially those with the power of judicial review of legislation – constitutional courts. Consequently, they have spoken about the 'global expansion of judicial power', 'governing with judges', and the rise of 'juristocracy'.[2] Judicialization was conceived mostly as a linear, intensifying trend. However, the recent rise of authoritarian populism has brought new dialectical dynamics to the judicialization narrative. Backed by an ideology resenting technocratic tendencies and seeking unmediated enforcement of the popular will, populist rulers targeted constitutional courts which had allegedly constrained the will of the real people.

The aim of this article is to analyse the relation between the populist rule and the judicialized structure of governance. The ideological underpinnings of populism suggest that populists should seek de-judicialization.[3] However, the analysis of Central and Eastern Europe (CEE) – a 'real-world laboratory' of checks and balances limitations[4] – shows a different experience. Drawing on the study of Hungary and Poland, this article argues that the relation between the (authoritarian) populist rule and judicialization is much more complex. Populists resort to a mixture of techniques targeting different components of judicial power, aiming for de-judicialization of politics or extreme politicisation of the constitutional court, depending on the scope of populists' political power and developments in time, particularly on the level of consolidation of the populist regime. Accordingly, marginalising constitutional courts is not the only strategy employed by populists. They also seek to take advantage of the judicialized structure of governance, tame and coopt constitutional courts for achieving their own goals.

A pattern emerges where the early unconsolidated populist regime first tries to prevent constitutional courts from blocking their early policies. Different de-judicialization techniques ranging from jurisdiction stripping and access restrictions to paralysis of the court facilitate this goal. Yet, complete de-judicialization is too costly to achieve and, moreover, unnecessary since courts can serve illiberal regimes as legitimising devices. Accordingly, populists then seek to tame the constitutional court – strip it of autonomous veto status by harmonising the court's ideological position with the government's preferences. The crucial technique is extreme politicisation of the bench through large-scale personnel changes. Consequently, constitutional courts captured by populists are not 'muted' all the time; they can also be actively exploited for legitimisation of the government's policies and as swords against political opponents.

Populism does not invent brand new court-curbing techniques. Compared to earlier authoritarian regimes, however, it provides a different context and justification for court-curbing – one disguised in democratic parlance. This results in important novelties regarding the framing of court-curbing, its resonance within the public and long-term consequences. I argue that these features of populist court-curbing increase the likelihood of the charade triadic structure emergence (see below) and of gradual erosion of the public demand for judicial independence. Populist court-curbing also differs from politicisation of the judiciary that regularly occurs in established democracies. Although the line may be blurred, sequencing, scope and unilateral nature of the court-curbing measures taken by populists make them tools of *extreme* politicisation. Populists seem to denounce the established rules of the game and seek to twist or even change appointment mechanisms in order to make possible the capture of a court by a single faction, which significantly compromises the standard functions of judicial review.

The novel contribution of this article is conceptual and theoretical. Several authors have already demonstrated curtailing and weaponizing of courts by populists (see below). This article, however, analyses these trends in the context of judicialization of politics – a highly influential umbrella theory of judicial politics. The theory claims that the introduction of judicial review of legislation shifted the previously dyadic structure of politics (government v. opposition) toward a triadic structure headed by a third impartial actor – the constitutional court. This article revisits these theories and takes into account the momentary and long-term challenges the populist rule poses to judicialization. Specifically, I distinguish several possible transformations of the judicialized triadic structure of governance. De-judicialization techniques weaken the triad and (partially) return the system to a dyadic structure. Extreme politicisation techniques produce a deformed triadic structure skewed toward the populist camp's preferences. In the long-term, these practices can lead to a 'charade' triadic structure, where the constitutional court turns into an inferior actor with a shifting ideological position depending on the preferences of its principals. In sum, the article revisits the judicialization of politics theories and updates them by providing a conceptual toolkit for the analysis of the populist backlash against judicialization and for constitutional courts' behaviour in populist-governed polities, which acknowledges the dynamic element in the lives of populist regimes.

The article proceeds in six parts. Part 2 summarises the judicialization of politics scholarship. Part 3 explains the ideological underpinnings of populism and the populist irritation with judicialized politics. Part 4 examines the various court-curbing techniques employed in Hungary and Poland. Building on these two cases, Part 5 (the core part of this article) provides a generalised account of the dynamics of populist court-curbing strategies, their rationale and effects on the structure of governance. Part 6 concludes.

2. Judicialization of politics

Hirschl defines judicialization of politics as 'the reliance on courts and judicial means for addressing core moral predicaments, public policy questions, and political controversies'.[5] According to Vallinder, judicialization of politics denotes

> the expansion of the province of the courts or the judges at the expense of the politicians and/or the administrators, that is, the transfer of decision-making rights from the legislature, the cabinet, or the civil service to the courts or, at least, the spread of judicial decision-making methods outside the judicial province proper.[6]

Judicialization of politics is a broad phenomenon encompassing the operation of various courts to various extents. This article focuses on constitutional courts for the following reasons. First, the most influential judicialization theories are centred around constitutional courts due to their direct interventions in the legislative process based on their power to strike down legislation (see below). Second, constitutional courts belong among the first targets of populist court-curbing. Third and related, attacks on constitutional courts are particularly detrimental to constitutional resilience since they make the subsequent capture of other institutions easier.[7]

Judicialization of politics by constitutional courts notably affects the politics of lawmaking and shifts it from a dyadic to a triadic structure.[8] Before the introduction of judicial review of legislation, lawmaking took place within a dyadic environment. It would be characterised by mutual negotiations among political parties. Although bills of rights may have existed even then, they were mostly viewed as political declarations lacking legally enforceable status. However, the introduction of written constitutions and judicially enforceable fundamental rights gradually shifted the lawmaking environment toward a triadic structure.[9] It was complemented with a third actor – a court with the power of judicial review of legislation. Once new legislation is adopted, several actors – such as the parliamentary opposition or individual citizens – can challenge the law in court on the grounds of its alleged unconstitutionality. Courts can strike down an unconstitutional statute, but they can also provide guidelines of constitutionally conform interpretation binding on other state authorities. Some courts even formulate directives ordering the lawmakers how the unconstitutionality shall be remedied.[10]

Thus, when a weaker political actor (usually the opposition party)[11] loses the battle over new legislation in the parliament, it can still achieve its goal through judicial means. A pre-condition is the ability to transform the political issue into legal terms. With respect to the current state of constitutionalisation across the world, this task does not seem too difficult.[12] Aharon Barak, the former Chief Justice of the Israeli Supreme Court, even argued that 'nothing falls beyond the purview of judicial review; the world is filled with law; anything and everything is justiciable'.[13]

The possibility of continuing a political battle by legal means has further consequences. Since the costs of transferring the policy issue to a court are usually low and the gains potentially high, the losing group of lawmakers has the incentive to activate a court frequently. That tends to intensify the level of judicialization. According to several authors, judicialization is somewhat of a one-way street, 'an inescapable fact'[14] – the triadic dispute resolution mechanism 'appears, stabilises, and develops authority over the normative structure'.[15] In some countries, political actors start taking preventive account of the constitutional court's case law when drafting new legislation and try to anticipate how the court will respond to it. Stone Sweet speaks about the pedagogical function of constitutional adjudication,[16] and conceives judicialization of politics as a process 'by which triadic lawmaking progressively shapes the strategic behaviour of political actors engaged in interactions with one another'.[17] As a result, the purely political dyadic structure of lawmaking is 'inevitably placed in the shadow of triadic rule making'.[18]

In sum, judicialization affects the politics of lawmaking in the following ways. First, it imposes substantive constraints on lawmakers as constitutional courts rule out certain policies as unconstitutional. Second, in the long-term perspective judicialization reinforces de-politicisation of certain constitutionalised spheres of law. This feature may be stronger in jurisdictions where courts apply the unconstitutional constitutional amendment doctrine and reserve the right to assess the constitutionality of constitutional amendments.[19] Third, through the pedagogical effect constitutional courts' judgments affect lawmaking also prospectively when political actors anticipate the courts' reaction when drafting new legislation. Fourth, the rhetoric of lawmaking tends to change. One can witness the influence of constitutional language on parliamentary debates and the spread of human rights vocabulary.

According to many scholars, these effects tend to intensify throughout time – the more constitutional case law exists, the more constraints arise and the more opportunities emerge to transfer the political dispute to a court. As a result, the mainstream theories of judicialization of politics are construed as linear narratives of progress and continuing judicialization.[20] Although several authors have warned that extreme judicialization can lead to politicisation of the judiciary,[21] many approaches to judicialization of politics do not acknowledge that there may emerge social and political processes, which lead to pushbacks or backlashes against judicialization, or, at least, do not provide conceptual space for analysing effects of such processes. Additionally, they are largely uni-dimensional and fail to fully recognise that judicial power is a composite of several institutional and political features.[22]

This article argues that populism disrupts the judicialization teleology, and brings about a dialectical dynamic to the judicialization narrative. In some jurisdictions, the populist rule manifested, *inter alia*, as a backlash against excessive technocratization and judicialization of democracy.[23] Part 3 further explains that the populist ideology suggests that populism in practice should lead to de-judicialization efforts and re-politicisation of the public sphere.

3. Populist irritation with judicialization of politics: ideational dimension

The listed effects of judicialization of politics are at odds with the ideological underpinnings of populism. Populism is a thin political ideology which explains how democracy should work and how the political leaders should relate to the people.[24] Mudde introduced an influential definition of populism as 'an ideology that considers society to be ultimately separated into two homogeneous and antagonistic groups, "the pure people" versus "the corrupt elite", and which argues that politics should be an expression of the volonté générale (general will) of the people'.[25]

The idea of a united ordinary people implies that there is one united popular will.[26] The goal of populist politics is to enforce such a popular will in an *authentic* way, without the compromising effects of non-majoritarian checks on the popular will.[27] Populists criticise the endless litigiousness stemming from the rule of law constraints on majoritarian democracy and aim to repoliticize the public sphere.[28] Accordingly, populists hold the position that the people's constituent power is still present to be exercised, which means that constitutional law is not necessarily supreme to politics.[29] In addition, populist leaders claim direct and unmediated connection with and support from the people.[30]

Müller adds that populists are also anti-pluralist and claim exclusive representation of the 'real' people.[31] Yet, there is a debate whether the anti-pluralist features are attributable to all varieties of populism. Nowadays, authoritarian versions of populism dominate.[32] And some authors argue that the authoritarian consequences are inherent in populism as such.[33] Others claim that some kinds of populism are not authoritarian and can be squared with constitutional democracy: 'The antiestablishment part of populism can be empirically and logically unbundled from its authoritarian and xenophobic dimensions'.[34] Since this article is more narrowly focused, I cannot do justice to this big question. I leave it aside and concentrate on the the type of populism that currently dominates politics in CEE, specifically in Hungary and Poland, i.e. populism tied with significant ethnonationalist, anti-pluralist, and illiberal elements.[35] Accordingly, my conclusions apply to this type of populism, usually referred to as authoritarian populism. More empirical work needs to be done to find out to what extent the patterns identified in this article are applicable beyond CEE authoritarian populism.

4. Populist irritation with judicialization of politics: practical politics dimension

Müller points out that authoritarian populists in government use three main strategies of governing: occupation (or colonisation) of the state, mass clientelism and discriminatory legalism, and repression of civil society.[36] The first feature is crucial for the focus of this article – populists tend to 'occupy' the state by perpetuating their power through centralisation and capturing state institutions.[37] Employment of the state colonisation strategy in populist-governed polities can be very broad and include institutions of civil society, electoral institutions, free media, parliamentary platforms for the expression of opposition, civil service, educational and cultural institutions.[38] Yet, the judiciary with constitutional courts in the first line often belongs among the early targets.

The operation of constitutional courts tends to bring about high levels of judicialization and its constraining effects, which are at odds with the populist ideology. According to the populist ideology, judicialized politics does not authentically represent the will of the ordinary people. Autonomous constitutional courts create a major obstacle for the realisation of the people's political sovereignty, since they possess significant veto capacity.[39] This part examines the populist assaults on constitutional courts in Hungary and Poland. The aim is not to retell all the details of the story of dismantling these two courts,[40] but rather to focus on the major points which help to understand the populist resentment against judicialization of politics in context.

4.1. Hungary

In 2010, the Fidesz party won the Hungarian parliamentary election, gaining a constitutional majority. Since then, the populist regime led by Viktor Orbán has thoroughly consolidated its power, using, *inter alia*, the state occupation strategy.[41] One of the first targets was the Hungarian Constitutional Court (HCC). Although a poster child among post-communist constitutional courts in the past,[42] the HCC was circumscribed in competences, packed and disciplined to a large extent. Initially, the new government's idea was to abolish the HCC and merge it with the Supreme Court.[43] Although the HCC maintained its existence in the end, the government took several steps to gradually weaken it and essentially 'tame' its veto capacity.

First, mechanisms affecting the HCC's composition were addressed. The system for electing the HCC's judges was changed in 2010. Originally, Hungary had relied on a parliamentary model of appointing HCC judges, which aimed at a consensual selection of the candidates by political parties, similarly to the German system. The selection was made by a two-third majority in an *ad hoc* parliamentary committee composed of one representative of each parliamentary party, irrespectively of its number of seats in the parliament. Since 2010, however, the committee's composition has had to respect the parties' weight in the parliament, which gives the government a dominance in the selection process.[44] With a two-thirds majority in the parliament, the new government got an opportunity to select its own preferred candidates without cooperating with the opposition.[45] Moreover, the government enlarged the number of vacancies by implementing a court-packing plan. The number of judges was increased from eleven to fifteen, and their term was extended from nine to twelve years. And since there were two vacancies at the time of court-packing, the government had the freedom to fill six seats.[46] During its first three years, the government managed to select nine HCC judges in total.[47]

These personnel changes affected the HCC's case law. Sólyom reported that the HCC got into a 'survival mode', facing a division between the new and the old judges: 'A clearly identifiable block of the new judges has never voted for unconstitutionality of a law issued by the present majority or the government'.[48] This was augmented by shuffling with the composition of HCC's panels. Scheppele reported that the panels were composed so that 'each panel of judges ha[d] a predictable post-2010 Fidesz majority'.[49]

Second, the government restricted access to the HCC. Most importantly, it quashed the Hugarian constitutional law's signature (and, admittedly, extraordinary) feature – *actio popularis*. Under this mechanism, anybody was entitled to file a motion for constitutional review of legislation, which assisted the HCC in developing its case law and involved the people in constitutional interpretation.[50] Instead, the government introduced a system of more traditional constitutional complaints, including the German type (*Verfassungsbeschwerde*), which allowed the HCC to review the constitutionality of ordinary courts' decisions in individual cases.[51] Thus, although access by an individual was preserved, the HCC's activation channels were restricted.[52] Although other channels of initiating review of legislation remained in place, state officials are not active in initiating review of legislation, probably because most of the offices are held by the government's nominees.[53]

Third, the Fidesz government resorted to jurisdiction stripping. The HCC was barred from reviewing financial laws.[54] Furthermore, the so-called Fourth Amendment to the new constitution restricted review of constitutional amendments exclusively to the procedural issues. The substance of constitutional amendments was immunised from judicial review.[55] That does not sound too controversial, as the unconstitutional consitutitonal amendment doctrine is not universally accepted. However, for the Fidesz government, which possessed the constitutional majority in the Parliament, constitutional amendment became a routine means of lawmaking used to override the HCC's rulings.[56]

Fourth, the Fourth Amendment also voided all the HCC's pre-2012 case law. That was a major blow to the HCC's authority as even the 'packed' HCC declared continuity with the previous case law. Yet, the Fourth Amendment stated that case law made before the coming into effect of the new constitution ceases to be in force. That meant a setback for the twenty years of constitutional developments in Hungary and, moreover, it erased the mandatory force of the judge-made constitutional law of Hungary.[57] This step effectively removed even the limitations on the government's will 'inherited' from the pre-Fidesz times.

In sum, these measures have had far-reaching consequences for the HCC and the rule of law in Hungary. Although the HCC fought back for about three years,[58] the constraints on lawmaking resulting from judicialization by the HCC were largely eliminated. An essential part of the government policies was entirely exempted from the HCC's review.[59] The remaining parts were strengthened by the possibility of constitutional override of the HCC's decisions. Moreover, the discontinuity with the previous constitutional jurisprudence implies that the populist government managed to get rid even of the HCC's previous jurisprudence. Finally, the installation of new judges through court packing and replacement of old judges led to the 'taming' of the HCC. Overall, as Bugarič and Ginsburg put it, 'the Fidesz government drastically revised the Hungarian constitutional and political order by systematically dismantling checks and balances, thereby undermining the rule of law and transforming the country from a postcommunist democratic success story into an illiberal regime'.[60]

4.2. Poland

Orbán's illiberalism provoked international reaction. Beside a lot of criticism, a supportive voice came from Poland. In 2011, Jarosław Kaczyński (Poland's former Prime Minister) admired Orbán's governance strategy: 'The day will come when we will succeed, and we will have Budapest in Warsaw'.[61] Kaczyński's prediction was right. In 2015, his Law and Justice party (PiS) won the parliamentary elections and gained the absolute majority of seats, yet was short of a constitutional majority.

PiS started governing the country in a manner which showed they did not want to repeat the scenario from 2005 to 2007. In that period, Kaczyński's populist government was quite successfully countered by independent actors, especially the Polish Constitutional Tribunal (PCT).[62] This time, the PiS government did not want to make the same mistake and attacked the PCT soon after taking office. Kaczyński was very open about his motives. He described the Tribunal as a potential obstacle to the realisation of PiS's electoral promises,[63] and stated he wanted to break up the 'band of cronies' who allegedly made up the Tribunal.[64]

The first phase of dismantling led to the PCT's paralysis.[65] The initial step was the battle over the former parliament's appointees to the Tribunal. Shortly before the end of its term, the prior parliament filled three vacancies with new judges. Yet, the MPs took a controversial step when they also elected two more appointees in the place of judges whose mandate would run out two months later, i.e. after the end of the parliament's term. Apparently, this was done deliberately to prevent the incoming parliament from choosing the judges.[66] Accordingly, the PCT declared these two appointments unconstitutional but confirmed the previous three.[67] Nevertheless, the PiS-backed President refused to swear in the three judges. The new PiS government declared all five appointments invalid and installed its own nominees at the PCT. However, the 'old' judges refused to hear cases with these new PiS-elected judges.[68] Yet, the PiS government later managed to instal one of the 'new' judges to the position of the PCT's acting and later regular President. One of her first steps was to include all the new controversial appointees in the PCT's panels.[69]

Soon after, the Parliament adopted several amendments to the Constitutional Tribunal Act, among them the so-called repair bill. Sadurski points out that these amendments had three main goals and effects – to exempt the new PiS legislation from effective constitutional review, to paralyse the court, and to enhance the powers of the political branches *vis-à-vis* the PCT.[70] To name but a few examples, the new legislation introduced a requirement of strictly respecting the sequence of judgments according to the time of the motion, a requirement of considering a case no earlier than 3 months (6 months in cases decided by the full bench) after notification of the parties about the proceedings. As for the paralysing provisions, the major change was the increase of the quorum – 13 out of 15 judges had to be present for the case to be heard. Regarding the third group of changes, the most striking was that the amendments increased the political branches' disciplinary powers over the PCT's judges.[71]

Although the repair bill seemed to be 'custom-made to paralyse the court' and left the Tribunal 'largely impotent',[72] the PCT managed to strike back in a series of judgments which Koncewicz labels as 'existential judicial review'.[73] The PCT declared the repair bill unconstitutional as it prevented the court from carrying out reliable and efficient work. Nevertheless, the government refused to implement or even publish several of these judgments.[74]

Meanwhile, by mid-2016, the PiS government had managed to appoint a majority of its judges to the bench. According to Sadurski, the judges nominated by PiS – except one – have so far shown themselves to be loyal to the government in all cases.[75] This effect was even augmented as the new PCT President reshuffled the composition of the panels and removed the 'old' judges from judge rapporteur positions.[76] By that time, the government had abandonded most of the changes in the procedure before the PCT as they had become unnecessary. New laws on the PCT more or less resemble the pre-crisis legislation. In Sadurski's interpretation, '[t]he earlier rules which seemed so defective to PiS when it did not have a majority on the Tribunal turned out to be perfectly satisfactory once it captured the majority'.[77]

5. Populist court-curbing: de-judicialization *and* extreme politicisation

The Hungarian and Polish examples have many similarities, but also important differences. Both Orbán and Kaczyński had previous governmental experience within a judicialized framework of politics. In the 1990s, Orbán was a member of the parliament and the Prime Minister (1998–2002). Accordingly, he experienced the very activist 1990s' HCC. Especially under Sólyom's presidency, the HCC was labelled as 'the most powerful constitutional court in Eastern Europe' and beyond.[78] The HCC became the leader of democratic transition and was virtually rewriting the constitutional theory of the country.[79] During the first six years of its existence alone, it quashed about two hundred statutes.[80] Kaczyński has also been a stable figure on the Polish political scene. PiS won the 2005 parliamentary election and he became a Prime Minister in 2006. In this period, the PCT was one of the major opponents of Kaczyński's reforms and, for example, annulled a statute altering media oversight, and the government's efforts to toughen lustration mechanisms.[81] Nevertheless, both Orbán and Kaczyński failed to win the subsequent election and were forced to retreat into opposition.

Some authors have argued that the activism and bold approach of CEE constitutional courts in the 1990s and 2000s leading to extensive judicialization of politics have been a part of the current problems.[82] Kosař, Baroš and Dufek even argued that 'super-strong constitutional courts' emerged in CEE that were 'not responsive to the electorate and unreflective of the views of the majority of the population'.[83] Accordingly, they depict the recent populist attacks on CEE constitutional courts as an 'overreaction to an overreaction' since populists shifted technocratic judicialized governance to another extreme by removing most checks on their government.[84] No matter if one accepts this narrative or not, it seems that the constitutional courts' past trajectory and the populist leaders' hands-on experience with their veto capacity – combined with many more socio-economic and political causes – form a part of the story.

After getting their second chance in the 2010s, Orbán and Kaczyński seemed to be determined to implement their political projects without the restraints resulting from strong and independent constitutional courts. Using the underpinnings of the populist ideology, both Orbán and Kaczyński were rather open about their efforts and targeted the respective constitutional courts. Yet, the techniques differed, mostly due to the different political backing of Orbán's and Kaczyński's governments. Whereas Orbán gained a constitutional majority in the parliament, Kaczyński had to operate with a 'mere' legislative majority.

Hungary and Poland represent two recent examples of illiberal turns and rule-of-law backsliding.[85] They have attracted a lot of attention as the backsliding is particularly shocking within the EU. However, they are not isolated cases and populist attacks against courts have taken place all over the world and have included both domestic and international courts.[86] Therefore, analysis of the Hungarian and Polish cases provide important insights regarding more general strategies of populist court-curbing with important repercussions for the theories of judicialization of politics. This part shows that the relation between (authoritarian) populist rule and judicialization of politics is much more complex than usually assumed. Court-curbing techniques employed by populists combine strategies of de-judicialization of politics *and* extreme politicisation of the judiciary, and target different components of judicial power depending on the scope of populists' political power and developments in time, particularly on the level of consolidation of the populist regime.

The following sections proceed according to the phases of the populist regimes. These phases constitute an analytical simplification as there are no clear lines separating them. In fact, there can be significant overlaps between the first (de-judicialization) and second (extreme politicisation) phases, especially if the ruling populists quickly gain an opportunity to appoint a considerable number of new constitutional court judges. Accordingly, there was a notable overlap between the de-judicialization and extreme politicisation phases in the Hungarian case. Still, I keep the two phases separate since changing judicial personnel usually takes time and, therefore, less time-consuming de-judicialization techniques play a separate role even in regimes that can start staffing constitutional courts with loyalists soon after coming to power.

5.1. Initial phase: de-judicialization

Generalising from the two cases, the populist court-curbing includes various aims, depending on the phase and consolidation of the populist regime. In the short-term perspective, populist governments need to exclude the constitutional court's power to block the initial reforms necessary to consolidate the regime.[87] The goal is de-judicializing politics.[88] This can be achieved by different ways, depending on the political power of the populist party.[89] If the party is powerful enough, it can employ hard de-judicialization techniques. The hardest one is the abolition of the constitutional court. This option was considered but not implemented in Hungary.[90] A less intensive option is restricting the channels used for transferring political issues to a court. This can be done through jurisdiction stripping and access restrictions. If the court is not competent to decide about certain types of issues, it will not be able to judicialize them. In this respect, the HCC was stripped of the competence to review financial laws and constitutional amendments. In those areas, therefore, politics became largely de-judicialized and returned to the dyadic logic. However, even if the court has the competence, it is difficult to judicialize the area if it is seldom (or never) activated by other actors. In this vein, the Hungarian government abolished *actio popularis*, which had previously represented a crucial activation mechanism for constitutional review of legislation.[91]

Techniques of hard de-judicialization are nonetheless very costly and demanding since they often require constitutional changes and likely result in higher reputational costs due to their tension with the principle of judicial independence.[92] The Polish scenario, however, exemplifies that less powerful and less consolidated populist regimes[93] can achieve de-judicialization too. The Polish playbook is a prime example of achieving de-judicialization through paralysis.[94] A combination of several subtle procedural and organisational changes led to de facto de-judicialization since it made it impossible for the PCT to effectively block the populist reforms. Deciding cases strictly according to when they reached the PCT, increasing the quorum, introducing a qualified majority requirement for quashing statutes and not publishing the court's decisions belong among the most effective techniques, the combination of which secures that the court will not be able to block the new legislation, at least for some time.[95] That is why these measures lead to provisional de-judicialization.[96]

The employment of de-judicialization techniques has grave consequences for the structure of governance. It implies weakening of the triad and a (partial)[97] shift to the dyadic structure. Hard de-judicialization techniques disrupt the links between the constitutional court and the opposition actors that are not able to initiate constitutional review due to access restrictions or jurisdiction stripping. Provisional de-judicialization techniques disrupt the link between the constitutional court and the government since they (partially) block the constitutional court from issuing consequential decisions through different paralaysis techniques.

5.2. Advanced phase: extreme politicisation

Provisional de-judicialization is arguably less costly than hard de-judicialization techniques. Still, its effects have limited durability since the court cannot be held in paralysis forever. Even hard de-judicialization techniques do not completely eliminate the constraints stemming from judicialization. Jurisdiction stripping and access restrictions are unlikely to completely block the court's activities. De-judicialization efforts in an early stage of a populist regime are thus not an endgame. In the more advanced stages of populist regimes, de-judicialization techniques are regularly coupled with extreme politicisation of the constitutional court,[98] which reflects a long-term aim of harmonising the ideological position of the court's majority with the government. Thereby, the government can diminish limitations stemming from the judicialized structures by absorbing the court's veto capacity.

That can be achieved by ideological approximation of the court to the government's preferences through large-scale personnel changes, in particular by hand-picking nominees who are likely to remain loyal to the government. Such measures crucially affect the court's power, which is a compound of several features including the court's autonomy. As Brinks and Blass put it, a consequential court 'must be capable of (i) developing and (ii) expressing preferences that are substantially distinct [...] from those of a single dominant outside actor [...]'.[99] The following scenarios demonstrate how personnel changes can affect the court's autonomy and veto capacity.[100]

Immediately after the populists' electoral victory, the court will likely be ideologically distant from the populist government. Imagine a scenario where an authoritarian populist political party (P) wins the election for the first time and takes over the government. Judges of the constitutional court (CC) were originally (t_0) appointed by the previous, non-populist political actors (A and B). Accordingly, the court's preferences and visions of proper constitutional interpretation should be on the non-populist side of the spectrum (CC in t_0 and t_1). Figure 1 illustrates the situation when two political actors (e.g. the government and the opposition party) have to agree on appointees for a constitutional judgeship. If the populist party subsequently forms the government, the ideological distance between the court and the government is likely to be great, which results in a strong veto position of the constitutional court.

Since the populist government aims to prevent the court from blocking its policies, it seeks to absorb the veto status of the court. The main aim is to bring the court's ideological position closer to that of the populist government. Several steps can be taken – separately or in combination – to do that. First, populists can pack the court – increase the size of the constitutional court and appoint loyal judges to the bench. The size of the constitutional court's bench is usually entrenched in the constitution. Therefore, this technique is often available only to the actors who control constitutional amendment, i.e. possess a constitutional majority. Packing the court with loyalists shifts the ideological position of the court. Figure 2 shows a hypothetical scenario where a nine-member court is packed and the number of judges is increased to fifteen.[101] It shows that the median judge will be closer to the position of the populist government in such a case.

Another technique is the replacement of incumbent judges with loyalists or nominating new loyal judges to vacant positions. Depending on the number of judges replaced, the effect is the approximation of the court to the position of the government. The median judge will, again, be closer to the populist position. Figure 3 exemplifies a scenario where four incumbent judges of a nine-member court are replaced by four judges nominated by the populists.

If the number of new judges appointed by the populists is too low, the ideological distance may remain considerable. The combination of court-packing and replacement thus seems to be the most effective. Figure 4 illustrates a scenario where four incumbent judges are replaced by populist-appointed judges and, moreover, the court's size is increased from nine to fifteen members. The median judge of the 'new' court will be ideologically considerably closer to the populist government.[102] Furthermore, the situation is more complex since constitutional courts often decide in smaller panels. Consequently, the engineering of the panels' composition can be particularly important for the absorption techniques.[103]

Finally, all the listed techniques can be accompanied by the populists' efforts to reduce the court's long-term ability to defend itself and to defend liberal democratic values. An important technique is reducing the constitutional court's authority through delegitimizing rhetorical attacks. The instruments of populist ideology and style can be particularly useful here as they provide the basis for justifying the anti-court behaviour.[104]

These models are crucial for understanding the populist attitude to judicialization of politics. Although the populist ideology seeks re-politicisation of the public sphere by reducing judicialization and technocratization in general, the populist actual rule shows that extreme politicisation of constitutional courts can be less costly and more profitable than complete de-judicializiation of politics. Acknowledging that the court's power consists of jurisdictional reach[105] *and* autonomy helps to understand this. A

Figure 1. Government alteration and ideological distance of the constitutional court.

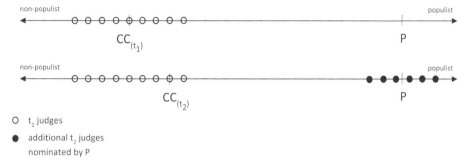

Figure 2. Shifting the ideological position of a court through court-packing.

court with broad jurisdictional reach and high autonomy is a major obstacle for the populist reform. But a court with low autonomy, which is unlikely to impose major restrictions on the governing actors, can serve a valuable legitimisation role. The populist regimes therefore preserve the constitutional courts' existence but aim to politicise the bench through nominating loyalists. That results in the legitimisation of the regime without the danger of the costly limits stemming from the judicialization of lawmaking because the court's veto status is absorbed. Due to large-scale personnel changes driven by extreme politicisation and unilateral control over judicial appointments, it is unlikely that the court will 'speak with a different voice than its legislative and executive counterparts (either because the judges are hand-picked ideological allies of the regime or because they fear the consequences of challenging powerful interests)'.[106] The government's control over the constitutional court is rarely total, thus the court may sometimes counter the majority. Still, it is unlikely in the case of the government's major interests.

Depending on the court-curbing techniques employed, the court can be (partially) muted – either through hard de-judicialization, or temporarily through provisional de-judicialization techniques – or turned into a 'regime ally court' through extremely politicised large-scale personnel change.[107] The latter option seems to be attractive across populist regimes, but it is particularly important for the less powerful populist

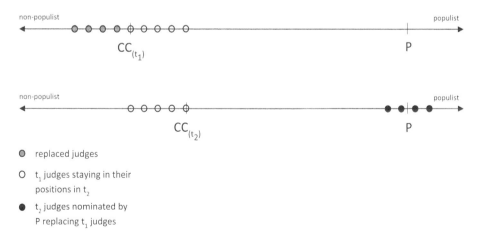

Figure 3. Shifting the ideological position of a court through replacement.

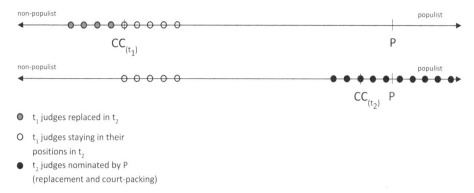

Figure 4. Combining court-packing and replacement.

regimes which lack alternative instruments to achieve their constitutional goals.[108] Accordingly, the PCT is extensively exploited in this manner as the government lacks a constitutional majority in *Sejm*. Sadurski thus titled the PCT in its current composition as a 'governmental enabler' and a 'protector of the legislative majority'.[109] After PiS gained a majority on the PCT, the ruling party itself brought several cases to the PCT seeking justification for its reforms.[110] Koncewicz argued that the PCT's rulings reach beyond mere rubber-stamping of the government's policies, and amount to 'weaponizing judicial review' to be used against the opposition.[111] Some authors coin this phenomenon as 'abusive judicial review'.[112] Castillo-Ortiz speaks about 'inverted courts' that become devices used by illiberal actors, rather than checks on their power.[113] The PCT's rulings on the Polish National Council of the Judiciary (NCJ) and on abortion policy illustrate this.

The NCJ was established as a crucial actor of court administration in Poland, a guardian of judicial independence, playing an important role in appointing judges of ordinary courts.[114] Accordingly, the NCJ became a strategic target of the PiS government. The Minister of Justice (acting as the Prosecutor General) challenged the NCJ before the PCT on the grounds of the NCJ's unrepresentative composition and individual mandates of the NCJ members. The PCT sided with the government's view and concluded that the existing system discriminates against lower court judges and that the Constitution requires a collective term of office for all the NCJ members.[115] Polish commentators argued that the PCT's judgment was designed to 'pave the way'[116] for the NCJ's reform by PiS, which significantly increased political control over the NCJ at the expense of judicial self-governance.

In 2019, Polish MPs – mostly PiS parlamentarians who had previously called for abortion restrictions – asked the PCT to assess constitutionality of abortion laws. The Tribunal delivered a controversial ruling claiming that abortion due to foetal defects is unconstitutional. Thereby, the PCT critically limited abortion in Poland, rejecting the most frequent ground for pregnancy termination as unconstitutional.[117] These two cases show that ideological approximation of the court by extreme politicisation might be more effective for the populists than de-judicialization efforts.

The governmental-enabler function of captured constitutional courts has a supranational dimension too. Even populists possessing a constitutional majority have troubles setting aside supranational legal constraints. Both the Hungarian and Polish governments used their constitutional courts to water down constraints stemming from EU law. In Hungary, the HCC used the concept of constitutional identity to legitimize the government's resistance against the EU's refugee policy.[118] In Poland, the Prosecutor General submitted a motion arguing that the preliminary reference procedure at the Court of Justice is unconstitutional to the extent it allows domestic courts to question domestic judicial design. Although the proceedings are pending, according to several commentators, it is not totally unlikely that the PCT will declare the unconstitutionality of Article 267 TFEU in the given scope.[119] These cases suggest that captured constitutional courts can be used not only against domestic opposition, but also against populists' supranational opponents.[120]

The described strategy of consolidating populist regimes has implications for the structure of governance. The constitutional court nominally exists and the triadic structure remains. Given the ideological approximation of the court through extreme politicisation, however, the triad is skewed toward the governmental camp. Nonetheless, judges do not necessarily become absolute agents of the government. Depending on the scope of the government's power and the personalities of particular judges,[121] we should speak about various levels of deformation of the triadic structure across coutries and issue areas. For instance, the deformation might not be visible in cases with low political salience, which may still appear in the court's docket. Generally, however, the government's increased control over the court casts doubt on the court's position of the *superior* third actor in the triadic structure of governance.

5.3. Declining phase: strategic defection or hegemony preservation through courts?

The time factor begs a question about the future scenario. Given the average length of constitutional judges' mandates, the duration of an extremely politicised court can be quite long. It may happen that a court ideologically attuned to the populist constitutionalism 'survives' longer than the populist government. Even if the populists eventually lose the election, the new majority will face the populist-picked constitutional judiciary. Since this has not happened (yet) neither in Hungary or Poland, we can only hypothesise how the courts would behave. Experiences from the Latin America suggest there are two main options. Judges may 'strategically defect' from their populist nominators once they begin losing power.[122] But they can also keep on fighting for the populists' interests and counter the non-populist actors' policies.[123] In the latter case, the populist politicisation strategy might eventually lead to the preservation of the deformed triadic structure of governance and the populists' power even after their electoral demise.[124]

Figure 5 summarises the previous scenarios and graphically expresses the analytical model of court-curbing strategies and their effects on governance in different phases of the populist rule. The model assumes the populist government's substantial control over the legislature. Yet, it does not mean that the opposition is necessarily a passive actor. The parliamentary opposition can try to prevent some court-curbing measures or, at least, increase the costs of court-curbing by voicing criticism. Still, authoritarian populists in government often limit oppositional rights in the legislature and deform the parliamentary processes.[125]

5.4. Long-term peril: 'charade' triadic structure

From the long-term perspective, however, the employment of de-judicialization and extreme politicisation techniques is likely to have detrimental effects for the constitutional courts' social legitimacy and their perceived independence. The deformation of the triadic structure in the phase of populists' decline may encourage further interferences in the constitutional courts' design or personnel even by the newly elected actors. Efforts to bring the situation back to normal can extend to a cycle of retribution, which is extremely troublesome for the stability of a constitutional order and for confidence in the constitutional structure. From the long-term perspective, such repeated interferences imply a threat of inverting the triadic structure upside-down and turning the constitutional court – originally thought of as a third superior impartial actor – into an inferior actor with a shifting ideological position subject to the preferences of the ruling majority. Hence, there is a risk of creating a 'charade' triadic structure, where the constitutional court nominally retains the position of a third actor, but is largely subordinate to the preferences of one or another political faction.

The 'charade' triadic structure is a consequence of eroding political norms of non-interference with the judiciary. In general, judicial independence has two major sources – legal safeguards and shared political culture of non-interference.[126] As demonstrated above, many of the legal safeguards can be twisted, deformed or eliminated. Still, the political norms of non-interference with judicial independence create 'soft guardrails'[127] and a critical precaution for the healthy functioning of checks and balances. The abovementioned court-curbing suggests that populists do not accept these norms and view judicial independence as an obstacle to their political projects that should be minimised by taming the judges of constitutional courts. The practice leading to the charade triadic structure endangers the social perceptions of judicial independence and may reduce the respect for judicial independence even further in the long term. Low decisional independence of courts (i.e. judicial ouput that systematically reflects the preferences of a particular political faction) leads to loss of their social legitimacy.[128] And if the general public loses confidence in the independence of the constitutional court, a vicious circle begins. Lower legitimacy of a court implies lower political costs

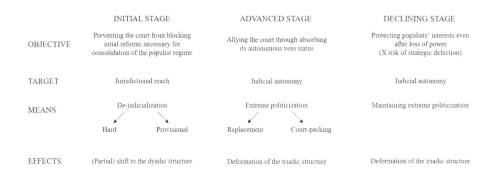

Figure 5. Populist court-curbing and (de-)judicialization.

of eventual court-curbing and of using courts for political domination, which increases the likelihood of further court-curbing and destruction of norms of non-interference with judicial independence. This effect can even be multiplied as populists regularly couple court-curbing with campaigns denigrating the judiciary.[129] As the next section argues, these features make the populist challenge distinctive.

5.5. Populism as a specific challenge to judicialization?

Is there anything specific about court-curbing *by populists*? After all, courts have been attacked by various actors, not just populists. The Nazis, Communists, military and other authoritarian regimes[130] have all interfered heavily with the independence of their judiciaries. The previous part showed that populists use similar techniques to the earlier authoritarians, such as jurisdiction stripping, court-packing and the replacement of judges. These techniques are not distinctively populist. They can be employed by actors of any political affiliation.

Still, there seem to be important specifics underlying populist court-curbing. Military coups or other forms of fast authoritarian reversion were typical methods of power-grabbing by the twentieth century totalitarian and authoritarian leaders.[131] Also the subsequent endurance of these regimes was based on physical and/or psychological violence. The twentieth century totalitarian and authoritarian ideologies were openly anti-democratic.[132] The current populist regimes are different.[133] Populist attacks on the rule of law and the separation of powers are more subtle and incremental.[134] Moreover, rather than relying on violence, populists use legal means of gaining power (or at least try to create such impressions).[135] Populist regimes are based on some form of democratic legitimacy, derived from popular sovereignty and elections. As Barber put it, '[p]opulists subvert constitutional government, but do so in a manner that brings much of the people along with them, and which allows – and requires – the basic structures of a democratic state to remain in place'.[136]

At the same time, populist ideology is built on a specific understanding of the vocabulary of constitutional democracy. Terms such as democracy, constituent power, popular will, and popular sovereignty are crucial for populists' political claims. Yet, as Part 3 showed, the populist constitutional vision gives a specific reading to these concepts, which also affects the context of populist court-curbing. Populist understanding of the named constitutional concepts allows for significant contempt for prior institutional boundaries while maintaining the appearance of democracy. In the realm of the judiciary, this translates to populists' skill in depicting judicial independence not as a means to ensure effective government, to protect the rule of law and fundamental rights, but rather as a bulwark allowing elitist judges to deform the genuine will of the real people.

Populists are thus able to explain their court-curbing under cover of constitutional-democratic vocabulary. Surely, the democratic parlance may be just a cloak covering authoritarian tendencies.[137] But it still allows populists to argue that breaking the existing formal boundaries and rejecting the hitherto 'soft guardrails' is justifiable or even necessary for achieving true democracy and popular sovereignty. Indeed, Viktor Orbán saw the constitutional reform as a part of Hungary's shift toward illiberal democracy.[138] Kaczynski even titled the pre-capture PCT as 'the bastion of everything in Poland that is bad'.[139] These quotes illustrate that the combination of the ideological basis of populism and populists leaders' aggressive communication style implies a powerful challenge to judicialization and to (constitutional) courts' social legitimacy.

As mentioned, populism does not invent brand new court-curbing techniques. Compared to earlier authoritarian regimes, however, the populist ideology and practice provide a very different context and justification for court-curbing – one disguised in democratic parlance. In sum, differences thus rest in the framing of court-curbing, its resonance within the public and long-term consequences. Although these may seem subtle details, they may increase the likelihood of the charade triadic structure emerging and the gradual erosion of public demand for judicial independence. Ignoring these specifics and treating contemporary populist court-curbing identically to earlier authoritarian attacks on judicial independence would miss the most critical point of the current populist challenge.

On the other hand, the democratic parlance seems to have a constraining effect too. The harshest de-judicialization techniques attacking the court's core competences (such as abolishing a court, severe jurisdiction stripping, etc.) might be hard to justify. The democratic disguise may limit the populists in how far they can go since the expectations of their voters and other actors are somewhat based on the liberal democratic past.[140] This even increases the likelihood of quickly advancing to the second phase seeking the capture of a court through personnel politics. Indeed, the de-judicialization phase in Poland was quite a short transitional period of provisional paralysis, which ended once PiS managed to gain a majority within the PCT. Even in Hungary, the government dropped the harshest de-judicialization plans (abolishing the HCC) and replaced them with partial jurisdiction stripping. Even the access restrictions (abolishing *actio popularis*) were compensated for by introducing new access mechanisms to the HCC (constitutional complaints). This constraining effect of using the constitutional democratic vocabulary, however, is no victory for the rule of law advocates. On the contrary, it increases the significance of the extreme politicisation strategy and, thereby, the likelihood of the deformed or even charade triadic structure emerging.

One may also ask whether there is anything specific about the populist court-curbing as compared to the situation in standard democracies. After all, some degree of politicisation of the judiciary is natural, even in established democracies. Similarly, court-curbing measures are also proposed in established democracies.[141] The line between legitimate measures aimed at making the judiciary more responsive and undesirable measures seeking unchecked power is blurred. Political actors are regularly involved in the procedure of selecting constitutional courts' judges, which is desirable from the viewpoint of constitutional courts' democratic accountability. Yet, it also implies that political considerations are regularly taken into account during the selection process. Accordingly, judicial appointments tend to reflect the balance of political power at the given time. As a result, the composition and orientation of constitutional courts shift in established democracies too.[142] These processes, however, should not regularly translate into *extreme* politicisation of constitutional courts. Institutional safeguards are supposed to prevent a unilateral takeover of a court. A plurality of actors is usually necessary for agreeing on the appointment and/or the appointments are diffused in time so that no single faction can capture the court. Yet, the court-curbing that took place in Hungary and Poland is qualitatively different from the instances of regular politicisation. Whereas the latter takes place within the established rules of the game, the populists sought to twist[143] or even change[144] the rules in order to make the capture by a single faction possible. Not only the timing, but also the combination of various amendments to the laws on constitutional courts suggests the bad faith of these measures. In sum, although some of the measures taken by populists can be justifiable under certain conditions, it is the sequencing, scope and unilateral nature of the court-curbing measures that make them tools of *extreme* politicisation.[145] Moreover, authoritarian populists' attacks on constitutional courts are often just an initial step in broader reforms seeking to get rid of institutional checks.[146]

6. Conclusion

Judicialization of politics represents one of the major recent developments in the system of democratic governance. This trend is not an unqualified good. Constitutional courts have been criticised from many positions for decades – for their counter-majoritarian logic and an uneasy relationship with democracy,[147] for promoting excessive individualism and flattening the collective identity necessary for a democratic polity,[148] and for lacking institutional capacity to decide complicated moral and empirical issues.[149] Yet, this article demonstrated the actual fragility of constitutional courts, especially in new democracies where the endurance of a sincere commitment to judicial independence and constitutionalism cannot be taken for granted.

Populism is a major challenger of the judicialized triadic structure of governance in such polities. The examination of Hungary and Poland, however, showed that CEE authoritarian populism does not seek principled de-judicialization for the sake of giving voice to the people. Authoritarian populists rather instrumentally mix court-curbing techniques targeting different components of judicial power, aiming for de-judicialization of politics or extreme politicisation of the court, depending on the scope of populists' political power and developments in time, particularly on the level of consolidation of the populist regime. In the early stage, populists seek (partial) return to the dyadic structure of politics in order to prevent courts from vetting their reforms necessary for initial consolidation of the regime. Subsequently, populists seek to tame courts and absorb their factual veto power by extremely politicised appointments. In the case of large-scale personnel changes through replacement and/or court-packing, the court majority will consist of judges loyal to the government. This produces a deformed triadic structure skewed towards populists' preferences.

In the long term, such developments endanger the political culture of non-interference with judicial independence, which creates the backbone of judicial authority. Such a scenario implies a risk of transforming the regular triadic structure of governance into a charade triadic structure. In the charade triadic structure, the constitutional court turns from a third impartial actor into an inferior actor with a swinging ideological position depending on the preferences of its principals. Such a transformation is extremely problematic. The loss of autonomous status and the deformation of the triadic structure make compliance with considerable parts of constitutional law subject to the government's preferences, which make politics supreme over these constitutional norms.[150] That raises serious concerns from the viewpoint of the rule of law principles, and protection of fundamental, especially minority, rights. Moreover, it endangers the competitiveness of the party system. The deformation of the triadic structure strips constitutional courts of their 'democratic hedging' function, which protects polities from 'one-party-ism'[151] – efforts to centralise power and reduce the government's democratic accountability – and, ultimately, from converting the system to a monist structure of governance, which excludes political opposition.

Notes

1. See Christoph Hönnige, 'Beyond Judicialization: Why We Need More Comparative Research about Constitutional Courts', *European Political Science* 10, no. 3 (2011): 346.
2. Neil Tate and Torbjörn Vallinder, eds., *The Global Expansion of Judicial Power* (New York: NYU Press, 1995); Alec Stone Sweet, *Governing with Judges* (Oxford: OUP, 2000); Ran Hirschl, *Towards Juristocracy* (Cambridge: Harvard University Press, 2004).
3. I understand de-judicialization as a process aimed at preventing a court from reviewing a policy and from intervening in political issues which were previously judicialized.
4. David Kosař, Jiří Baroš, and Pavel Dufek, 'The Twin Challenges to Separation of Powers in Central Europe: Technocratic Governance and Populism', *European Constitutional Law Review* 15, no. 3 (2019): 429.
5. Ran Hirschl, 'Judicialization of Politics', in *The Oxford Handbook of Law and Politics*, eds. G. Caldeira, R.D. Kelemen, and K. Whittington (Oxford: OUP, 2008), 119.
6. Torbjörn Vallinder, 'When the Courts Go Marching In', in *The Global Expansion of Judicial Power*, eds. N. Tate and T. Vallinder (New York: NYU Press, 1995), 13.
7. Yaniv Roznai and Tamar Hostovsky Brandes, 'Democratic Erosion, Populist Constitutionalism and the Unconstitutional Constitutional Amendments Doctrine', *Law and Ethics of Human Rights* 14, no. 1 (2020).
8. Alec Stone Sweet, 'Judicialization and the Construction of Government', *Comparative Political Studies* 32, no. 2 (1999): 148.
9. Ibid.; Martin Shapiro, *Courts* (Chicago: University of Chicago Press, 1981), 1–2.
10. Allan Brewer-Carías, ed., *Constitutional Courts as Positive Legislators* (Cambridge: CUP, 2013), 153–64.
11. Other political actors, however, may have their interest in using judicial review of legislation too. See Lubomír Kopeček and Jan Petrov, 'From Parliament to Courtroom: Judicial Review of Legislation as a Political Tool in the Czech Republic', *East European Politics and Societies* 30, no. 1 (2016): 140.
12. Ran Hirschl, 'The New Constitutionalism and the Judicialization of Pure Politics', *Fordham Law Review* 75, no. 2 (2006–2007): 721.
13. Ibid.
14. Luís Roberto Barroso, 'Countermajoritarian, Representative, and Enlightened: The Roles of Constitutional Courts in Democracies', *American Journal of Comparative Law* 67, no. 1 (2019): 114.
15. Stone Sweet, 'Judicialization', 164.
16. Alec Stone Sweet, *Governing with Judges* (2000), 194–204.
17. Stone Sweet, 'Judicialization', 164.
18. Ibid., 158.
19. See Yaniv Roznai, *Unconstitutional Constitutional Amendments* (Oxford: OUP, 2017).
20. See, critically, Daniel Abebe and Tom Ginsburg, 'The Dejudicialization of International Politics?', *International Studies Quarterly* 63, no. 3 (2019): 524; Karen Alter, Emily Hafner-Burton and Laurence Helfer, 'Theorizing the Judicialization of International Relations', *International Studies Quarterly* 63, no. 3 (2019): 458; Doreen Lustig and Joseph Weiler, 'Judicial Review in the Contemporary World—Retrospective and Prospective', *ICON* 16, no. 2 (2018): 369.
21. E.g. John Ferejohn, 'Judicializing Politics, Politicizing Law', *Law and Contemporary Problems* 65, no. 3 (2002): 42; Stephen Gardbaum, 'Are Strong Constitutional Courts Always a Good Thing for New Democracies?' *Colum.J.Transnat'l L.* 53, no. 2 (2015): 306.

22. See the critique by Daniel Brinks and Abby Blass, 'Rethinking Judicial Empowerment: The New Foundations of Constitutional Justice', *ICON* 15, no. 2 (2017): 298; and Björn Dressel, 'Courts and Governance in Asia', *Hong Kong Law Journal* 42, no. 1 (2012): 95.
23. Andrea Pin, 'The Transnational Drivers of Populist Backlash in Europe: The Role of Courts,' *German Law Journal* 20, no. 2 (2019): 225; Yascha Mounk, *The People vs. Democracy* (Cambridge: Harvard University Press, 2018), 73.
24. Aziz Huq, 'The People against the Constitution', *Michigan Law Review* 116 (2017): 1132.
25. Cas Mudde, 'The Populist Zeitgeist', *Government and Opposition* 39, no. 4 (2004): 543.
26. Luigi Corrias, 'Populism in a Constitutional Key: Constituent Power, Popular Sovereignty and Constitutional Identity', *European Constitutional Law Review* 12, no. 1 (2016): 11.
27. Ben Stanley, 'The Thin Ideology of Populism', *Journal of Political Ideologies* 13, no. 1 (2008): 101.
28. Mudde, 'The Populist Zeitgeist', 555; Heike Krieger, 'Populist Governments and International Law', *EJIL* 30, no. 3 (2019): 971; Nadia Urbinati, 'The Populist Phenomenon', *Raisons Politiques* 51, no. 3 (2013): 147.
29. Oran Doyle, 'Populist Constitutionalism and Constituent Power', *German Law Journal* 20, no. 2 (2019): 162.
30. Kurt Weyland, 'Clarifying a Contested Concept: Populism in the Study of Latin American Politics', *Comparative Politics* 34, no. 1 (2001): 14.
31. Jan-Werner Müller, *What Is Populism?* (Philadelphia: University of Pennsylvania Press, 2016), 20.
32. Pippa Norris and Roger Inglehart, *Cultural Backlash: Trump, Brexit and the Rise of Authoritarian Populism* (Cambridge: CUP, 2018).
33. Andrew Arato, 'Socialism and Populism', *Constellations* 26, no. 3 (2019): 469.
34. David Fontana, 'Unbundling Populism', *UCLA Law Review* 65 (2018): 1482. See also Bojan Bugarič, 'Could Populism Be Good for Constitutional Democracy?', *Annual Review of Law and Social Science* 15 (2019): 41.
35. See Bojan Bugarič, 'Central Europe's Descent into Autocracy: A Constitutional Analysis of Authoritarian Populism', *ICON* 17, no. 2 (2019): 597; Tímea Drinóczi and Agnieszka Bień-Kacała, 'Illiberal Constitutionalism: The Case of Hungary and Poland', *German Law Journal* 20, no. 8 (2019): 1140.
36. Jan-Werner Müller, 'Populism and Constitutionalism', in *The Oxford Handbook of Populism*, C. Rovira Kaltwasser et al. (Oxford: OUP, 2017), 596.
37. *Id.*
38. Wojciech Sadurski, *Poland's Constitutional Breakdown* (Oxford: OUP. 2019), 132.
39. See Ben Stanley, 'Confrontation by Default and Confrontation by Design: Strategic and Institutional Responses to Poland's Populist Coalition Government', *Democratization* 23, no. 2 (2016): 273–4.
40. In this respect, see writings of the Hungarian and Polish authors cited below.
41. Müller, *What Is Populism?*
42. László Sólyom, 'The Rise and Decline of Constitutional Culture in Hungary', in *Constitutional Crisis in The European Constitutional Area*, eds. Armin von Bogdandy and Pál Sonnevend (London: Bloomsbury, 2015), 24.
43. Ibid., 23.
44. Katalin Kelemen, 'Appointment of Constitutional Judges in a Comparative Perspective – with a Proposal for a New Model for Hungary', *Acta Juridica Hungarica* 54, no. 1 (2013): 16.
45. Kim Lane Scheppele, 'Understanding Hungary's Constitutional Revolution', in *Constitutional Crisis in The European Constitutional Area*, eds. Armin von Bogdandy and Pál Sonnevend (London: Bloomsbury, 2015).
46. Gábor Halmai, 'Dismantling Constitutional Review in Hungary', *Rivista di Diritti Comparati* 3, no. 1 (2019): 35.
47. Scheppele, 'Understanding Hungary's', 115.

48. Sólyom, 'The Rise and Decline', 23. See also Zoltán Szente, 'The Political Orientation of the Members of the Hungarian Constitutional Court between 2010 and 2014', *Constitutional Studies* 1 (2016): 123.
49. Kim Lane Scheppele, 'Constitutional Coups and Judicial Review: How Transnational Institutions Can Strengthen Peak Courts at Times of Crisis', *Transnational Law and Contemporary Problems* 23 (2014): 72.
50. Scheppele, 'Understanding Hungary's', 116.
51. Article 24 (2) d) of the Fundamental Law of Hungary.
52. Fruzsina Gárdos-Orosz, 'The Hungarian Constitutional Court in Transition – from Actio Popularis to Constitutional Complaint', *Acta Juridica Hungarica* 53, no. 4 (2012): 302.
53. Halmai, 'Dismantling', 33–4.
54. Scheppele, 'Understanding Hungary's', 117.
55. Ibid.
56. Sólyom ('The Rise and Decline', 27) described the practice as 'permanent constitution-making'.
57. Ibid., 29.
58. See Scheppele, 'Constitutional Coups', 72 ff.
59. Sólyom, 'The Rise and Decline', 24.
60. Bojan Bugarič and Tom Ginsburg, 'The Assault on Postcommunist Courts', *Journal of Democracy* 27, no. 3 (2016): 73.
61. Neil Buckley and Henry Foy, 'Poland's New Government Finds a Model in Orban's Hungary', *Financial Times*, 6 January 2016, https://www.ft.com/content/0a3c7d44-b48e-11e5-8358-9a82b43f6b2f.
62. Stanley, 'Confrontation by Default'.
63. R. Daniel Kelemen and Mitchell Orenstein, 'Europe's Autocracy Problem: Polish Democracy's Final Days?', *Foreign Affairs*, 7 January, 2016, https://www.foreignaffairs.com/articles/poland/2016-01-07/europes-autocracy-problem.
64. 'Poland's Government Carries Through on Threat to Constitutional Court', *The Guardian*, 23 December 2015, https://www.theguardian.com/world/2015/dec/23/polands-government-carries-through-on-threat-to-constitutional-court.
65. Sadurski, *Poland's Constitutional Breakdown*, 61–79.
66. Wojciech Sadurski, 'How Democracy Dies (in Poland): A Case Study of Anti-Constitutional Populist Backsliding', *Revista Forumul Judecatorilor* 10, no. 1 (2018): 122.
67. Kelemen and Orenstein, 'Europe's Autocracy'.
68. The battle over the appointments was actually even more complicated. For details see Lech Garlicki, 'Constitutional Court and Politics: The Polish Crisis', in *Judicial Power*, ed. Christine Landfried (Cambridge: CUP, 2019), 146.
69. Wojciech Sadurski, 'Polish Constitutional Tribunal Under PiS: From an Activist Court, to a Paralysed Tribunal, to a Governmental Enabler', *Hague Journal on the Rule of Law* 11, no. 1 (2019): 68.
70. Ibid., 71.
71. Ibid., 72–3.
72. Bugarič and Ginsburg, 'The Assault', 73 and 74.
73. Tomasz Tadeusz Koncewicz, 'Understanding the Politics of Resentment', *Indiana Journal of Global Legal Studies* 26, no. 2 (2019): 501.
74. Tomasz Tadeusz Koncewicz, 'Of Institutions, Democracy, Constitutional Self-Defence and the Rule of Law', *Common Market Law Review* 53, no. 6 (2016): 1785; R. Daniel Kelemen, 'Europe's Other Democratic Deficit: National Authoritariansim in Europe's Democratic Union', *Government and Opposition* 52, no. 2 (2017): 228.
75. Sadurski, 'Polish Constitutional Tribunal', 71.
76. Ibid.
77. Ibid., 74.
78. Herman Schwartz, *The Struggle for Constitutional Justice in Post-Communist Europe* (Chicago: University of Chicago Press, 2000), 75, 106.

79. Radoslav Procházka, *Mission Accomplished: On Founding Constitutional Adjudication in Central Europe* (Budapest: CEU Press, 2002), 118–19.
80. Schwartz, *The Struggle*, 106.
81. Wojciech Sadurski, *Rights before Courts* (Dordrecht: Springer, 2014), 360.
82. Wen-Chen Chang, 'Back into the Political? Rethinking Judicial, Legal, and Transnational Constitutionalism', *ICON* 17, no. 2 (2019): 455; Gardbaum, 'Are Strong Constitutional Courts'. See also *supra* note 27.
83. Kosař, Baroš, and Dufek, 'The Twin Challenge', 444.
84. Ibid., 430.
85. Some court-curbing advocates argue that the actions taken against the HCC and the PCT merely mark a shift from legal to political constitutionalism, which stresses the parliamentary rule at the expense of strong judicial review. Others, such as Castillo-Ortiz and Halmai, however, have persuasively shown that the concept of political constitutionalism was simply hijacked to legitimize the populist attacks on constitutional courts. See Pablo Castillo-Ortiz, 'The Illiberal Abuse of Constitutional Courts in Europe', *European Constitutional Law Review* 15, no. 1 (2019): 63; Gábor Halmai, 'Populism, Authoritarianism and Constitutionalism', *German Law Journal* 20, no. 3 (2019): 302.
86. See Andrew Arato, 'Populism, Constitutional Courts, and Civil Society', in *Judicial Power*, ed. Christine Landfried (Cambridge: CUP, 2019), 318; Erik Voeten, 'Populism and Backlashes against International Courts', *Perspectives on Politics* 18, no. 2 (2020): 407.
87. Theoretically, constitutional courts can also decide to 'voluntarily' leave the field clear for populists and self-impose a self-restraint approach. However, I do not hypothesise if this would avoid populist court-curbing since both analysed courts initially fought against the populist regimes (see above). On courts' strategic considerations when facing a populist backlash see Yaniv Roznai, 'Who Will Save the Redheads? Towards an Anti-Bully Theory of Judicial Review and Protection of Democracy', *William & Mary Bill of Rights Journal* 29, no. 2 (2020): 327.
88. For my understanding of de-judicialization see *supra* note 4.
89. Such power includes not only the number of seats in the parliament, but also the level of public support, and the government's concern over international reputation.
90. *Supra* note 59.
91. Katalin Kelemen, 'Access to Constitutional Justice in the New Hungarian Constitutional Framework: Life after the Actio Popularis?', in *Law, Politics, and the Constitution: New Perspectives from Legal and Political Theory*, eds. Antonia Geisler, Michael Hein, and Siri Hummel (Frankfurt: Peter Lang, 2014), 64.
92. See the critical reactions of international actors summarised in Scheppele,'Constitutional Coups', 87–114.
93. I consider the Polish regime less consolidated than the Hungarian one since PiS possesses 'merely' a legislative majority. Moreover, there is a greater political and social plurality in Poland, and greater public support for the EU, therefore a greater concern for reputational costs. See Wojciech Sadurski, 'So, It's the End of Liberal Democracy? Think Again', *Euronews*, 16 April 2019, https://www.euronews.com/2019/04/16/so-it-s-the-end-of-liberal-democracy-think-again-view.
94. A legislative majority is sufficient for the paralysis technique if the procedural and organisational rules are enshrined in an ordinary statute and have not been constitutionalised.
95. Some of these measures, of course, can remain permanent.
96. For the sake of completeness, it should be noted that other techniques exist which might eventually lead to provisional de-judicialization, e.g. starving the court out by budgetary constraints. Effects of courts' interventions can also be evaded by serial non-compliance with their decisions or, alternatively, with overriding case law with constitutional amendments.
97. Depending on the scope and intensity of the techniques employed.
98. I understand politicisation as a process of parties capturing a state institution by party patronage [Petr Kopecký et al., *Party Patronage and Party Government in European*

Democracies (Oxford: OUP, 2012), 7]. The result of high politicisation is that 'judicial decision-making tends to become politics carried on by other means' (Ferejohn, 'Judicializing Politics', 64). For me, the crucial element leading to politicisation is *unilateral* control of judicial appointments by a particular faction outside the court (see also Brinks and Blass, 'Rethinking Judicial Empowerment', 307).

99. Brinks and Blass, 'Rethinking Judicial Empowerment', 299.

100. Following Brinks and Blass (ibid., 299), I understand autonomy as 'the extent to which a court is designed to be free from control by an identifiable faction or interest outside the court, both before the judges are seated, through the formal process of appointment [...], and after the judges have been seated, by formal means of punishing or rewarding judges'.

101. Scenarios in figures no. 2–4 presuppose that the populist party has enough power to choose the new judges on its own, without the necessity to seek agreement with another actor.

102. See Sólyom's ('The Rise and Decline', 23) and Sadurski's ('Polish Constitutional Tribunal', 71) assessements of the loyal judicial behaviour of the new judges appointed to HCC and PCT.

103. See above the reshuffling of the PCT's and HCC's chambers.

104. See Jan Petrov, 'The Populist Challenge to the European Court of Human Rights', *ICON* 18, no. 2 (2020): 499.

105. I have in mind *de facto* jurisdictional reach comprising the range of competences, access rules and factual operability of the court (capacity to reach a decision).

106. Brinks and Blass, 'Rethinking Judicial Empowerment', 299.

107. Ibid., 301; Dressel, 'Courts and Governance', 6.

108. See similarly David Landau and Rosalind Dixon, 'Abusive Judicial Review: Courts against Democracy', *UC Davis Law Review* 53 (2020): 1313.

109. Sadurski, 'Polish Constitutional Tribunal'.

110. Stanisław Biernat and Monika Kawczyńska, 'Though this Be Madness, Yet there's Method in't: Pitting the Polish Constitutional Tribunal against the Luxembourg Court', *Verfassungsblog*, 26 October 2018, https://verfassungsblog.de/though-this-be-madness-yet-theres-method-int-the-application-of-the-prosecutor-general-to-the-polish-constitutional-tribunal-to-declare-the-preliminary-ruling-procedure-unconstitut/.

111. Tomasz Tadeusz Koncewicz, '"Existential Judicial Review" in Retrospect, "Subversive Jurisprudence" in Prospect', *Reconnect*, 17 October 2018, https://reconnect-europe.eu/blog/existential-judicial-review-in-retrospect/.

112. Landau and Dixon, 'Abusive Judicial Review'. See also Raul Sanchez Urribarri, 'Courts between Democracy and Hybrid Authoritarianism: Evidence from the Venezuelan Supreme Court', *Law and Social Inquiry* 63, no. 4 (2011): 855 (referring to 'courts as instruments of political domination').

113. Castillo-Ortiz, 'The Illiberal Abuse', 67. See also Wojciech Brzozowski, 'Can the Constitutional Court Accelarate Democratic Backsliding? Lessons from the Polish Experience', in *The Role of Courts in Contemporary Legal Orders*, ed. Martin Belov (Hague: Eleven, 2019), 371, at 377 (referring to the PCT as a 'silent helper of the political branches of government').

114. Anna Śledzińska-Simon, 'The Rise and Fall of Judicial Self-Government in Poland', *German Law Journal* 19, no. 7 (2018): 1848.

115. PCT, judgment of 20 June 2017, no. K 5/17.

116. Sadurski, 'Polish Constitutional Tribunal', 78.

117. Aleksandra Kustra-Rogatka, 'Populist but Not Popular: The Abortion Judgment of the Polish Constitutional Tribunal', *Verfassungsblog*, 3 November 2020, https://verfassungsblog.de/populist-but-not-popular/.

118. HCC, judgment of 5. 12. 2016, no. 22/2016. See Gábor Halmai, 'Abuse of Constitutional Identity. The Hungarian Constitutional Court on Interpretation of Article E) (2) of the Fundamental Law', *Review of CEE Law* 43, no. 1 (2018): 23.

119. Kacper Majewski, 'Will Poland, With Its Own Constitution Ablaze, Now Set Fire to EU Law?', *Verfassungsblog*, 17 October 2018, https://verfassungsblog.de/will-poland-with-its-

own-constitution-ablaze-now-set-fire-to-eu-law/; Biernat and Kawczyńska, 'Though this Be Madness'.

120. On populists' resistance to international law and international courts see Voeten, 'Populism and Backlashes'; Petrov, 'The Populist Challenge'; Tamar Hostovsky Brandes, 'International Law in Domestic Courts in an Era of Populism', *ICON* 17, no. 2 (2019): 576; Mikael Madsen, Pola Cebulak, and Micha Wiebusch, 'Backlash against International Courts', *International Journal of Law in Context* 14, no. 2 (2018): 197.

121. Szente, for example, showed that most post-2010 appointees in Hungary usually do not vote against the government, yet there is some variance among them. See Szente, 'The Political Orientation'.

122. Gretchen Helmke, 'The Logic of Strategic Defection: Court-Executive Relations in Argentina under Dictatorship and Democracy', *American Political Science Review* 96, no. 2 (2002): 291.

123. The Venezuelan Supreme Tribunal, for instance, guarded the populist president Maduro against the oppositional majority in the National Assembly. See Landau and Dixon, 'Abusive Judicial Review'. However, it should be noted that this is a specific case since Venezuela is a presidential system. Therefore, the government does not have to leave when it loses the parliamentary majority. Moreover, the pro-presidential forces won the controversial election to the National Assembly in 2020.

124. See Hirschl's ('Towards Juristocracy') hegemonic preservation theory.

125. I am thankful to the anonymous reviewer for pointing my attention to the role of the opposition. On deformation of the parliamentary processes by authoritarian populists see e.g. Viktor Kazai, 'Le renforcement du contrôle de la procédure législative. Une stratégie proposée aux Cours constitutionnelles opérant dans un système populist', *Annuaire International de Justice Constitutionnelle* 34 (2019): 765.

126. R. Daniel Kelemen, 'The Political Foundations of Judicial Independence in the European Union', *Journal of European Public Policy* 19, no. 1 (2012): 43–4.

127. Steven Levitsky and Daniel Ziblatt, *How Democracies Die* (New York: Crown, 2018), 101.

128. Maria Popova, *Politicized Justice in Emerging Democracies* (Cambridge: CUP, 2012), 23–4.

129. Fryderyk Zoll and Leah Wortham, 'Judicial Independence and Accountability: Withstanding Political Stress in Poland', *Fordham International Law Journal* 42, no. 3 (2019): 904–7.

130. Tom Ginsburg and Tamir Moustafa, eds., *Rule by Law: The Politics of Courts in Authoritarian Regimes* (Cambridge: CUP, 2008).

131. Aziz Huq and Tom Ginsburg, 'How to Lose a Constitutional Democracy', *UCLA Law Review* 65, no. (2018): 93.

132. Adam Przeworski, *Crises of Democracy* (Cambridge: CUP, 2019), 134.

133. Kim Lane Scheppele, 'The Opportunism of Populists and the Defense of Constitutional Liberalism', *German Law Journal* 20, no. 3 (2019): 314.

134. Tom Ginsburg and Aziz Huq, *How to Save a Constitutional Democracy* (2019), 43.

135. Accordingly, scholars refer to abusive constitutionalism [David Landau, 'Abusive Constitutionalism', *UC Davis Law Review* 47, no. 1 (2013): 189], legal instrumentalism [Paul Blokker, 'Populism as a Constitutional Project', *ICON* 17, no. 2 (2019): 535], and autocratic legalism [Kim Lane Scheppele, 'Autocratic Legalism', *University of Chicago Law Review* 85, no. 2 (2018): 545] as typical features of populist constitutionalism.

136. N.W. Barber, 'Populist Leaders and Political Parties', *German Law Journal* 20, no. 2 (2019): 130.

137. Halmai, 'Populism, Authoritarianism and Constitutionalism'.

138. 'Full text of Viktor Orbán's speech at Băile Tuşnad (Tusnádfürdő) of 26 July 2014', *Budapest Beacon*, 29 July 2014, https://budapestbeacon.com/full-text-of-viktor-orbans-speech-at-baile-tusnad-tusnadfurdo-of-26-july-2014/.

139. Christian Davies, 'Poland Is "On Road to Autocracy", Says Constitutional Court President', *The Guardian*, 18 December 2016, https://www.theguardian.com/world/2016/dec/18/poland-is-on-road-to-autocracy-says-high-court-president.

140. See Urribarri, 'Courts between Demcoracy', 858.

141. Clark, 'The Separation of Powers'; David Kosař and Katarína Šipulová, 'How to Fight Court-Packing?', *Constitutional Studies* 6 (2020): 133.
142. See Mark Tushnet, 'After the Heroes Have Left the Scene: Temporality in the Study of Constitutional Court Judges', in *Judicial Power*, ed. Christine Landfried (Cambridge: CUP, 2019), 300.
143. See Part 4 (describing the messy personnel situation at the PCT in late 2015 and 2016).
144. See Part 4 (describing the change of the appointment procedure to the HCC).
145. See Renáta Uitz, 'Can You Tell When an Illiberal Democracy Is in the Making? An Appeal to Comparative Constitutional Scholarship from Hungary', *ICON* 13, no. 1 (2015): 279.
146. Arato, 'Populism, Constitutional Courts', 322.
147. Jeremy Waldron, 'The Core of the Case Against Judicial Review', *Yale Law Journal* 115, no. 6 (2006): 1346.
148. See Lustig and Weiler, 'Judicial Review', 339–41.
149. Paul Yowell, *Constitutional Rights and Constitutional Design* (Oxford: Hart, 2018).
150. Castillo-Ortiz ('The Illiberal Abuse', 70) depicts captured constitutional courts as devices of 'de-normativisation of the constitution'.
151. Samuel Isacharoff, 'Constitutional Courts and Democratic Hedging', *Georgetown Law Journal* 99 (2011): 961.

Acknowledgements

I am grateful to Nick Barber, John Ferejohn, Gábor Halmai, Ondřej Kadlec, David Kosař, Hubert Smekal, to the participants in 2019 Law in Context Workshop (Oxford University), JUSTIN Research Meeting (Masaryk University), and PopCon conference on Populist Transformation of Constitutional Law (2021) for their comments, which have significantly improved this text. I am also thankful to the YCC Scholarship Exchange Program organised by the American Society of Comparative Law. The research leading to this article has received funding from the European Research Council (ERC) under the European Union's Horizon 2020 research and innovation programme (grant number 678375 JUDI-ARCH ERC-2015-STG).

Disclosure statement

No potential conflict of interest was reported by the author(s).

Funding

The research leading to this article has received funding from the European Research Council (ERC) under the European Union's Horizon 2020 research and innovation programme (grant number 678375 JUDI-ARCH ERC-2015-STG).

ORCID

Jan Petrov http://orcid.org/0000-0001-9445-596X

Authoritarian populism, conceptions of democracy, and the Hungarian Constitutional Court: the case of political participation[*]

Max Steuer ⓘ

ABSTRACT

Authoritarian populist actors rhetorically embrace a conception of democracy as unconstrained majority rule. The majoritarian conception of democracy challenges the role of independent constitutional courts as institutions safeguarding fundamental rights and the rule of law beyond majority rule. This article highlights how the tension between the countermajoritarian rationale of constitutional courts and them embracing a majoritarian conception of democracy provides an opening for the political success of authoritarian populists. The tension is particularly pertinent in decisions on petitions submitted by authoritarian populists, who themselves tend to invoke majoritarian democracy. Empirically, the article studies how the Hungarian Constitutional Court conceptualised democracy in the context of political participation leading up to the pivotal 2010 elections, which paved the way towards the rise of authoritarian populism in Hungary. Employing contextual analysis of decisions referring to democracy in relation to political participation, it shows that, even before the changes adopted by the post-2010 parliamentary majority, the Hungarian Court embraced a majoritarian conception of democracy in this segment of its decision making. Consequently, the Court's conception of democracy fed into authoritarian populist rhetoric. The findings caution courts when interpreting the meaning(s) of democracy and emphasise the potential and limits of judicial responses to authoritarian populism.

1. Introduction

> Every year new books and articles appear on democracy and constitutional judicial review. The stream is not going to stop because many people who like democracy also like judicial review, and try as many of them might, it is not possible to render the two compatible. (Martin Shapiro)[1]

Contemporary constitutional courts (CCs) went well beyond the roles envisioned for them by their ideational father, Hans Kelsen.[2] Today, a CC[3] is the last resort that can

---

[*]All translations from Hungarian are the author's, unless indicated otherwise.

ⓘ Supplemental data for this article can be accessed https://doi.org/10.1080/13642987.2021.1968379.

reverse human rights violations at the domestic level. Such violations include exclusion from participation in the decisions of the community that the individual is a member of through elections and other forms of political involvement.[4] Yet, as Martin Shapiro's statement, articulated by others as the 'countermajoritarian difficulty',[5] emphasises, the range of competences some CCs have at their disposal[6] raises doubts about the compatibility of CCs' operations with democracy. In this picture, the rights-protecting function of the CCs is in tension with further democratisation and with the prevention of deterioration of democracy, mirroring a broader 'decoupling' between human rights and democracy.[7]

If democracy is sharply separated from human rights, the door is left wide open for challengers of CCs and constitutionalism (which builds on the centrality of human rights protection in a democratic context) more broadly. Prominent among these challenges are authoritarian populists: actors who rhetorically invoke the 'rule of the people' as the founding pillar of democracy while, in fact, they aim to gain control over state institutions and remove the possibility for the people to vote them out of office.[8] Independent CCs can considerably complicate authoritarian populists' strategies,[9] and hence they are a prime target.[10] Moreover, in the European Union context, an alliance between CCs and authoritarian populists might be particularly useful for the latter to challenge the rule of law and fundamental rights claims stemming from supranational courts such as the European Court of Human Rights[11] or the Court of Justice of the EU.[12]

Existing scholarship overwhelmingly focuses on what other actors (authoritarian populist or not) can 'do' to CCs.[13] While this literature brings important insights on the capacity of other actors to resist these trends, there is a gap in examining the CCs' capacities (or lack thereof) to resist authoritarian populists' advances, both before and after constitutional transformations that contribute to autocratisation.[14] This article contributes to filling this gap by exploring how particular conceptions of democracy as embraced by the CCs in their decision-making may advance or hamper (1) the success of authoritarian populists and (2) the CCs' own standing as guardians of democracy understood in conjunction with fundamental rights. The key conceptual claim, rooted in scholarship of interpretive institutionalism, is that minimalist, majoritarian conceptions of democracy advanced by CCs tend to undermine CCs' own standing in the political regime. Even more, embracing these conceptions may help authoritarian populists to gain or retain access to power. Consequently, a CC willing to maximise its capacity to prevent authoritarian populists' advances should turn to more robust conceptions of democracy.

The empirical support for this claim is provided by an analysis of the conceptions of democracy embraced by the Hungarian Constitutional Court (HCC) since its establishment until 2017[15] in cases concerning political participation (predominantly elections and referenda). These cases are examined because they overlap precisely with the components of democracy frequently emphasised by authoritarian populists as based on the principle of majority rule: elections and other forms of expression of the popular will.[16] Hungary is placed centre-stage because it provides a 'living experiment' of a democratic regime that underwent an autocratic transformation.[17] The HCC itself has been hailed as a crucial institution of democratic transition in the 1990s,[18] but has significantly departed from that image since then. Was the HCC indeed powerless to respond to authoritarian populist advances before the adoption of the Hungarian Fundamental Law by the Orbán-led coalition, and does it have any remaining leeway to challenge authoritarian populism? Cases concerning political participation, some of which concerned initiatives of the supporters of PM Viktor Orbán, provide important evidence for the purpose of answering these questions.

Utilising a contextual approach, the article finds that the HCC has embraced a majoritarian understanding of democracy close to the one presented by authoritarian populists[19] ahead of the crucial 2010 Hungarian parliamentary elections. As a result, the Court made it easier for an unchecked majority to arise and make opportunistic use of referenda as an important avenue of political participation. In the subsequent years, the HCC continued to embrace a majoritarian conception of democracy, but, somewhat self-contradictorily, it coupled this conception with a wide leeway for governmental action in political participation cases. What could have started as an honest ideational disagreement over the role of the Court and the conceptions of democracy that should prevail in Hungary resulted in the judicial majority embracing a majoritarian, rather than countermajoritarian stance, that proved detrimental for resisting authoritarian populists and for the Court's capacity to act as a guardian of democracy.

2. Constitutional courts, political participation and conceptions of democracy

Democracy is a fundamental, if not even founding, principle for constitutional interpretation. As Gottlieb put it, 'the fact that everyone's theory of interpretation is based on democracy implies that courts should protect democracy'.[20] The popularity of the 'democracy talk' has generated a virtually unending variety of conceptions of democracy that make general references to the concept possible in excessively different contexts.[21] Consequently, it is necessary to lay down at least a foundational framework for analysis of the differences between key conceptions of democracy with an emphasis on the role of participation rights in these conceptions.

Existing indexes trying to measure the type and quality of political regimes today[22] provide inspiration for this endeavour. Most of them apply minimalist conceptions of democracy, that revolve around the centrality of open political contestation for public offices.[23] However, minimalist conceptions allow too many divergent cases to use the label 'democracy', resulting in the need to 'add attributes to a concept as a way to give it more content and thus better address relevant theoretical concerns and discriminate among cases'.[24] From the perspective of studying CCs' decision-making, the emphasis on political contestation only fails to account for a broader space of CC action, and feeds into the 'countermajoritarian rhetoric' of CCs undermining open democratic contestation by exercising their powers. Consequently, a broader and more inclusive conception of democracy is needed for one to analyse CCs' capacity to address their competing interpretations. This article relies on middle-range conceptions that go beyond equating democracy with majority rule.[25] These conceptions are far from exhausting the full content of democracy that a maximalist conception could bring forward; yet, the maximalist conception faces criticisms of 'overburdening the concept'[26] and introduces output-based elements to democracy[27] that go beyond the political participation cases discussed in this article.

Middle-range conceptions establish a vital connection between democracy, rule of law and fundamental rights protection as well as acknowledge that institutionalised political participation is vital for democracy.[28] If individuals were not willing to get involved in politics through electing their representatives and deciding on key public matters submitted to them, those few with access to most resources would retain unchecked control over the direction of the polity (if such a constellation could be considered a polity at all). Elections are the bedrock of democracy, and so invoking the principle of free and fair decision-making procedure on the representatives of the polity remains a key component of democratic theory and fundamental rights standards, even if, on their own, elections do not exclude majority tyranny.[29]

Thus, elections are a necessary, but insufficient component of participatory democracy. If a CC understands democracy only in the context of free and fair elections, it embraces a minimalist (majoritarian) conception, at the detriment of minority opinions which, at times, might advocate for more robust standards of fundamental rights protection. The challenge with not connecting democracy to participation other than elections is precisely the impossibility of the minorities to win them, and realise their ideas for political reform.[30] Moreover, the disconnect might lead to artificial separation of arguments about participation as a component of democracy in the CCs' reasoning. If democracy does not end at the ballot box, but encompasses constant popular involvement in decision making, political participation between elections comes to the surface as its substantial component as well.[31] Referenda are a key instrument for fostering the involvement of citizens in decision making in addition to election. Yet they do not exhaust the conception of participatory democracy, which includes rights-related decisions that broaden the freedom of information, assembly, speech, emphasising the collective rather than individual features of these rights.[32]

The majoritarian conceptions as well as the participatory conception can be grouped under the umbrella term of direct democracy. The dispute between direct democracy and its counterpart, representative democracy, goes back thousands of years to ancient Greece, where democracy unbound was perceived by philosophers such as Plato and Aristotle as one of the bad forms of government.[33] When dealing with agendas such as the permissibility of certain questions to be asked through a referendum, or the scope of electoral rights (censuses based on age, criminal conviction or education), CCs need to engage in finding a balance between these two components and their justification might have wide-ranging consequences given the significance of many cases related to elections (sometimes up to deciding on who gets to govern the country) or referenda (that might go as far as to deciding on the form of constitutional order). Notably, only minimalist democracy can be used by authoritarian populists to advance unconstrained majoritarianism; participatory democracy is resilient to such advances because it is equally concerned with participation of minorities and assesses it in the context of the available avenues for meaningful involvement in the public sphere of the given political regime (see Figure 1).

Before summing up, a brief note on deliberative democracy as a conception of democracy that has achieved a prominent position in the literature is in order.[34] Deliberation as 'mutual communication that involves weighing and reflecting on preferences, values, and interests regarding matters of common concern'[35] is a stand-alone concept that can be employed in other than democratic realities. In a democracy, however, equal concern

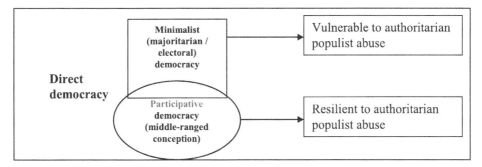

Figure 1. The distinction between minimalist and participative conceptions of direct democracy in terms of their proneness to abuse by authoritarian populist actors. The spheres of minimalist and participatory democracy partially overlap because participatory democracy includes elections within the conception of democracy. Source: author.

and respect must guide the deliberative process, enabling all voices to be heard and different viewpoints (at least as long as they do not incite violence) to be heard and be potentially influential.[36] The relationship between participative and deliberative democracy is a contested one.[37] Nonetheless, for the purposes of examining CCs' engagement with democracy on questions of political participation, it is not necessary to separate the participative and deliberative 'faces' of democracy. Following Pateman,[38] participation alone entails more than voting and majoritarian calculation of preferences, and can accommodate a range of other instruments helping to realise citizens' political rights (such as participatory budgeting).

What kind of reasoning of the CCs, then, confirms their falling for a minimalist perception of democracy, as opposed to a robust commitment to free and fair elections combined with additional elements of the democratic regime? How should we expect CCs to talk about democracy in the context of, say, review of electoral complaints, so that they avoid the 'majoritarian' label? A distinction should be made between perceiving participation as a tool for pushing through the majority will as opposed to the means for improved equality of the involvement of all members of the political community in the decision making. In other words, if participation is perceived as an amplifier of political rights and equality, then it would be unjustified to 'accuse' CCs of going 'the majoritarian way' in their reasoning just because they connect democracy to participation in cases that by all means relate to participation more than to other dimensions of democracy. In this sense, political participation builds on minimalist accounts which 'can accommodate a broader notion of participation than is typically supposed'.[39] At the same time, minimalist accounts remain confined to majority rule of the citizens (including in processes such as participatory budgeting), and so conceptualisations of democracy placing fundamental rights and the rule of law centre-stage are equally important for developing a participatory conception of democracy.

3. Constitutional courts' conceptions of democracy: an interpretive institutionalist framework

Studying conceptions of democracy by the CCs is important because it provides insights into how the CCs perceive their institutional role which may pose a significant constraint for their capacity to identify and enhance democracy. The theoretical perspective of interpretive new institutionalism is particularly helpful in supporting this claim. Interpretive institutionalism is a strand of 'new institutionalism'[40] that recognises the ability of independent political action by institutions. Institutions (such as CCs), defined as 'collections of interrelated rules and routines' have capacity to substantially influence political development, for instance, by 'chang[ing] the distribution of political interests, resources and rules by creating new actors and identities [...]'.[41] The actors in these institutions, such as the judges of the CCs, can shape these rules through various mechanisms including judicial review of legislation, constitutional interpretation or decisions on complaints of individual citizens and associations about alleged human rights violations. Yet, the basic competences and decision-making procedures are set outside the CCs' purview and even CCs have a hard time to explicitly deviate from them.

This institutional logic underpins theorising in the fields closely related to public law. 'Public law institutionalists' are interested in both long-term and short-term 'causal processes' that may lead to 'transformative moments' on the one hand and 'responses of political institutions, actors and voters to the challenges these processes throw up' on the other hand.[42] Key decisions of CCs at these transformative moments are a fruitful object of study in this tradition. Interpretive institutionalism can be useful with regard to the role of ideas that emerge in the decision-making processes in and by political institutions. This institutionalist theory attempts to capture the subtle processes of change which unfold not only within institutions themselves but also with regard to their impact on polities. Such a perspective recognises that 'certain settings hold a sense of appropriateness about what kinds of behaviors or motivations are considered acceptable under certain circumstances'.[43]

Applying interpretive institutionalism to identify these contexts and norms, then, implies the recognition of a 'constitutive conception of law',[44] where legal rules and principles are able to shape individual beliefs and actions. This, while it may seem as a step towards returning to the formal-legal analysis carried out by 'old' institutionalisms,[45] is a step forward because it places law and politics not into a hierarchical relationship of dependence of the former on the latter, but into a mutually constitutive relationship between the legal rules and outcomes.

That CCs may have impact on the political regimes can hardly be doubted but it remains far from clear how this impact works and what channels it is transmitted through. Still, focusing on the fundamental justification of their existence (safeguarding and enhancing democracy) makes it possible to formulate questions able to elucidate this impact. Such questions start with identification of the approach of the courts, allegedly possessing only output and procedural, but not input legitimacy,[46] to democratic regime in its varieties. Subsequently, they continue with searching for the reasons for having such an approach, its shifts in time (understood as changes in the composition of judges and electoral terms, but without ignoring potentially critical single, non-repeatable events) and from country to country.

Using this framework, this article zooms in on the Hungarian Constitutional Court's understandings of political participation in relation to democracy to evaluate its capacity to respond to or, vice versa, facilitate majoritarian readings of democracy presented by authoritarian populists. It uses a sample of 49 HCC majority decisions and 27 separate opinions concerning political participation out of the full population of 231 HCC majority and separate opinions explicitly including the keyword 'democracy' between

1990 and September 2017.[47] The cases typically pertain to competences specific to elections,[48] particularly the review of the certification of referendum petitions as decided by the National Electoral Commission (NEC). Yet, as participation-related disputes might also occur when CCs execute some of their standard competences such as individual complaints or constitutional review of legislations, some cases (e.g. the interpretation of electoral legislation) belong to this traditional domain of CC activity.

The results show that the HCC, on balance, leaned towards a majoritarian notion of democracy in the context of political participation cases during the period under scrutiny. Moreover, at a crucial moment, it endorsed a conception of democracy advantageous to authoritarian populists in their quest for unchecked majorities to decide on behalf of 'the people'. The analysis provides an alternative to the countermajoritarian difficulty discourse and refocuses scholarly attention on the capacities of CCs to be central actors in struggles for democracy.

4. The Hungarian Constitutional Court's struggle for participative democracy: openings for authoritarian populist abuse

During the 1990s, the Hungarian Constitutional Court came to be known as one of the most powerful institutions of its kind worldwide, thanks to its extensive review powers that it was willing to use to advance robust notions of international human rights compatible with (and sometimes going beyond) international standards.[49] Its decision making became synonymous with judicial activism[50] and the model of 'legal' as opposed to 'political' constitutionalism.[51] It was composed of eleven judges until the increase to 15 judges in the aftermath of the post-2010 constitutional changes. These changes prompted concerns by several authorities including the Venice Commission.[52] Several competences of the Court have gradually been curtailed, including the competence to substantively review the constitutionality of referendum questions.[53] The appointment procedure was changed significantly in 2011 from a model supporting the influence of all parliamentary parties on the composition of the Court (even in case of a constitutional majority held by a single party) to one that significantly favours the influence of the parliamentary majority.[54] This means that before and in the years immediately after 2010 the majority of the judges were still appointed according to the previous model. The newly appointed judges gradually gained majority and have constituted the full composition of the Court since 2013.

Because of this political context, Hungary represents a suitable case to study how a CC might respond to situations in which authoritarian populist notions of democracy are invoked that restrict the meaning of democracy to majority rule through elections and referenda. Even if the terminology and interpretations invoked by the Court at the time of writing are sometimes seen as affected by all its judges having received the endorsement of Viktor Orbán's Alliance of Young Democrats (Fidesz),[55] this was not the case in the years leading up to the enactment of the new Hungarian Constitution (Fundamental Law) and in the years thereafter. The following analysis embraces the distinction between pre-2010 and post-2010 case law not because of a fundamental change in the composition of the Court, but because of the change of the political context—the constitutional majority obtained by Viktor Orbán, who was a key actor in some of the most difficult cases concerning the scope and context of popular participation in a democracy that Court had engaged with. The period before the landmark parliamentary elections can, for the purposes of explication, be split to that of the 1990s, dominated by the Constitutional Court presided by László Sólyom, and the new millennium, in which the Court had to grapple with President Sólyom's legacy. Last but not least, while majority opinions contain the legally binding verdicts of the Court, separate opinions are essential in highlighting the differences between the reasoning of individual judges, and are the source of alternative arguments and case outcomes that may be used in the future.[56] Consequently, a separate subsection is devoted to the latter, highlighting how the readiness of the Court to embrace a majoritarian conception of democracy favourable to Orbán's populist rhetoric was not a result of unanimous views on the bench.

4.1. Majority decisions before 2010

The evidence from the HCC case law of the 1990s shows a priority for representative democracy, with limited space for a participatory conception. Thus, already in 1990, the Court explained that the purpose of direct democracy is 'the direct influence of the citizen over the matters of her concern'.[57] Hence, a 'democratic institutional system' operates as a conundrum of the proper function of the parliament, the referendum, public initiatives and constitutional judging.[58] Subsequently, the Court advocated a 'trusteeship model' of representation by prohibiting the possibility to organise referenda on recalling acting deputies.[59] In Halmai's view, 'this approach essentially reflects the liberal position that in a democratic state governed by rule of law the power derived from the people is exercised through constitutional organs, primarily representative bodies'.[60] The arguments of a multiparty system and parliamentary (i.e. representative) democracy justified the approval of the dissolution of a political party which does not propose any candidates for two subsequent general elections.[61] The free execution of the mandate of deputies was enhanced by a subsequent decision on the right to establish parliamentary party groups, that emerges from the 'two pillars of parliamentary democracy: the free mandate and equality of the deputies on the one hand and the specific tasks of the parties on the other hand'.[62] None of these decisions can be argued to advance an excessively minimalist conception of democracy; they simply show the appeal of the conception of democracy in its representative mutation, with a key role for the legislature and the political parties, as opposed to calls for the people's direct, unconstrained rule.

In a second, smaller set of decisions before 2000, the Court broadened the notion of democracy in relation to participation, but only in very specific and limited ways. One pertained to local democracy, where, for the Court, 'democracy under the rule of law[63] entailed a 'functional democracy' with certain powers reserved for local self-governance.[64] The other concerned the significance of obligatory before facultative referendum in case of a conflict between the two.[65] But even here, the reasoning showed signs of concern on the abuse of the instrument of (facultative) referendum by political parties which would aim to undermine an obligatory referendum.[66]

These contradictory directions can be observed post-2000 as well but with only very few new ideas. Firstly, references to 'party democracy' in terms of the essential role of political parties[67] and to the primacy of representative democracy (especially in cases affirming the rejection of proposals for referenda)[68] have been frequent in the case law of the HCC led by János Németh and, subsequently, András Holló.[69] A second, more original argument, was on elections as a cornerstone of democracy. In a decision concerning campaign silence periods, the Court argued that 'an indispensable condition of a political regime based on democracy is a stable, lawful and predictably functioning electoral system'.[70] Thirdly, in addition to the significance of the elections for the formation of the government, the Court also recognised the significance for an electoral participation for '[…] a successful outcome [of] the elections [in] a representative democracy'.[71] While these cases underscore the significance of elections, they do not signal a move towards participatory democracy approached through the lens of equality or fundamental rights.

After 2005, the initiatives of two political parties, Fidesz and the Christian Democratic People's Party (KDNP), prompted the Court to specify its conception of the relationship between direct and representative democracy.[72] The referendum-related cases that included at least a single reference to democracy form just a fraction of all cases the HCC had to deal with. This absence of more frequent references is evidence in itself; the HCC was able to justify and discuss complex decisions evaluating the certification or rejection of referendum petitions submitted to the NEC without discussing democracy. Moreover, references to democracy tend to appear in those cases that enhanced the scope for referendum in the Hungarian legal system, a change which Halmai reads as inconsistent with earlier HCC practice and potentially 'politically motivated'.[73]

When democracy was invoked, however, it tended to be in a way that placed the Court's verdicts and reasoning into an unresolvable tension. While the reasoning of the Court did not challenge the prioritisation of representative democracy, the verdicts themselves were largely supportive of the realisation of the referenda. For example, the Court quashed the NEC's decision that refused to validate the referendum petition on the abolishment of the daily hospital fee for hospitalised patients.[74] Along similar lines, it narrowly interpreted the prohibition to launch a referendum on the government manifesto (in relation to a question concerning the financing of higher education) and ordered the NEC a new proceeding.[75] The Court also ordered a new proceeding after the NEC had rejected a petition for public referendum on a special fee paid for visitation of physicians, dentists and home treatment of patients by medical staff.[76] Last but not least, it endorsed a Fidesz-KDNP-initiated referendum on the state or local government ownership of healthcare institutions.[77]

As a consequence of such decisions, the 'dormant mine' of the referenda went off in 2008 with the 'Social Referendum' that helped the Fidesz-KDNP coalition led by Viktor Orbán succeed in the 2010 elections.[78] Albeit the Court gave effect to more favourable view of direct democracy in these decisions,[79] it did not accompany these with substantive justifications, giving rise to a peculiar 'doublespeak' between the two components of the decisions. Hence, it was simple to read direct democracy in a minimalist, majoritarian fashion, as opposed to advancing a more participatory conception that would incorporate safeguards against partisan abuse of the referenda.

The subsequent years under President Paczolay continue to document this tension between referring to democracy as a means of limitation of popular decision-making between elections and verdicts often favourable to majoritarian democracy via referenda. In 2009, the HCC asserted that the so-called 'approval referendum'[80] does not permit the citizens to bind the National Assembly to repeal an act or some of its parts.[81] The HCC embedded the referendum in representative democracy elements by attributing constitutional significance to the fact that the provisions regulating the referendum were part of the section of the Constitution dealing with the National Assembly.[82]

A similar prevalence of majoritarian, minimalist democracy, though without the tension between direct and representative iterations of democracy is observable in the Court's majority decision on campaign financing. Here, the judges reiterated the crucial position of political parties and the free and fair competition among them, in a parliamentary democracy.[83] Similar arguments appear in a few other cases in this period.[84] Yet, at this point, the basis for authoritarian populist claims had been laid down in the key cases that permitted the Fidesz-KDNP-orchestrated referenda to go ahead. The general lesson emerging from this development is that inconsistencies in a few key cases have the potential to undermine more than a decade of consistent reasoning (in this case, for the prevalence of representative democracy).

4.2. Majority decisions after 2010

As of 2010, the Court had to deal with petitions trying to stop Viktor Orbán's transformation of the constitutional system with the help of the judicial power. On the subject of referenda, the Court approved the rejection of a petition for a referendum on the new Hungarian Constitution where the petitioners pleaded for using direct democracy to give a public affirmation to the basic law.[85] Admittedly, it would have been difficult for the Court to reach an opposite conclusion, given that, between the submission of the petition and the decision making of the HCC, the possibility to decide via referenda on amendments to the constitution was explicitly banned in the new Fundamental Law. Nevertheless, it remains striking that the judges did not engage with the issue more thoroughly; the substantive discussion in the decision has barely two pages. Via this petition, the HCC had the opportunity to explore, at least *obiter dictum*, the implications of a constitutional ban on referendum on constitutional amendments for the relationship between direct and representative democracy in the Hungarian constitutional order.[86]

In 2016, the Court first approved the decision of the National Assembly on the public consultation on 'migration' and then invalidated the Supreme Court's verdict on the financing of the public consultation. In the former decision, it referred to the right of the National Assembly to decide for some questions to be regulated by 'direct democracy'.[87] Starting as a *tabula rasa,* without discussion of its previous case law on the subject, the Court did not cover the factual implications and eventually inconsistencies in the decision on the public consultation itself, not to mention the procedural rules surrounding it. In the decision on financing the public consultation, it sided with the NEC instead. Here, public broadcasting on behalf of the government before the consultation served 'the public interest [so that] the institution of public consultation fulfils its function [and] in the given question direct democracy can be realised'.[88] The HCC, therefore, did not see an issue with those opposing the public consultation (including the formulation of the questions) not having equal broadcasting space and public resources available for presenting their position.[89] In short, in both decisions, the 'doublespeak' of supporting direct democracy in the verdict and representative democracy in the justification has given way to a conception where direct democracy is free to be shaped and moulded by the executive.

The case law on electoral affairs referring to democracy confirms the view that the Court appeared ready to place the 'management of direct democracy' into the hands of the ruling majority. Its January 2013 decision declaring the unconstitutionality of the voter registration and the restrictions on political campaigns was hailed as the triumphant 'return' of the Court despite the advances of authoritarian populism.[90] The Judge Rapporteur, István Stumpf, argued extraconstitutionally that the decision on voter registration 'should have created a balance in the system of the separation of powers between the forces of political constitutionality and legal constitutionality'.[91] The decision was seen as successful in that the government did not adopt voter registration as a constitutional provision. Yet, the compartmentalisation of the rule of law principle (associated with 'legal constitutionality') and the democracy principle (associated with 'political constitutionality') in the verdict remains conducive to a majoritarian, minimalist conception of democracy.[92] Similarly, a later case that invalidated elements of the electoral regime for elections of some members of the Budapest capital city council[93] featured a reference to democracy through the articulation of the 'one person, one vote' principle.[94] In sum, the HCC developed continuous support for the prevalence of parliamentary democracy together with putting forward a number of arguments for allowing decisions through the instruments of direct democracy.

As a core takeaway, the differences between and therefore the limits of direct and representative democracy were blurred in the core decisions concerning the referenda, resulting in the tilting of the conception of democracy towards a simple majority principle. This allowed authoritarian populist actors to carry through questionable agendas via submitting them to referenda and to public consultations. The referenda were not always successful as to the result desired by these parties, but they managed to carry the attention of the public and the media. Later, the HCC extended the gap between majority rule and equal participation in a democracy by avoiding the discussion on the inherent connection between the management of political campaigns and democracy, thus weakening ideas of inclusive participation as a component of democracy even further. This development points to the dangers of connecting representative democracy with majoritarian or electoral conceptions of direct democracy as opposed to conceptions of participatory democracy. The latter would enable, for example, more thorough considerations of a possibility of a referendum on a new constitution, or of equal access to the media by proponents of different responses to questions posed at an ongoing referendum.

4.3. Separate opinions

Even if a CC's majority opinions present an incoherent, or ineffective conception of democracy from the perspective of preventing the rise of authoritarian populism, separate opinions (provided that they are allowed and published in the given system) might offer an opportunity to challenge the dominant narrative. Such challenges are limited in the separate opinions to the HCC's decisions pertaining to political participation. Firstly, in the electoral complaints case (invalidation of excessively short time frame to submit complaints against the electoral results), Judge Kiss joined by Judge Tersztyánszkiné Vasadi advocated for a more extensive verdict on unconstitutionality by noting that 'the principle and requirement of democracy is not a feather on the hat,[95] but such a claim that needs to be safeguarded with real options for material validation'.[96] Secondly, two other dissents, one concerning the possibility of voting in local elections for Hungarians who are not located in their permanent residence or registered location[97] and the other the definition of organisations that may nominate candidates for regional elections,[98] featured clashes with the majority's more restrictive views on issues of local democracy and electoral participation. Yet, these slightly more robust conceptions of democratic participation did not occur frequently.

The trend in separate opinions shifted in the period shortly before and after 2007, when these started to advocate more restrictive interpretations of participation in cases where the Court's majority decided in favour of a referendum. These views offered a deeper dive into the constitutional boundaries of the referendum in Hungarian democracy. While they did not offer more robust participatory conceptions of democracy, they highlighted the danger of embracing direct democracy in a majoritarian fashion. Appendix 1 summarises key arguments presented by the judges in these cases.

After 2010, with the parliament initiating the new 'national consultations' to boost illiberal sentiments across the country,[99] the HCC could not avoid addressing the question of direct democracy in the new realities, and, as discussed, did so in two decisions concerning the public consultation in 2016.[100] The separate opinions in one of these decisions make for a relevant case study of the subtle differences in the opinions of the judges appointed by the Fidesz-led majority.[101] Thus, Judge Czine adopted a rights-based position, stating that the HCC was not entitled to quash the decision of the Supreme Court that questioned the disproportionate access of the government to the media to promote the national consultation and its preferred position to the questions. Judges Pokol and Stumpf and President Sulyok disagreed with the verdict as well, but their justification was rooted more in the Court's limited competences in the context of the case. President Sulyok specifically highlighted the absence of rights-based considerations at the level of the CCs' review and advocated the rejection of the petition on that basis. Even though the rejection would essentially have strengthened the rights-based position, as it would have upheld the Supreme Court's objection towards unequal access to the media, the contrasting justifications indicate that it is not merely strategic considerations but ideational diversity, that was at play here. Yet, despite these ideational differences, the potential negative implications of the consultation for the system of representative democracy appears to have escaped all the dissenters' attention—perhaps because the very fact that it had been initiated by the parliamentary majority defies the idea of popular initiative that can counterbalance the parliament.

In other than referendum-related disputes after 2010, the separate opinions indicate a trend of lack of strong elaborations of the meaning of democracy in context of the constitutional challenges at hand (see Appendix 2). Perhaps the most notable remarks concern the expressions of support for a strong, protective state, that prevents the abuse of the tools of electoral campaigns or of superficial information of the voters (Judge Lenkovics, Judge Szívós). Judge Pokol confirmed his consistency in advocating for a deferential CC[102] but his proposed decisions would have had a restrictive effect on 'the people' as they would have introduced restrictions in the right to vote and prevented a functioning local administration until the next elections. The second tendency is the 'covert' utilisation of the concept of democracy—some judges used it to signal their commitment to it (at the local level and/or during elections), but the merit of their reasoning in the particular case would either have made no difference, or even introduced new restrictions in one or both areas.

All in all, there are few separate opinions operating with democracy arguments in the context of political participation cases. The HCC's thinking on participation as a fundamental component of democracy had been rather underdeveloped even before the changes of 2010, and more opinions on the topic were only triggered by the initiatives of Fidesz and its collaborators after the scandals of the centre-left government. With popular initiatives being blatantly employed for the ends of electoral victories and consequent autocratisation of the regime, the HCC found itself between two fires—standing up for enhanced citizen participation as a feature of functioning democracy and the inability of the legal system to address the abuses of such enhanced tools. This resulted in contradictory signals about the desirability of free, equal and inclusive participation as a constitutive element of democracy. Coupled with the absence of a more holistic conception of democracy, the discussion about democracy in the context of participation transformed into a discussion about minimalistic electoral democracy, disconnected from checks and balances, the value of public deliberation or the educational effects of participation. Some of the most recent cases included in the analysis (referenda initiated by the ruling majority) indicate, however, that this jurisprudence remains far from insignificant, and the Court's arguments have not infrequently supported the justification of the majority transforming the means used for direct democracy into its private tool for power concentration.[103]

4.4. Towards explaining the HCC's choice of conceptions of democracy

Once recognising the choice of the HCC of a majoritarian notion of democracy at the expense of a robust understanding of political participation encompassing minority rights, the question arises why this has been the case. Sceptical voices could argue that there was no alternative available for the Court, because CCs, by the virtue of their institutional setup, are 'far from preeminent actors in the system of democratic deliberation'.[104] In this picture, the HCC would be structurally unable to overcome the shadow of the limitations posed by its position, and hence advance a conception of democracy that matches with it. After 2010, these limitations have just amplified due to the executive's clear ambition to reduce the centrality of the Court in the Hungarian institutional system and the adoption of a Constitution that (by restricting referenda on constitutional amendments, for example)[105] is not conducive towards a participatory conception of democracy. If the CCs' capacity to represent a bulwark against autocratisation is proportional to the quality of democracy that is already present in the system,[106] the HCC's capacities got reduced merely by the transformation of authoritarian populists into governing power after the 2010 elections.

Yet, an explanation of this kind would neglect the internal resources that CCs might have at their disposal even under circumstances of autocratisation. The significance of judicial philosophies in constitutional adjudication,[107] as well as the role of public opinion[108] and strategic calculations by the courts[109] have long been acknowledged, and offer partly conflicting and partly overlapping explanations. Case law data do not suffice to provide a fully-fledged response,[110] and the pre-2010 referendum cases should not be seen in isolation from other cases before and shortly after the 2010 elections, such as the key ruling on the Transitional Provisions to the Fourth Amendment of the Fundamental Law.[111] However, there is no reason to believe that pre-2010, the Court was manipulated by public or political elite pressures: it possessed extensive competences and the selection process for constitutional judges continued to require the collaboration between coalition and opposition parties. Hence, authoritarian populists could not just take over. Considering that neither expert nor popular support for the Fidesz-KDNP-initiated referenda was overwhelming,[112] the strategic account is likely to struggle with explaining the Court's choices, particularly in terms of the inconsistency between the verdict and the justification in key cases. At the least, it would have to demonstrate that the perceived negative consequences on the HCC's authority by rejecting the Fidesz-KDNP initiatives were, in the eyes of the deciding judges, greater than the inconsistent reasoning applied by the Court. An alternative promising explanation speaks to ideational divides, particularly between judges favouring representative democracy with a limited role for direct democracy, and those eager to enhance the significance and impact potential of the referendum in the Hungarian constitutional system. The referendum cases could then be read as a conflict between different conceptions of democracy, in which direct democracy, occasionally and in an inconsistent manner, prevailed over representative democracy. In either case, in the peculiar Hungarian context, the enhancement of direct democracy provided an opening for the partisan monopolisation of referenda in Hungary and the subsequent weakening of the HCC.[113]

5. Conclusion

For constitutional courts, it is difficult to counter the charges of the illegitimacy of their decision-making on substantive policy issues and the talks about the primary responsibility of other political actors for the future of the democratic regime. However, if they embrace a majoritarian conception of democracy that supports authoritarian populist actors' claims, they are cutting down the branch they are sitting on. Indeed, a majoritarian conception of democracy is at odds with the CCs' constitutional position and hence enables their further marginalisation, if public actors invoke them in support of curtailing the CCs' competences or similar measures. This article has attempted to show that even when defending free and fair elections and other instruments of direct democracy which embrace majority rule, there is a difference between defending political participation and majoritarianism. Only in the former does democracy go beyond elections to ensure safeguards that everyone (at least all citizens) have a chance to participate in political decision making, and so only the former is a viable conception of direct democracy for CCs with an ambition to contribute to the safeguarding of democracy read in conjunction with human rights and the rule of law.

The focus of this article has been on authoritarian populism. There is an extensive debate whether 'other populisms' might be compatible with (some conceptions of) democracy. Accepting Müller's argument on the incompatibility between populism and pluralism[114] would result in a negative answer; siding with the diverse views that leave room for 'emancipatory populism'[115] would imply a positive response. Further research could explore whether such 'democratic populisms' would be compatible with a robust role of CCs or whether some of them use the label to conceal 'essentially anti-democratic trends'.[116] This question might not have an either-or response. CCs may be in tension with 'democratic populism' when they decide on particular policy matters. Simultaneously, they may be conducive to populist reforms if the latter are understood as supporting guarantees of equal political participation and enhancing the means through which 'the people' may decide on the future of their political community. Facing authoritarian populists, however, CCs going down the populist track seems to be a doomed path: the voices of the authoritarian populists are louder, and they can use the legitimation provided by the CCs to further their antidemocratic ambitions.

Before the 2010 elections, the Hungarian Constitutional Court had a particularly suitable position within the constitutional system of Hungary to offset populist rhetoric thanks to its extensive powers and international recognition. While it formally embraced representative democracy restrictive to the direct decision making by the people, this reasoning nevertheless conflicted with the majority opinions that supported the realisation of the referenda initiated by Viktor Orbán and his supporters.[117] Further research is needed into the determination of the actual impact of the Court's decisions on the success of the Fidesz-KDNP coalition in 2010, including the public reflections of the Court's judgments as an essential avenue for influence of constitutional courts. Nevertheless, this article highlights the limited capacity of the HCC to recognise the drawbacks of associating itself with authoritarian populist rhetoric, even before the judicial majority became composed of nominees of the Fidesz-KDNP coalition. Regardless of the societal response to the Court's decision making, this finding indicates the conditioning of CCs' as bulwarks against autocratisation by them introducing conceptions of democracy in their case law that leave space for a robust role of the courts.

The application of the interpretive institutionalist approach to the conceptions of democracy introduced in this article would benefit from being studied in relation to CCs other than in Hungary (both as individual and comparative case studies), and in relation to dimensions of democracy other than political participation. Yet, even though the article discusses only cases pertaining to political participation, it introduces the foundations of a new strategy for a more effective exercise of constitutional guardianship. The strategy, in its foundations, consists of two related steps. Firstly, CCs should develop and consistently pursue conceptions of democracy beyond mere majoritarianism. Secondly, when doing so, they should be sensitive to the political context of the cases they are called to adjudicate on.

Notes

1. Martin Shapiro, 'Judicial Power and Democracy', in *Judicial Power: How Constitutional Courts Affect Political Transformations*, ed. Christine Landfried (Cambridge: CUP, 2019), 21.
2. Hans Kelsen and Carl Schmitt, *The Guardian of the Constitution: Hans Kelsen and Carl Schmitt on the Limits of Constitutional Law*, trans. Lars Vinx (Cambridge: CUP, 2015), 43–78.
3. This paper empirically studies centralised CCs which have gained prominence gradually after World War I. After World War II, this form of constitutional review was adopted globally in different legal systems. See Tom Ginsburg, 'The Global Spread of Constitutional Review', in *The Oxford Handbook of Law and Politics*, ed. Keith E. Whittington, R. Daniel Kelemen, and Gregory A. Caldeira (Oxford: OUP, 2010), 81–98. Yet, there is

no obvious reason for why most of the conceptual considerations raised would not apply to the decentralised model of judicial review as well, the most known example of which is the United States.

4. Carole Pateman, 'Participatory Democracy Revisited', *Perspectives on Politics* 10, no. 1 (2012): 7–19, https://doi.org/10.1017/S1537592711004877.

5. David Robertson, 'The Counter-Majoritarian Thesis', in *Comparative Constitutional Theory*, ed. Gary Jacobsohn and Miguel Schor (Cheltenham: Edward Elgar, 2018), 189–207. The original formulation of the thesis comes from Alexander M. Bickel, *The Least Dangerous Branch: The Supreme Court at the Bar of Politics*, Second edition (New Haven: Yale University Press, 1986).

6. This is especially the case with abstract constitutional interpretation which allows to 'read meanings' into virtually any constitutional provision. For a classification of competences in the Central and Eastern European context, see Wojciech Sadurski, *Rights Before Courts: A Study of Constitutional Courts in Postcommunist States of Central and Eastern Europe*, Second edition (Dordrecht: Springer, 2014), 13–27.

7. Lin Chun, 'Human Rights and Democracy: The Case for Decoupling', *The International Journal of Human Rights* 5, no. 3 (2001): 19–44, https://doi.org/10.1080/714003726.

8. Gábor Halmai, 'Populism, Authoritarianism and Constitutionalism', *German Law Journal* 20, no. 3 (2019): 298–301, https://doi.org/10.1017/glj.2019.23.

9. David Prendergast, 'The Judicial Role in Protecting Democracy from Populism', *German Law Journal* 20, no. 2 (2019): 245–62, https://doi.org/10.1017/glj.2019.15.

10. Pablo Castillo-Ortiz, 'The Illiberal Abuse of Constitutional Courts in Europe', *European Constitutional Law Review* 15, no. 1 (2019): 48–72, https://doi.org/10.1017/S1574019619000026. The aim of authoritarian populists is not necessarily to eliminate CCs altogether; some intend to make CCs work in their favour via a range of strategies. For examples of these strategies, see Kim Lane Scheppele, 'Autocratic Legalism', *University of Chicago Law Review* 85 (2018): 545–83; David Kosař and Katarína Šipulová, 'How to Fight Court-Packing?', *Constitutional Studies* 6, no. 1 (2020): 133–64.

11. David Kosař and Katarína Šipulová, 'The Strasbourg Court Meets Abusive Constitutionalism: Baka v. Hungary and the Rule of Law', *Hague Journal on the Rule of Law* 10, no. 1 (2018): 83–110, https://doi.org/10.1007/s40803-017-0065-y.

12. Peter Van Elsuwege and Femke Gremmelprez, 'Protecting the Rule of Law in the EU Legal Order: A Constitutional Role for the Court of Justice', *European Constitutional Law Review* 16, no. 1 (2020): 8–32, https://doi.org/10.1017/S1574019620000085.

13. For example, Bojan Bugarič and Tom Ginsburg, 'The Assault on Postcommunist Courts', *Journal of Democracy* 27, no. 3 (2016): 69–82, https://doi.org/10.1353/jod.2016.0047; Jan Petrov, '(De-)Judicialization of Politics in the Era of Populism: Lessons from Central and Eastern Europe', *The International Journal of Human Rights*, 2021, 1–26, https://doi.org/10.1080/13642987.2021.1931138.

14. For the concept of autocratisation as a regime transformation brought about by authoritarian populists (among others), see Anna Lührmann and Staffan I. Lindberg, 'A Third Wave of Autocratization Is Here: What Is New about It?', *Democratization* 26, no. 7 (2019): 1095–1113, https://doi.org/10.1080/13510347.2019.1582029.

15. Data were collected up to this point that incorporates the decision on the national consultation on 'immigration and terrorism' of 2016 (22/2016 [12. V.] AB). For a broader context see Gábor Halmai, 'Abuse of Constitutional Identity. The Hungarian Constitutional Court on Interpretation of Article E) (2) of the Fundamental Law', *Review of Central and East European Law* 43, no. 1 (2018): 23–42, https://doi.org/10.1163/15730352-04301002. This particular case did not include a reference to democracy in relation to political participation (it addresses the concept of 'constitutional identity' against the background of the discussion of the relationship between the European Union and the Hungarian legal order). Hence, it is not included in the empirical analysis.

16. See, in the Hungarian context, András Körösényi, Gábor Illés, and Attila Gyulai, *The Orbán Regime: Plebiscitary Leader Democracy in the Making* (London: Routledge, 2020).

17. From the voluminous literature, see the views of János Kis, 'The Puzzle of "Illiberal Democracy"', in *Rethinking Open Society: New Adversaries and New Opportunities*, ed. Michael Ignatieff and Stefan Roch (Budapest; New York: Central European University Press, 2018), 179–93; Tímea Drinóczi and Agnieszka Bień-Kacała, 'Extra-Legal Particularities and Illiberal Constitutionalism – The Case of Hungary and Poland', *Hungarian Journal of Legal Studies* 59, no. 4 (2018): 338–54, https://doi.org/10.1556/2052.2018.59.4.2. A debate in this literature pertains to whether 'illiberal democracy' and 'illiberal constitutionalism' are standalone conceptions of constitutionalism and democracy or oxymoronic, meaningless terms where the adjective undermines the substance of the noun.

18. Herman Schwartz, *The Struggle for Constitutional Justice in Post-Communist Europe* (Chicago: University of Chicago Press, 2002).

19. See, e.g., Emilia Palonen, 'Performing the Nation: The Janus-Faced Populist Foundations of Illiberalism in Hungary', *Journal of Contemporary European Studies* 26, no. 3 (2018): 308–21, https://doi.org/10.1080/14782804.2018.1498776.

20. Stephen E. Gottlieb, *Unfit for Democracy: The Roberts Court and the Breakdown of American Politics* (New York: NYU Press, 2016), 239.

21. Jean-Paul Gagnon, '2,234 Descriptions of Democracy: An Update to Democracy's Ontological Pluralism', *Democratic Theory* 5, no. 1 (2018): 92–113, https://doi.org/10.3167/dt.2018.050107. This article uses the term 'conceptions of democracy' to capture subjectively perceived understandings of democracy. Here, 'conceptions' represent a middle ground between 'understandings' and 'meanings' of democracy, the former denoting more 'objective' and the latter more 'subjective' conceptions. Given that CCs provide legally binding interpretations of constitutional principles, their conceptions have a significance beyond subjective perceptions of individual or collective actors. On the distinction between 'understandings' and 'meanings' of democracy see Norma Osterberg-Kaufmann, Toralf Stark, and Christoph Mohamad-Klotzbach, 'Challenges in Conceptualizing and Measuring Meanings and Understandings of Democracy', *Zeitschrift Für Vergleichende Politikwissenschaft* 14, no. 4 (2020): 299–320, https://doi.org/10.1007/s12286-020-00470-5.

22. Freedom House, Varieties of Democracy, Bertelsmann Transformation Index (BTI), Polity IV, The Economist Intelligence Unit Democracy Index, to mention several well-known indexes. Of course, each of them has a more narrowly defined purpose and uses different methodologies, but they all pay attention to (specifically defined) characteristics of political regimes.

23. Michael Coppedge, Angel Alvarez, and Claudia Maldonado, 'Two Persistent Dimensions of Democracy: Contestation and Inclusiveness', *The Journal of Politics* 70, no. 3 (2008): 632–47, https://doi.org/10.1017/s0022381608080663.

24. Gerardo L. Munck and Jay Verkuilen, 'Conceptualizing and Measuring Democracy: Evaluating Alternative Indices', *Comparative Political Studies* 35, no. 1 (2002): 9, https://doi.org/10.1177/001041400203500101.

25. See, e.g., Marc Bühlmann et al., 'The Democracy Barometer: A New Instrument to Measure the Quality of Democracy and Its Potential for Comparative Research', *European Political Science* 11, no. 4 (2012): 519–36, https://doi.org/10.1057/eps.2011.46.

26. Munck and Verkuilen, 'Conceptualizing and Measuring Democracy', 9.

27. Wolfgang Merkel, 'Is There a Crisis of Democracy?', *Democratic Theory* 1, no. 2 (2014): 13–14, https://doi.org/10.3167/dt.2014.010202.

28. An example is Wolfgang Merkel's embedded democracy, see, e.g., Merkel, 14–17.

29. Alexander Hamilton, James Madison, and John Jay, *The Federalist Papers* (New York: Signet Classic, 2003).

30. This is especially the case in majoritarian electoral systems whereby for some constituencies it may become impossible to have any representation of their political views e.g. Thomas Quinn, 'Throwing the Rascals out? Problems of Accountability in Two-Party Systems', *European Journal of Political Research* 55, no. 1 (2016): 120–37, https://doi.org/10.1111/1475-6765.12118. In systems of proportional representation (with some exceptions, such

as the single transferable vote system), representation might improve through coalitions but is not guaranteed either.

31. Cf. Pateman, 'Participatory Democracy Revisited', 14. Pateman hints at an important point that cannot be satisfactorily discussed here: the democratic ideal cannot be implemented by restricting participation to citizens, considering global migration and mobility. A modern notion of participation requires innovative tools for proportionately involving non-citizens as well in the decision making of states and political communities at a sub-state or supra-state level.

32. David Held, *Models of Democracy*, Third edition (Cambridge: Polity Press, 2006), 209–16.

33. The invention of representation is the key difference that, in Cartledge's slightly exaggerated terms, ensures that '"We, the People", in any mass-popular sense are kept well away from any direct access to—let alone the regular daily exercise of—governmental power.' Paul Cartledge, *Democracy: A Life* (Oxford: OUP, 2018), 306.

34. Such as in the over 800-page long Oxford handbook on the subject. André Bächtiger et al., eds., *The Oxford Handbook of Deliberative Democracy* (Oxford: OUP, 2018).

35. Andre Bächtiger et al., 'Deliberative Democracy: An Introduction', in *The Oxford Handbook of Deliberative Democracy*, by Andre Bächtiger et al., ed. Andre Bächtiger et al. (Oxford: OUP, 2018), 2, https://doi.org/10.1093/oxfordhb/9780198747369.013.50.

36. For more substantive accounts of deliberation, the philosophy of Jürgen Habermas, *Between Facts and Norms: Contributions to a Discourse Theory of Law and Democracy*, trans. William Rehg (Cambridge, Mass.: The MIT Press, 1998) provides a source for further exploration.

37. Stephen Elstub, 'Deliberative and Participatory Democracy', in *The Oxford Handbook of Deliberative Democracy*, ed. Andre Bächtiger et al. (Oxford: OUP, 2018), 186–202, https://doi.org/10.1093/oxfordhb/9780198747369.013.5.

38. Pateman, 'Participatory Democracy Revisited'.

39. Thamy Pogrebinschi and David Samuels, 'The Impact of Participatory Democracy: Evidence from Brazil's National Public Policy Conferences', *Comparative Politics* 46, no. 3 (2014): 329.

40. Peter A. Hall and Rosemary C. R. Taylor, 'Political Science and the Three New Institutionalisms', *Political Studies* 44, no. 5 (1996): 936–57, https://doi.org/10.1111/j.1467-9248.1996.tb00343.x.

41. James G. March and Johan P. Olsen, *Rediscovering Institutions: The Organizational Basis of Politics* (New York: The Free Press, 1989), 160, 164.

42. Rogers M. Smith, 'Historical Institutionalism and the Study of Law', in *The Oxford Handbook of Law and Politics*, ed. Gregory A. Caldeira, R. Daniel Kelemen, and Keith E. Whittington (Oxford: OUP, 2008), 50, https://doi.org/10.1093/oxfordhb/9780199208425.001.0001.

43. Howard Gillman and Cornell W. Clayton, 'Introduction. Beyond Judicial Attitudes: Institutional Approaches to Supreme Court Decision-Making', in *Supreme Court Decision-Making: New Institutionalist Approaches*, ed. Cornell W. Clayton and Howard Gillman (Chicago: University of Chicago Press, 1999), 4.

44. Cornell W. Clayton, 'The Supreme Court and Political Jurisprudence: New and Old Institutionalisms', in *Supreme Court Decision-Making: New Institutionalist Approaches*, ed. Cornell W. Clayton and Howard Gillman (Chicago: University of Chicago Press, 1999), 21.

45. R. A. W. Rhodes, 'Old Institutionalisms', in *The Oxford Handbook of Political Institutions*, ed. Sarah A. Binder, R. A. W. Rhodes, and Bert A. Rockman (Oxford: OUP, 2008), 90–108.

46. Mark Thatcher and Alec Stone Sweet, 'Theory and Practice of Delegation to Non-Majoritarian Institutions', *West European Politics* 25, no. 1 (2002): 18–19, https://doi.org/10.1080/713601583.

47. These decisions were identified via keyword search and their list is on file with the author. The advantages of a keyword search as a basis for selection of the population of decisions under study is that it transcends the usual limitations posed by the types of proceedings or the judicial composition of the court. The keyword under study is 'democracy', based on the logic that an explicit reference to 'democracy' (rather than something else with the

attribution 'democratic') is necessary to safely assume that the court thought about the particularities, or at least one selected issue within a broader case, in the context of democracy. The conceptions identified are then subject to scrutiny through a contextual analysis with the help of the particularities of the case in question and their juxtaposition with other key concepts.

48. For a discussion of this and other 'ancillary' CC powers, see Tom Ginsburg and Zachary Elkins, 'Ancillary Powers of Constitutional Courts', *Texas Law Review* 87 (2009): 1431–61.

49. László Sólyom and Georg Brunner, eds., *Constitutional Judiciary in a New Democracy: The Hungarian Constitutional Court* (Ann Arbor: University of Michigan Press, 2000); see also overview in Katalin Kelemen and Max Steuer, 'Constitutional Court of Hungary', in *Max Planck Encyclopedia of Comparative Constitutional Law*, ed. Rainer Grote, Frauke Lachenmann, and Rüdiger Wolfrum (Oxford: OUP, 2019), https://oxcon.ouplaw.com/view/10.1093/law-mpeccol/law-mpeccol-e802.

50. Gábor Halmai, 'The Hungarian Approach to Constitutional Review: The End of Activism? The First Decade of the Hungarian Constitutional Court', in *Constitutional Justice, East and West: Democratic Legitimacy and Constitutional Courts in Post-Communist Europe in a Comparative Perspective*, ed. Wojciech Sadurski (The Hague; London: Springer, 2010), 189–212.

51. Paul Blokker, *New Democracies in Crisis? A Comparative Constitutional Study of the Czech Republic, Hungary, Poland, Romania and Slovakia* (London: Routledge, 2013).

52. Venice Commission, 'Opinion on the Fourth Amendment to the Fundamental Law of Hungary', 15.6 2013, 17–29, https://www.venice.coe.int/webforms/documents/?pdf=CDL-AD(2013)012-e.

53. László Sólyom, 'The Constitutional Court of Hungary', in *The Max Planck Handbooks in European Public Law: Volume III: Constitutional Adjudication: Institutions*, ed. Armin von Bogdandy, Peter Huber, and Christoph Grabenwarter (Oxford: OUP, 2020), 416–17.

54. Katalin Kelemen, 'Appointment of Constitutional Judges in a Comparative Perspective — With a Proposal for a New Model for Hungary', *Acta Juridica Hungarica* 54, no. 1 (2013): 5–23, https://doi.org/10.1556/AJur.54.2013.1.2.

55. Gábor Halmai, 'A Coup Against Constitutional Democracy: The Case of Hungary', in *Constitutional Democracy in Crisis?*, ed. Mark A. Graber, Sanford Levinson, and Mark Tushnet (Oxford: OUP, 2018), 243–56.

56. Katalin Kelemen, *Judicial Dissent in European Constitutional Courts: A Comparative and Legal Perspective* (London: Routledge, 2017).

57. 28/1990 (XI. 22.) AB, 2.

58. 28/1990 (XI. 22.) AB, 2.

59. 2/1993 (I. 22.) AB; see also András Szalai, 'Manipuláció vagy korrekció? A népszavazás mint a parlamentáris kormányzat ellensúlya [Manipulation or Correction? The Referendum as a Counterweight to Parliamentary Governance]', *Pro publico bono - Magyar közigazgatás*, no. 3 (2013): 140–42.

60. Gábor Halmai, 'Referendum and Representative Democracy', *Fundamentum* 12, no. 5 (2008): 5.

61. 53/1996 (XI. 22.) AB, 2.

62. 27/1998 (VI. 16.) AB, 5; see also Erdős Csaba, 'Az országgyűlési képviselők szabad mandátumának alapjai és az intézménnyel kapcsolatos legfontosabb kihívások [The Fundamentals of the Free Mandate of the Parliamentary Representatives and the Most Important Related Challenges]', *Parlamenti Szemle* 2, no. 2 (2017): 16.

63. *Jogállam demokráciája* as referenced in Hungarian.

64. 67/1992 (XII. 21.) AB, 3.

65. 52/1997 (X. 14.) AB. See also Halmai, 'Referendum and Representative Democracy', 6–7.

66. 52/1997 (X. 14.) AB, 11.

67. 844/B/2002 AB, 6; 441/H/2001. AB, 5, with reference to 27/1998 (VI. 16.) AB; 1/2002 (I. 11.) AB, with reference to 27/1998 (VI. 16) AB.

68. 6/2000 (III. 17.) AB, 2: '[…] the tools of direct democracy serve to add to, and influence, the exercise of power by [parliamentary] representatives.' This was a reference that the Court reproduced from the reasoning of the National Electoral Commission. A few minor cases are not elaborated here.

69. A somewhat new argument can be found in 2001, where the HCC explained that the certification procedure by the National Electoral Commission (NEC) for referendum petitions is a 'legal guarantee' served to 'stabilise the constitutional democracy'. 32/2001 (VII. 11.) AB, 7. This term appeared in a technical (and politically uncontroversial) decision that invalidated the NEC's verdict on the ground that the signature forms for the petition to launch such a voting contained all proposed questions at once, not one by one. Hence, it does not counter the overall direction of the Court's case law towards a representative democracy with a strong partisan component.

70. 39/2002 (IX. 25.) AB, 6.

71. 59/2003 (XI. 26.) AB, 4. In this case, the Court invalidated the excessively short period for submitting complaints against electoral results by unsuccessful candidates (in that context, in a mayoral election).

72. According to two political scientists, this has become 'the main politically – as well as theoretically – relevant problem of the year'. Gabriella Ilonszki and Sándor Kurtán, 'Hungary', *European Journal of Political Research* 47, no. 7–8 (2008): 998, https://doi.org/10.1111/j. 1475-6765.2008.00795.x. The period of increased concern for the impact and relevance of referenda begins in 2004, with the referendum held that year. See Zoltán Pozsár-Szentmiklósy, 'Direct Democracy in Hungary (1989–2016): From Popular Sovereignty to Popular Illusion', *Acta Universitatis Sapientiae Legal Studies* 6, no. 1 (2017): 111.

73. Halmai, 'Referendum and Representative Democracy', 16.

74. 33/2007 (VI. 6.) AB, 8. Here, the Court argued that there is no need to modify the calibration of direct and representative democracy in the Hungarian system for the referendum to be permitted.

75. 15/2007 (III. 9.) AB.

76. 34/2007 (VI. 6.) AB.

77. 13/2007 (III. 9.) AB. Unlike in the previous three cases, here the Court referred to its more pro-participation reasoning from the 1990s (28/1990 [XI. 22.] AB), thus slightly reducing the tension between the verdict and the reasoning.

78. László Komáromi, 'Milestones in the History of Direct Democracy in Hungary', *Iustum Aequum Salutare* 9, no. 4 (2013): 55.

79. Zoltán Tibor Pállinger, 'Citizens' Initiatives in Hungary: An Additional Opportunity for Power-Sharing in an Extremely Majoritarian System', in *Citizens' Initiatives in Europe: Procedures and Consequences of Agenda-Setting by Citizens*, ed. Maija Setälä and Theo Schiller (Basingstoke: Palgrave Macmillan, 2012), 128; see also 119.

80. On the classification of these types of referenda in a comparative perspective, see Komáromi 'Az országos népszavazás és az Alkotmánybíróság: Reflexiók az elmúlt negyedszázad gyakorlatára [The National Referendum and the Constitutional Court. Reflections on the Practice of the Last Twenty-Five Years]', *Alkotmánybírósági Szemle*, no. 2 (2015): 80–81.

81. 64/2009 (VI. 18.) AB, 8. This petition for an 'approval referendum' began with a popular initiative asking for the approval of an act already enacted by the National Assembly, which the Court found to be a prohibited subject for a referendum.

82. 84/2010 (V. 20.) AB, 3. The decision approved a denial of the NEC to certify a petition.

83. 63/2008 (IV. 30.) AB, 9, 12, 14, also Péter Smuk, 'Pluralism Confined? Party Law Case Studies from Hungary', in *Constitutionalism in a Plural World*, ed. Catarina Santos Botelho, Luís Heleno Terrinha, and Pedro Coutinho (Porto: Universidade Católica Portuguesa, Centro Regional do Porto, 2018), 99.

84. 967/E/2006, 3-4. In this case, the Court understands the whole mechanism of Hungarian parliamentary democracy to be based on political party representation in the legislature.

85. 2/2012 (II. 10.) AB, 2. This case is different in significance from a number of others in which the Court approved the NEC's negative decision on petitions asking to submit very specific

legislative amendments to a popular vote in a referendum (1/2012 [II. 10.] AB, 2; 9/2012 [III. 9.] AB, 2).

86. No separate opinions were submitted to the decision either.

87. 12/2016 (VI. 22.) AB, 6; for a more holistic overview of the Court's reasoning in the case, see Kriszta Kovács, 'Hungary', *East European Yearbook on Human Rights* 1, no. 1 (2018): 166–7.

88. 19/2016 (X. 28.) AB, 3.

89. See Eszter Bodnár, Fruzsina Gárdos-Orosz, and Zoltán Pozsár-Szentmiklósy, 'Developments in Hungarian Constitutional Law', in *The I·CONnect-Clough Center 2016 Global Review of Constitutional Law*, ed. Richard Albert et al. (Boston: I•CONnect and the Clough Center, 2017), 79.

90. Maximilian Steinbeis, 'The Return of the Hungarian Constitutional Court', *Verfassungsblog* (blog), 2013, https://verfassungsblog.de/the-return-of-the-hungarian-constitutional-court-2/; see also Katalin Kelemen, 'Hungary: Voter Registration Declared Unconstitutional', *Diritti Comparati* (blog), 5 February 2013, http://www.dirittticomparati.it/hungary-voter-registration-declared-unconstitutional/.

91. István Stumpf, 'Rule of Law, Division of Powers, Constitutionalism', *Acta Juridica Hungarica* 55, no. 4 (2014): 313–4, https://doi.org/10.1556/AJur.55.2014.4.1; István Stumpf, 'The Hungarian Constitutional Court's Place in the Constitutional System of Hungary', *Polgári Szemle* 13 (2017): 249, https://doi.org/10.24307/psz.2017.0314.

92. 1/2013 (I. 7.) AB, 14, 15. The majority referred to an earlier decision of the Court about the importance of the stability of the electoral system (39/2002 [IX. 25.] AB).

93. *Fővárosi közgyűlés* in original.

94. 26/2014 (VII. 23.) AB, 17. The Court discovered a violation of electoral equality as districts with substantial differences in population had the same number of deputies eligible to represent them. The reference echoed an older case (22/2005 [VI. 17.] AB).

95. Denotes an ornament that has pure aesthetic but not material function.

96. 59/2003 (XI. 26.) AB, 9-10.

97. 783/E/2002 (Judge Lévay joined by Judge Bragyova), 8; see also Eszter Bodnár, 'Választójog és választási rendszer az Alaptörvényben [The Right to Vote and the Electoral System in the Fundamental Law]', *Magyar Közigazgatás – Szakmai fórum* 3 (2011): 106.

98. 755/B/1998 (Judge Kiss joined by Judge Balogh), 9.

99. Zoltán Tibor Pállinger, 'Direct Democracy in an Increasingly Illiberal Setting: The Case of the Hungarian National Referendum', *Contemporary Politics* 25, no. 1 (2019): 62–77, https://doi.org/10.1080/13569775.2018.1543924.

100. 12/2016 (VI. 22.) AB, 6; for a more holistic overview of the Court's reasoning in the case, see Kovács, 'Hungary', 166–7. The second decision is 19/2016 (X. 28.) AB.

101. In this case, Judges Czine, Pokol, Stumpf and President Sulyok dissented, with Judge Szalay joining the latter two dissents. I thank an anonymous reviewer for prompting me to expand on these separate opinions.

102. Béla Pokol, 'The Juristocratic Form of Government and Its Structural Issues', in *Verfassungsgerichtsbarkeit Und Demokratie: Europäische Parameter in Zeiten Politischer Umbrüche?*, ed. Tamara Ehs, Robert Kriechbaumer, and Heinrich Neisser (Vienna: Böhlau Verlag, 2017), 61–78.

103. Even though the article cannot derive conclusions on the practice after 2017, an HCC decision from July 2020 on the procedure of conducting referenda expresses a commitment to popular sovereignty and direct democracy but sees the latter as complementary to the exercise of power by the legislature. 22/2020. (VIII. 4.) AB, para. 21-22.

104. Cass R. Sunstein, *Legal Reasoning and Political Conflict*, Second edition (New York: Oxford University Press, 2018), 223; on the limited role of courts on social change, see Gerald N. Rosenberg, *The Hollow Hope: Can Courts Bring About Social Change?*, Second edition (Chicago: University of Chicago Press, 2008).

105. Drinóczi Tímea, *Az alkotmányos párbeszéd: A többszintű alkotmányosság alkotmánytana és gyakorlata a 21. században [Constitutional Dialogue: The Theory and Practice of Multi-Level*

Constitutionalism in the 21st Century] (Budapest: MTA Társadalomtudományi Kutatóközpont Jogtudományi Intézet, 2017), 221–2.

106. Tom Gerald Daly, *The Alchemists: Questioning Our Faith in Courts as Democracy-Builders* (Cambridge: CUP, 2017).

107. David Robertson, *The Judge as Political Theorist: Contemporary Constitutional Review* (Princeton: Princeton University Press, 2010).

108. Or Bassok, 'The Two Countermajoritarian Difficulties', *Saint Louis University Public Law Review* 31 (2012): 333–82; Two scholars specify the readiness to subordinate to public sentiment by judges as 'judicial populism'. Alon Harel and Noam Kolt, 'Populist Rhetoric, False Mirroring, and the Courts', *International Journal of Constitutional Law* 18, no. 3 (2020): 759–62, https://doi.org/10.1093/icon/moaa055. It is not obvious, however, that popular and populist views should be treated as the same when evaluating the 'degree of populism' of a particular court, especially in light of authoritarian populism not actually endorsing meaningful, broad popular participation.

109. Shannon Ishiyama Smithey, 'Strategic Activism: A Comparative View of Judges as Institution Builders', in *Open Judicial Politics*, ed. Rorie Spill Solberg, Jennifer Segal Diascro, and Eric Waltenburg (Corvallis: Oregon State University, 2020), 378–99, https://doi.org/10.5399/osu/1118; see also András Sajó and Renáta Uitz, *The Constitution of Freedom: An Introduction to Legal Constitutionalism* (Oxford: OUP, 2017), 364–6.

110. Interview data allow to penetrate more deeply into the deliberative environment at the Court in the respective periods.

111. Gábor Halmai, 'Unconstitutional Constitutional Amendments: Constitutional Courts as Guardians of the Constitution?', *Constellations* 19, no. 2 (2012): 182–203, https://doi.org/10.1111/j.1467-8675.2012.00688.x.

112. As Arato points out, many of the early reforms introduced by the Orbán government were subject to domestic and international criticisms, that could (and on occasion even did) embolden the HCC to rule against the governing majority. Andrew Arato, *Post Sovereign Constitution Making: Learning and Legitimacy* (Oxford: OUP, 2016), 213–22.

113. Pepijn van Eeden, 'Discover, Instrumentalize, Monopolize: Fidesz's Three-Step Blueprint for a Populist Take-over of Referendums', *East European Politics and Societies* 33, no. 3 (2019): 705–32, https://doi.org/10.1177/0888325418800548.

114. Jan-Werner Müller, *What Is Populism?* (Philadelphia: University of Pennsylvania Press, 2016).

115. Bojan Bugarič, 'Could Populism Be Good for Constitutional Democracy?', *Annual Review of Law and Social Science* 15, no. 1 (2019): 42, https://doi.org/10.1146/annurev-lawsocsci-101518-042927.

116. Sonja C. Grover, *Judicial Activism and the Democratic Rule of Law: Selected Case Studies* (Cham: Springer, 2020), 236.

117. Pállinger, 'Direct Democracy in an Increasingly Illiberal Setting', 69–70.

Acknowledgements

Earlier versions of this article benefitted from comments of the participants of the ECPR General Conference 2020, the IPSA World Congress 2021, research seminars at the Jindal Global Law School, Örebro University (School of Law, Psychology and Social Work), Washington State University (School of Politics, Philosophy, and Public Affairs) and WZB Berlin Social Science Center as well as of Darina Malová and several other members of the Comenius University in Bratislava (Department of Political Science). My appreciation goes also to the anonymous reviewers for their valuable feedback. The usual disclaimer applies.

Disclosure statement

No potential conflict of interest was reported by the author(s).

ORCID

Max Steuer http://orcid.org/0000-0001-7638-5865

ᵍ OPEN ACCESS

Through selective activism towards greater resilience: the Czech Constitutional Court's interventions into high politics in the age of populism

Hubert Smekal ⓘ, Jaroslav Benák ⓘ and Ladislav Vyhnánek ⓘ

ABSTRACT
With technocratic populist Andrej Babiš leading the Czech government coalition, the country has experienced some democratic backsliding. In contrast to its Hungarian and Polish counterparts, however, the Czech Constitutional Court has been spared from executive capture. This article argues that resilient constitutional courts may act as one of the key safeguards against illiberal populism. We demonstrate that resilient constitutional courts are products of an institutional framework, which prevents court-packing by loyal allies of populist leaders, and of courts' activities that increase their reputation with the public, thus making political attacks against them overly costly. We argue that the Czech Constitutional Court has exercised an approach of selective judicial activism that focuses on keeping political competition fair while avoiding involvement in controversial socially transformative judicial decision-making which would outrage large parts of the population. Moreover, by acting as a guardian of fair political competition, the Court contributed to the further fragmentation of the political landscape, which in turn prevented the accumulation of political power, and hence the Court shielded itself from political attacks.

Introduction

Czechia, Hungary, and Poland, once considered frontrunners in the post-communist transition,[1] have experienced a bumpy ride on the road to fully consolidated democracy in the last decade. The remaining Visegrád Four country – Slovakia – took an authoritative turn under Prime Minister Mečiar as early as the mid-1990s.[2] Slovakia witnessed, for example, the abduction of a President's son and still struggles with clientelistic networks – not even stopping short of killing an investigative journalist and his fiancée. Hungary and Poland currently face political proceedings for alleged breaches of the European Union's values. Despite experiencing some symptoms of illiberal populism recently, Czechia stands as the only country in the region spared from grave democratic excesses. We argue that an

---

This is an Open Access article distributed under the terms of the Creative Commons Attribution-NonCommercial-NoDerivatives License (http://creativecommons.org/licenses/by-nc-nd/4.0/), which permits non-commercial re-use, distribution, and reproduction in any medium, provided the original work is properly cited, and is not altered, transformed, or built upon in any way.

essential part of the explanation of Czechia's liberal democratic survival is provided by its Constitutional Court, which has remained, unlike its Hungarian, Polish, and Slovak counterparts, relatively free of political capture. Such a position has enabled the Court to employ a selectively activist approach that occasionally interferes in highly political issues. The Court focuses on the protection of fair political competition and separation of powers while remaining hesitant to push forward socially divisive values issues.

Central European constitutional courts, endowed with the hope to prevent illiberal democratic backsliding, have played an important part in democratic transitions.[3] However, in Hungary and, more recently in Poland, the constitutional courts have been largely packed by loyalists of the populist regime and do not fully exercise their function as a vital constraint on political power.[4] In contrast, the Czech Constitutional Court (hereinafter also 'the Court') has continued to maintain an image of an independent tribunal. This is especially noteworthy, given the Court's occasional interventions into the realm of 'mega-politics'. Hence, we ask how the Court remained resilient, able and willing to challenge democratic backsliding.

This article contributes to the literature on the role of constitutional courts in countries experiencing democratic backsliding. While most of the scholarship has analysed spectacular cases of populists' capture of the courts, we identify elements that support constitutional courts' resilience. In an environment of worsening quality of democracy both in the region (Hungary and Poland) and at home, the Czech Constitutional Court has remained surprisingly resilient. We argue that it results from an interplay between structural political elements and the Court's behaviour. Nevertheless, the picture is not all rosy – we analyse a number of issues of concern. Understanding the elements supporting and undermining constitutional courts' resilience contributes to the democratic regime's ability to face the populist challenge.

The case study of the Czech Constitutional Court's resistance to strengthening populism builds on elite interviews with the Court's judges themselves. The article uncovers how Czech constitutional judges perceive the influence of other branches of power and of the public, and judges' coping strategies with such influence. We build on extensive literature that has identified variables affecting a court's position in the political system, and discuss the impact of those variables in the Czech context.

After this introduction, a review of literature on constitutional courts and the populist challenge follows. Then, we zoom in on the Czech case and examine the twofold relationship between the Czech Constitutional Court and the populist challenge. First, we scrutinise structural factors that have contributed to the Court's relative resilience, thus contributing to its independent position even amidst the surge of populist attacks on Central European courts. At the same time, we recognise that the Court has played an active role in preserving those factors. We argue that the Court's activist judgements concerning the separation of powers and political process have contributed to political fragmentation in Czechia and bolstered judicial independence. This, in turn, has helped to sustain a relatively reasonable level of liberal democracy of a country in a tested region. In this regard, we elaborate more deeply on a string of activist 'mega-politics' judgements culminating with a 2021 election judgment, whereby the Court dramatically intervened in the political competition field by striking down crucial parts of the Electoral Law eight months before the general election. Finally, in the Conclusion, we draw broader lessons from the Czech case.

Making constitutional courts resilient

The dichotomy between democratic and authoritarian regimes has become increasingly blurred, and so has the role of courts.[5] On the one hand, judges in authoritarian regimes can become relatively independent and show some degree of assertiveness vis-à-vis the ruling elites. On the other hand, courts in hitherto democratic regimes can prove instrumental in abetting democratic backsliding once they are packed by loyal judges.[6] Courts can act as important actors in shaping the nature of a polity, but they are not a panacea. Democratic erosion results from a complex interplay between underlying economic, political, social, and cultural macrostructures, embedded in an international context. Current scholarship points both to successful and unsuccessful examples of courts countering democratic backsliding and has emphasised the importance of carefully thinking through and timing political interventions by judges.[7] Even though courts might enjoy momentary public support, elected actors typically have better access to media and can mobilise public opinion more easily.[8]

In the European Union context, democratic backsliding can be judicially resisted not only by litigation in national courts, but also by the European Commission or by another Member State starting infringement proceedings, or by a national court sending a preliminary question to the Court of Justice. However, supranational judicial interventions have so far been unable to turn the tide of democratic backsliding in Hungary and Poland. Moreover, overreliance on supranational judicial intervention to defend democracy risks politicising the EU judiciary and also creates an alibi for the lack of political will to intervene in EU Member States' governance of their judiciaries.[9]

The prospect of a successful defence against a populist government depends partly on a court's institutional design. A constitutional court needs to have the necessary powers as well as the opportunity to use them. This opportunity is very closely associated with the design of access to a court. For example, the Czechoslovak Constitutional Court established in 1920 had the authority to review legislation, but only very few state organs could initiate the proceedings, and petitions from the public were not allowed at all. This diminished the importance of the Court to such a level that the German occupation forces in 1939 did not bother to dissolve the court, seize its building, or arrest its personnel.[10]

Another crucial element includes the willingness of judges to protect liberal democracy. As Aziz Huq has pointed out, 'the robustness of democratic institutions under the rule of law cannot be disentangled from the character and motivations of those elected or appointed to high office'.[11] Even the most powerful court will refrain from taking any action if staffed with judges loyal to a government or sympathetic to the government's political ideology.

The two factors – ability and willingness to protect liberal democracy under the rule of law – combined will produce a 2×2 matrix of court positions, as indicated in Table 1.

Table 1. Court's positions towards the protection of democracy.

willing and able	willing but unable
unwilling but able	unwilling and unable

Source: the authors.

Courts unwilling and unable to protect democracy are entirely harmless for a populist government, as, for example, the Constitutional Court of Belarus shows. The President appoints all its judges, and also many members of the state bodies that have standing before the Court. As a consequence, the Court grants only few petitions. Apparently, none of the authorised petitioners wants to break the illusion of the rule of law in Belarus, and neither do the judges themselves, as they have considered even very problematic practices compliant with the Belarusian Constitution.[12]

Both 'hybrid situations' (i.e. willing but unable and unwilling but able) can arise independently from populism and serve as a reason why the court will be deemed harmless and thus left intact by a government. However, such situations may also come as a result of court-curbing attempts from a populist government. Some courts have been stripped of their powers, or their decisions were systematically overridden by constitutional revisions,[13] making these courts unable to constrain a government anymore. This happened to the Hungarian Constitutional Court in the first phase of Orbán's takeover. Alternatively, populist governments packed courts with their loyalists, thus shifting their power balances.[14] The Polish Constitutional Tribunal represents a prominent example of this latter trajectory.[15]

This article analyses how some courts have managed to stay willing and able to protect liberal democracy. Caserte and Cebulak use the concept of 'resilience' and define it as the 'capacity of courts to maintain the legal, political, and ideological ideas that justify their own existence'.[16]

A good starting position for creating a resilient court comprises its institutional design, including its powers and internal procedures, and personal composition.[17] The real challenge is to keep the courts able and willing to protect democracy, and prevent them from slipping either towards inability or unwillingness.

Some authors connect the greater success of Western democracies at fending off attacks on liberal institutions with better-developed traditions of independence and professionalism of Western courts, media, human-rights organisations, and ombudspersons, which all mutually reinforce one another. Conversely, weak and underdeveloped institutions invite a drift toward 'illiberal democracy'.[18] The illiberal approach to constitutional courts displays traits such as opportunistic instrumentalism (first framing courts as elitist bodies constraining popular will, and then exploiting them after coming to power), the transformation of a constitutional constraint into a legitimising tool (leverage of the ruling party over constitutional judges, the selective restriction of court powers), their use as tools of constitutional mutation (a new interpretation of the constitution), and the creation of perverse constitutional incentives (after court-packing occurs, the opposition does not trust it and stops using it).[19] In illiberal constitutionalism, constitutional interpretation shifts from the constitutional court towards the executive, who has leverage over the court. This allows the government to act without proper constraints while it can declare its actions fully constitutional, and, therefore, legitimate.[20]

Generally, populist governments do not welcome any constraints on their power, particularly not from independent courts. Hence, such governments seek to diminish judicial review or turn it to their advantage. The situation becomes especially worrying when the populist majority is large enough to revise the constitution. The government can then change both the court's design (the number of judges, terms of office, rules of appointment, voting rules, etc.) as well as the constitutional framework providing the yardstick for the review. The possibility to change the constitution allows the government to override unwelcome court decisions, making the court an unattractive option for exercising effective oversight. Political fragmentation preventing the formation of governments able to change constitutions is thus crucial for courts' resilience.[21] But as the Polish case shows, it might not be enough to shield the judiciary completely.

Direct attacks against courts usually get a lot of public attention, and tactics such as violent threats, forced resignations, or harassing judges can easily harm the government's reputation. Strong public support for the court considerably increases reputation costs for assaults on courts. On the contrary, unpopular courts invite political attacks.[22]

Table 2 summarises findings from the literature on various factors that affect courts' resilience. These factors usually have a synergic effect. The court's legal design offers little protection if all potential veto players side with the populist government, which can thus easily change the design. Similarly, even a relatively weak populist party can pack the court with loyal judges in the case of an improper institutional design. Finally, a robust design and fragmented political landscape do not necessarily prevent willing judges from becoming government allies. Courts's independence can be boosted by the public's backing. Courts build the reservoir of public trust by their decision-making and PR activities gradually, hence increasing the costs of potential political attacks. High judicial legitimacy can embolden courts to make more assertive decisions.[23]

Determinants of the Czech Constitutional Court's resilience

The previous section outlined the main findings of existing literature concerning the relationship of (constitutional) courts and their capacity and willingness to make assertive independent decisions on the one hand, and the attempts of populist regimes to subjugate independent courts on the other hand. Our introduction asserted that despite the Czech populist backsliding and the widespread experience of political attacks on other Central European courts, the Czech Constitutional Court has not (yet) been deprived of capacity and willingness to behave independently.

This section explains why the Court proved resilient to populist assaults, especially compared to its Polish and Hungarian counterparts, and how the resilient Court has contributed to a comparatively better quality of democracy, despite its recent deterioration. First, we briefly introduce the Czech constitutional-political context, focusing on the populist leanings of the current political leadership. Next, we discuss the nature of the Court's activism and how it has been influenced by the changing political landscape. Obviously, if the Court was extremely self-restrained, it would hardly present any challenge to the political

Table 2. Key factors affecting a court's resilience.

Political factors
• Level of political fragmentation[70] • Public support of the court[71]

The court's design
• Jurisdiction[72] • Framework for review (the conception of the constitution, the role of international law and/or EU law)[73] • Access to the court[74] • Legal effects of decisions[75] • Terms of office and their renewability[76] • Appointment and removal procedures[77]

Intra-court factors
• Preferences and attitudes of individual judges[78] • The ability of judges to persuade their colleagues[79]

Source: the authors.

institutions such as the Government or the Parliament, and the key question of this article (*How has the Czech Constitutional Court remained resilient, able and willing to challenge the political institutions?*) would lose much of its meaning. The Court has shown relatively high levels of activism and assertiveness towards other branches, and has continued to do so even in the last couple of years under populist Prime Minister Babiš.

Therefore, we follow up with an analysis of the determinants of the Court's resilience to populist influences. In this regard, we build on the existing literature and focus on the institutional design of the Court and the political fragmentation as the main explanatory factors. However, we go beyond the claims made in the literature and argue that the Court's ability to resist populist influences is not solely shaped by external factors. On the contrary, the Court's willingness to make activist decisions and to actively use its reservoir of public support for this purpose has played a significant role in keeping these external factors favourable.

The constitutional-political context of the Court's functioning

Czechia has tried to dissociate itself from the Visegrád Four label of democratically backsliding countries. Although Czechia has performed significantly better than Hungary and Poland on indices of democracy and human rights in the last decade,[24] the literature has pointed out a decisive shift towards a form of populist democracy,[25] characterised by a dominant party with a populist ideology, the decline of the traditional left, and the rise of minor parties on both fringes of the cultural spectrum.[26] Compared to the conservative national populism of Viktor Orbán and Jarosław Kaczyński, Andrej Babiš – a billionaire, leader of the ANO 2011 movement and the Czech Prime Minister since 2017 – has resorted to technocratic populism, which strategically uses the appeal of technocratic competence, anti-corruption rhetoric, and the ideology of expertise with a populist political appeal to ordinary people.[27] Babiš succeeded in constructing an image of corrupt, power-seeking and incompetent politicians undermining the hard work of ordinary people, who could instead rely on a successful businessman able to 'manage the state like a company'.[28]

The different nature of populism in Hungary and Poland on one side and in Czechia on the other side[29] has significant repercussions. Babiš's ANO 2011 counts among valence populist parties, overwhelmingly emphasising non-positional issues such as, e.g. performance, transparency and the fight against corruption.[30] Babiš's technocratic approach, with its thin ideology, arguably will not mobilise and polarise the public as much as Orbán's and Kaczyński's invocations of their nations' greatness. Moreover, Babiš clashing with expert institutions, such as the Constitutional Court and the Czech National Bank, would undermine his own emphasis on the technocratic rule.

The Czech Parliament consists of the Chamber of Deputies and the Senate, with the Chamber of Deputies holding the position of the main political battlefield and the Senate of a stabilising factor with partial veto powers. The political composition of both parliamentary chambers usually does not correspond because a proportional election system determines the composition of the Chamber of Deputies (200 deputies elected for four years as members of political parties), while 81 senators earn their seats for six years in a two-round majority staggered election (one-third of the Senate every two years). Moreover, the Senate is staffed not only by political parties' cadres but also by independent regional personalities outside mainstream parties or representatives of fringe parties. For these senators, a petition to the Constitutional Court represents one of the very few options how to achieve a substantive change.[31] The bicameral Parliament with often very different partisan compositions makes it difficult for populists to change the Constitution, which was the case in Hungary. The second important fragmentation occurs in both parliamentary chambers with a multitude of parties in the lower chamber and individual senators in the Senate, thus hindering a prospect of an easy compromise. The diverse composition of the Senate plays a crucial role in the appointment process of constitutional judges. This distinguishes Czechia from Poland, where Sejm, the lower chamber of the Polish Parliament, associated with the ruling Government, elects constitutional judges. The overall Czech constitutional structure hence contains more safeguards against the populist takeover, but at the expense of decision-making readiness.

Political institutions operate in the environment of diversified public trust, which we examine more in detail below. Generally, the public tends to support expert political bodies, such as the Court, and distrust central political institutions, such as the Parliament and the Government.

The Czech Constitutional Court as an activist court

Before analysing the relationship between the Court's activism and the potential threat to its independence from populist political forces, we have to answer the question to what extent is the Court activist. Only then we can turn to examine how its activism was influenced by populist threats to its independence.

Judicial activism, in general, is a contested concept, lacking a single dominant definition or approach.[32] For the purposes of labelling a judgement as 'activist', we work with several criteria. First, we take into account only politically significant cases. Furthermore, we consider whether the Court relied on a reasonably foreseeable constitutional standard. If the Court delivers a salient judgement with a politically significant impact and the judgment is based only on a vague constitutional standard (rather than a clear wording of the Constitution), we consider it an activist judgement. This is especially true if the Court relied on a purposive interpretation of the constitutional provision in question. As Lino Graglia put it: 'By judicial activism I mean, quite simply and specifically, the practice by judges of disallowing policy choices by other governmental officials or institutions that the Constitution does not clearly prohibit'.[33] The cases discussed below (such as *Melčák* or the *Grand Election* judgements) clearly fall within this category. Another important signal of activism is a judgement that in fact creates new rules and may be labelled as 'legislating from the bench', thus encroaching on the competences of other constitutional bodies, mainly parliaments.[34] Finally, we take into account the measure of comparative activism of a constitutional court (i.e. whether the Court stands out from a comparative point of view).

In comparative literature, activist constitutional courts tend to attract considerable attention. In this regard, the Czech Constitutional Court's case-law has never really made as big a splash as the Hungarian Constitutional Court did when it abolished capital punishment, or the South African Constitutional Court that was considered very activist and interventionist in its early days.[35] The most intriguing activist judgements of the Czech Constitutional Court have concerned issues of organisational constitutional law such as separation of powers or electoral process. With regard to substantive fundamental rights' interpretation, the Court has been relatively restrained. In the Czech context, powerful politicians and interest groups, seeking their own political agendas, have often accused the Court of undue activism. In 2006, for example, a think-tank founded by President Václav Klaus published a volume entitled 'Judgeocracy in the Czech Republic: Fiction, or reality', condemning various decisions of the Court and judicial review in general.[36] In 2011, Prime Minister Nečas criticised the allegedly activist *Building Savings* judgement[37] and accused some members of the Court of being biased.[38] Similar instances of politically motivated labelling abound.

Despite not being as famous as some other courts with judicial review powers, the Court has, in fact, shown a decent degree of activism. Its activism, however, seems to be rather selective. The Court has tended to lash out in certain types of cases, yet it has remained deferential in other areas.

It is important to note that the Czech Constitutional Court is endowed with virtually all the powers that a constitutional court can have.[39] Amongst other things, it can hear individual constitutional complaints, review all sorts of legislative acts, decide on competence conflicts, conduct a preventive review of international treaties, or try a President for high treason or gross violation of the constitutional order. Most of the Court's case-load consists of constitutional complaints that are heard by three-member chambers. However, the most significant cases, such as the review of legislation, are assigned to a 'plenum' consisting of all fifteen judges. For the purposes of our article, we must distinguish between the Court's activism in the individual constitutional complaint procedure from its activist approach in plenary cases, particularly plenary cases involving a review of the constitutionality of legislation. Even though the Court has been at times very activist when deciding on individual constitutional complaints, we will largely ignore these cases, as they are less relevant in the discussion concerning populism. In the individual constitutional complaint procedure, even activist judgements directly communicate only with the parties to the proceedings; they are usually not seen as a challenge to the ruling political powers, and thus typically fly under the radar. Consequently, we focus mainly on the activist plenary judgements in which the Court directly challenged the ruling majority and entered the political arena.

A further distinction can be made between cases involving substantive human rights issues, such as politically controversial cases concerning the rights of minorities, and cases dealing with organisational constitutional law issues, such as separation of powers, independence of the judiciary and the general rule-of-law issues. The Court has perhaps retreated towards self-restraint in substantive human rights cases,[40] but it does not seem to be the case in organisational constitutional law cases and electoral matters, which are of utmost importance for the purposes of our article. The latter category included the most prominent examples of the Court's activism, which we present here (*Euro-Amendment*, *Melčák*, the *Grand Election Judgements* and a line of case law concerning judicial independence, such as the *Brožová* judgement and the *Judicial Salaries* saga).

In the 2002 *Euro-Amendment* judgement,[41] the Court refused to acknowledge the impact of a constitutional amendment and unilaterally included international human rights treaties in the concept of constitutional order.

In 2009, in the midst of a political crisis, virtually all relevant political parties concluded that the best solution would be to shorten the term of office of the lower chamber of the Parliament and organise snap elections as soon as possible. They considered the standard constitutional procedure too slow. Therefore, copying the solution used almost 12 years earlier, the Parliament adopted an *ad hoc* constitutional act that would allow a unique reduction in the electoral term. However, this time, a member of the Chamber of Deputies used a constitutional complaint to challenge the constitutional act and the President's consequent decision to call snap elections. The Court's plenum (all fifteen judges sitting *en banc*) annulled the constitutional act in question by the *Melčák* judgment[42] because it was a non-general solution that contravened the principle of the generality of law and the prohibition of retroactivity. This judgment has had far-reaching consequences because it was the first time that the Court explicitly held that it had the power to review even constitutional amendments adopted by the Parliament. The judgment was thus a clear challenge to the Parliament's authority, and its competence to decide what is (and is not) part of the constitutional order. Arguably, the judgement influenced the outcome of the following 2010 parliamentary election. In response to the judgment, some senior members of the Parliament publicly suggested that it should be disregarded as an *ultra vires* exercise of the Court's power.[43] Still, the brewing constitutional crisis eventually petered out, and other constitutional actors accepted the judgment.

The 2001 *Grand Election Judgement*[44] did not deal with a constitutional amendment, but its political significance might be even greater. The Court declared unconstitutional an Election Law amendment that increased the number of voting districts, introduced a modified D'Hondt method and abolished the second scrutiny. The modifications to the electoral system, sponsored by the two strongest political parties at that time, would have drastically weakened smaller political parties and allowed the two strongest parties to control the Chamber of Deputies. Interestingly, the case was brought before the Court by President Václav Havel. The Court declared the reform unconstitutional because the amendment in question introduced too many majoritarian elements, although the Constitution prescribes for elections to the Chamber of Deputies a 'system of proportional representation'. This was a significant blow to the two strongest political parties and arguably started the animosity towards the Court on the part of Václav Klaus and Miloš Zeman, two of the most important political leaders in the post-1993 Czechia.

Finally, a series of cases concerning judicial independence has evidenced the Court's activism in the pre-2010 period. In addition to numerous judgements defending judicial salaries against an (allegedly) arbitrary reduction,[45] the Court delivered a string of decisions concerning a conflict between President Václav Klaus and Supreme Court President Iva Brožová. In 2006, when Václav Klaus dismissed Iva Brožová from the position of Supreme Court President, the Constitutional Court not only found this dismissal unconstitutional and *de facto* reinstated Iva Brožová at the helm of the Supreme Court, but also struck down Article 106 of the Czech Law on Courts and Judges, declaring that it was unconstitutional for the executive to dismiss court presidents.[46] However, the Czech Parliament fought back and introduced limited terms for all court presidents (ten years for presidents of apex courts and seven years for presidents of other courts).[47]

All the aforementioned judgements predate the populist turn in Czech politics, which is typically associated with Babiš's becoming the Prime Minister in 2017. They show the Court's determination to interfere with high politics, even up to invalidating a constitutional amendment. Even though the Court did not produce many judgements of a similar magnitude in the last decade, one clearly stands out – the 2021 *Grand Election Judgment II*.[48] The Court held that a particular combination of the key elements of the electoral system adopted in the aftermath of the *Grand Election Judgement I* violated the constitutional principle of proportional representation as well as the principle of equality of the right to vote. It annulled *inter alia* the legal threshold for coalitions. But much more importantly, it held that the combination of fourteen districts and the system of allocating seats (D'Hondt formula used at the level of districts) causes unequal and disproportionate seat allocation. However, the Court only formally annulled the system of seat allocation and not the existence of districts. It thus left the Parliament the task of coming up with a constitutionally valid solution. The *Grand Election Judgement II* went even further than the *Grand Election Judgement* 20 years ago, making it virtually impossible for any future electoral system to significantly favour stronger political parties. It took the Court three years to deliver the ruling, which was announced merely eight months before the election. Prime Minister Babiš responded furiously, accusing the Court of 'overstepping all boundaries' and not acting impartially.[49] Nevertheless, even this outburst eventually petered out and there have not seemed to be any consequences for the Court yet.

The presented Court's activist judgments concern mainly structural constitutional issues. Unlike its Polish and Hungarian counterparts, the Court has stayed away from the 'cultural wars', including, e.g. LGBT rights.[50] The Court can thus portray itself rather as a guardian of fair political competition that at the same time avoids dividing Czech society by advancing sensitive agendas. The *Grand Election Judgement II* shows that even in the current environment, the Court is not afraid to issue far-reaching judgements that might invite the ire of (populist) top political figures. We do not claim that the Court's emphasis on separation of powers, judicial independence and electoral process is a result of a conscious strategy. The Court simply reacted to emerging challenges to the young Czech constitutional system and the most significant challenges happened to concern these issues. Thus, as we develop in the following section, even without a clear strategy, the Court contributed to the resilience of the Czech constitutional system and arguably shielded itself from potential court-curbing. This would not be possible without the willingness of the Court to make these decisions at critical times. The composition of the Court proved crucial, which points to the importance of the appointment mechanism. New entrants then experience institutional socialisation and internalise the ethos of the Court.

What makes the Czech Constitutional Court resilient?

As shown above, the Court does not operate in an environment devoid of populist tendencies. At the same time, it does not share the headlines with its Polish and Hungarian counterparts as a victim of populist capture. Even after coming into power in 2017, Babiš's coalition government has not stripped the Court's powers, cut its budget, appointed a loyalist, or employed any other big trick from the populist repertoire.[51]

Following the structure presented in Table 2, we elaborate on reasons why the Court has remained resilient. We assume that Babiš, as a businessman used to managing and making decisions, prefers his governing not constrained by any checks, including judicial.

First of all, the Court's resilience might be partly explained by its institutional design and the inability of the appointing actors to exploit its inherent weaknesses we analyse below. Secondly, the Czech parliamentary majorities and governments, including the current populist-dominated coalition, are in a weak position to mount such an attack due to the significant fragmentation of the Czech political landscape. Moreover, the Court has accumulated a fair deal of public support that helps in shielding it from political attacks. Finally, the diverse composition of the Court and its persisting ethos of the original dissident Court safeguarding liberal democracy further strengthen resilience to populist assaults.

In general, the Court's design strongly builds on a template from the German Federal Constitutional Court in combination with a US-style appointment process. The Court consists of fifteen judges appointed by the Czech President upon approval of the Senate. Subsequently, out of these fifteen judges, the Czech President unilaterally[52] appoints the Court President and two Vice Presidents. Judges serve for ten years, and their term is, by convention, renewable. The pure 'American model', with a President nominating all judges and the Senate confirming all of them, is alien to parliamentary democracy and does not exist anywhere else in the European Union or even in the Council of Europe.[53] One of the 1993 Constitution drafters[54] suggested that the institutional setup of the Court was approved behind closed doors at the very last moments of the constitution drafting to increase the powers of Václav Havel, who was widely expected to be elected the first President of independent Czechia.[55]

Unless the Senate works as a real safeguard, the Czech President as the only nominating organ could *de facto* create his 'own' Court. The President's position is further strengthened by the fact that there is no staggered system of appointing judges, and thus virtually the entire Court is replaced every ten years. As a result of this peculiar institutional design, every Czech President (Václav Havel, Václav Klaus, and Miloš Zeman) appointed almost the entire Court at the beginning of his first five-year term.[56] Accordingly, the first Court (1993–2002) is often referred to as the 'Havel Court', the second (2003–2012) as the 'Klaus Court' and the third Court (2013–now) as the 'Zeman Court'. Despite these labels, none of the three Czech Presidents fully took advantage of his powers. Each of them relied on his advisors, who have always proposed a relatively balanced and diverse Court, including representatives of different legal professions, careers and political leanings.[57] Moreover, the Senate has worked as a reliable safeguard so far and rejected the most controversial candidates, sometimes even repeatedly, and thus effectively constrained the Czech President. As a result, the Court has never turned out to be a body consisting purely of the President's ideological allies.

The dynamics of selecting the Court's judges have changed profoundly over time. Anti-communist sentiments characterised the selection of the Havel Court. The appointment of the Havel Court went on relatively smoothly; still, two candidates were rejected due to ties with the communist regime, and one resigned during the appointment process after a critical press campaign pointing out his problematic writings during the communist era.

The formation of the Klaus Court ten years later turned out to be more difficult. The Senate had been established in the meantime and wanted to show that it had to be taken seriously. Moreover, the composition of the Senate was relatively hostile to Klaus during the first two years of his mandate. At the same time, Havel's era was coming to an end, and dissidents had lost their influence in Czech politics. The Senate rejected as many as eight Klaus' candidates.[58] This prompted severe tensions between the Senate and President Klaus, who became so frustrated that he refused to propose further candidates.[59] The first standoff occurred at the beginning of Klaus' first term in 2003. The Senate approved the first three candidates proposed by Klaus,[60] but in July 2003, it showed its teeth for the first time by rejecting Klaus' legal advisor, Aleš Pejchal. In the next confirmation round, the Senate rejected three out of four of Klaus' nominees. After this bitter defeat, Klaus slowed down in making further nominations, which incapacitated the Court deciding on the constitutionality of laws. Klaus became so desperate that he even nominated Pejchal for the second time, with the same negative outcome. The second impasse took place towards the end of Klaus's second term in 2012, as the term of the last Havel Justices was ending. This time, after the Senate rejected two of Klaus's candidates, Klaus proclaimed that he would not nominate anyone else and would leave this duty to the new President. The main victim was again the Court, which was short two Justices for a year.

Zeman's role was arguably easier than Klaus's for several reasons. Zeman became the first directly elected Czech President, which boosted his democratic legitimacy, and faced a friendly Senate, in which his former colleagues from the Social Democratic Party had the majority. Moreover, Zeman could discuss his choices with the Court's President, Pavel Rychetský, who had served in Zeman Government in 1998–2002. Despite these favourable circumstances, the Senate rejected three of Zeman's candidates and restaffing the Court eventually took almost three years.

In sum, while the law governing the selection of Court's judges has remained intact, the dynamics of this process, as well as external circumstances, have changed profoundly. During Havel's presidency, the public and the media largely ignored judicial nominations, but this started to change during Klaus's presidency and eventually resulted in a public spectacle during Zeman's term. Both Havel and Zeman faced a rather cooperative parliamentary chamber, while Klaus initially had to persuade a quite hostile Senate. Each Czech President also picked from a different pool of candidates and relied on different advisors. Havel discussed his choices broadly and listened to dissidents, Klaus relied exclusively on his friends and political advisors, and Zeman, to a large extent, outsourced the shortlisting to his friend, the Court's President, Rychetský. Miloš Zeman, however, either did not intend or failed to exploit the favourable situations fully and, in fact, helped in creating a court that has proven to be anything but his ally.

Even though the Court's composition has always turned out fairly balanced ideologically, its institutional design has some inherent weak spots that could be exploited in the future. The crucial one concerns the process of appointments. The Czech system allows – under a certain constellation – the President and the Senate to seize the whole Court with a carefully selected group of fifteen judges. So far, this scenario has not materialised. This is partly due to the second resilience factor, i.e. the existing political fragmentation in the Senate, whose diverse composition prevents a monochromatic Court, built solely on President's preferences.

For a Czech populist leader bent on getting the Court out of the way, the following scenario would be a dream one. First of all, populists would dominate the Chamber of Deputies and consequently the Government. Second, the President would be their ally. Finally, they would have at least a strong plurality in the Senate. The fulfilment of the first condition would allow the hypothetical leader to enforce her policies, while the President and the Senate would appoint a sympathetic Court. However, such conditions have never occurred, mainly because of two factors. The first one is the intentional constitutional design of the separation of powers; the second one is tied to the fragmented nature of the Czech political party system. The Senate was intentionally designed as a counterweight to the Chamber of Deputies, which is tied to the Government and everyday politics. This was one of the reasons why the Senate, rather than the Chamber, approves judicial candidates. In countries with a unicameral parliament, such as Hungary, the hijacking of a constitutional court is much easier. In unicameral systems, it is not only easier to change the constitution and important statutory law specifying the design of the political process, but usually also the appointments to a constitutional court will be dominated by the current majority.

At the same time, political fragmentation is not only apparent in the Chamber of Deputies – Senate relationship, but also in the composition of the Chamber of Deputies itself. With five to nine political parties sitting in the Chamber of Deputies, Czechia qualifies as an example of extreme pluralism[61] characterised by the notorious instability of the Governments.[62] For an unstable government in a pluralist system of checks and balances, it is a very complicated task to try and tame a constitutional court. Knowing this allows us to see the *Grand Election Judgements* in a new light. By emphasising the principle of proportional representation and forcing the Parliament to adopt closely proportional electoral systems, the Court contributed to political fragmentation and made it more difficult for future Governments and Parliaments to curb that fragmentation. The fact that the Court's activism manifested itself predominantly in the area of separation of powers, judicial independence, and electoral competition has had long-term consequences for the way the political process operates in Czechia and for the conditions in which the Court works. While substantive human rights activism by a non-resilient constitutional court might be easily countered by strong populist governments, as the Polish and Hungarian cases show, judicial activism that contributes to that court's own actual resilience makes this considerably more difficult.

Other possible weak spots in the Court's institutional design might impair its independence, but they are arguably manageable. The possibility of reappointment potentially undermines the independence of incumbent judges, who may want to increase their chances to be reappointed by strategic manoeuvring towards the end of their term. The problems burst out fully in the following Court's overhaul in 2013–2015 as four incumbent judges from the Klaus Court ran for reappointment to the Zeman Court, and two of them failed. Voting in the Senate followed a clear pattern. Those incumbent judges who voted on key judgments towards the end of their term along the lines with the Senate's majority were eventually rewarded by reappointment. In contrast, those who voted against the Senate's majority were *de facto* punished for their decision-making, and the Senate rejected them. This sends a clear signal to the current judges of the Zeman Court about what they are supposed to do if they want to have their term renewed in the early 2020s. Nevertheless, in our interviews, many current judges openly expressed their dislike for reappointment. If they stick to their words and voluntarily do not run for a second term, such practice might evolve into a constitutional convention.

Another possible problem is that even without a constitutional supermajority in both parliamentary chambers, the ruling majority in the Chamber of Deputies might change the statutory rules of the Court's procedure to limit its powers.[63] But with the *Melčák* judgement in mind, it is very probable that a mere statutory amendment would be annulled by the Court if it felt that such legislation would hinder its role as a guardian of the Constitution.

Finally, any aggressive steps towards the Court by political actors would have to overcome the fact that the Court enjoys a good deal of public trust, and that the voters tend to trust the Court and other expert public bodies more than the Government and the President, to say nothing about the notoriously unpopular Parliament. In July 2020, 57% of respondents trusted, and 31% mistrusted, the Court, which are comparable figures to other expert public bodies, such as the Supreme Audit Office or the Ombudsperson.[64] This trend has stretched from the 1990s until today. The Court carries a good deal of its legitimacy from its infancy in the 1990s, when the Havel Court built on the dissident ethos. The Court has repeatedly bolstered its legitimacy by its ability to correct the excesses of the lower courts and mainly by standing up to rather unpopular Governments and parliamentary majorities. While doing this, the Court was viewed by the public as an impartial expert institution. The loss of the appearance of impartiality might have a devastating effect on the Court's public support. Not surprisingly, the alleged lack of impartiality was the main rhetorical weapon that Prime Minister Babiš used against the Court after the 2021 *Grand Election Judgement II*. He relied on some political remarks of the Court's President Pavel Rychetský directed against Babiš and President Miloš Zeman.[65] It is extremely advisable that the Court's representatives stay away from politics in their public appearances because otherwise, they threaten their reputation as impartial experts, which has earned them public trust.

Our semi-structured interviews with Czech constitutional judges further support the argument that the Court judges do not (have to) take into account the possible threat of populist retribution. The interviews provided us with crucial information on the judicial perception of public and political influence on judicial decision-making. We interviewed ten out of fifteen constitutional judges. The remaining three explicitly refused to participate, and two repeatedly reported scheduling conflicts. The interviews were conducted between the years 2017 and 2019, usually lasted one hour and consisted of fifteen open questions, which enabled further probing. The project concerned generally extra-legal influences on judicial decision-making. We promised the interview partners strict confidentiality in order to facilitate their sincerity in answers.

The most fruitful question on the judicial perception of public pressure concerned a separate opinion by a Slovak constitutional judge, Ivetta Macejková, concerning a very closely watched case in which Slovak Prime Minister Mečiar gave amnesty to the kidnappers of the Slovak President's son. Asking about a case from a different jurisdiction should contribute to greater openness in the answers of Czech judges. Judge Macejková, President of the Slovak Constitutional Court at the time, composed a separate opinion in which she contemplated the position of a judge in modern society. A judge does not live in isolation and is well aware of public opinion polls, political and media discussions etc. However, wrote Macejková, judges should not follow public opinion but decide according to law;

this way, judges will be seen as independent, impartial and objective. Only then the public will respect the judgments, even though it may disagree with them.[66]

We asked Czech constitutional judges what they thought about Macejková's position. Two groups of respondents emerged. The first group rejected the idea of any influence of public opinion, while the second acknowledged its existence and reflected on it but also has tried to mitigate it. A good example of the first group's respondents was the statement: 'I would not be interested in [public opinion polls] at all. For example, when we decided on the restitution of churches' properties, 80% of respondents or so were against it. [Public opinion polls] do not play such a role here as it might seem from the outside. Being at the Constitutional Court is like being in an ivory tower'. Another judge pointed to the fact that he sometimes hears criticism of Court's decisions but strictly decides how he thinks the case should be decided. Yet another judge stressed that Constitutional Court judges have to be immune against public opinion. However, he conceded that, unlike its Slovak counterpart, the Czech Constitutional Court has been spared long-term media attacks, has enjoyed a great deal of respect and has never faced public resistance against its decision. Judges rationalised their resistance to public opinion by noting that 'vox populi is not always vox dei', and also pointed out to the majority society's bias against minorities.

The second group acknowledged pressure from the public; however, these judges have tried to actively mitigate its impact. They anticipate potential adverse reactions from the public and adjust their reasoning style or its presentation accordingly. This group of judges 'does not live in a bubble' (as opposed to the first group, which works in an 'ivory tower') and tries to be especially persuasive when they fear a popular backlash. Moreover, in case of very important judgments, these judges felt that it was vital to communicate actively with the public and explain the decision, because in such cases, 'to sell the decision to the public is as important as to issue a good decision'.

Regarding perceptions of political pressures, Czech constitutional judges see the potential risk in the possibility of renewable terms and point to past examples when Senators penalised the judges with whom they disagreed in the case of restitution of churches' properties by not approving them for a second term. On the other hand, Czech judges stated that they greatly appreciated the lack of political attacks on the Court for its judgments in highly political cases. Especially compared to other Visegrád countries, the judges praised politicians for staying away from the Court's powers, composition and budget. Some judges mentioned a certain basic level of political culture that, with certain exceptions, especially from the far-right, prevents politicians from contravening the Court. Judges explained politicians' restraint as a consequence of public support for the Court, which discourages politicians from open attacks. Judges also emphasised that they did not succumb to political pressure and, in return, they had striven to stay away from politics. Therefore, some disliked the lack of political restraint from Court President Rychetský, an ex-Minister of Justice with a long history in Czech politics, who does not hesitate to comment on political issues in his media appearances.

To sum up, Czech constitutional judges enjoy the support of the public, which makes open political attacks against them a risky option. Judges did not perceive any pressure from politicians and have also tried not to provoke any. Some judges, for this reason, criticised Court President Rychetský for unnecessary political comments for the media. As regards pressure from the public, some judges stated they did not consider it at all, while others tried to work strategically with the reasoning and its media presentation in order to persuade the public about their reasoning.

Conclusion

The Czech case serves as a significant counter-example to the cases of Poland or Hungary. Despite sharing a similar trajectory in the 1990s and the 2000s, all three countries have taken dramatically different turns in the last decade regarding the rule of law and the independence of top courts. The Polish and Hungarian constitutional courts have faced successful attacks by the ruling political powers. Czechia has also experienced populist turn and democratic backsliding; however, the situation differs in relation to its Constitutional Court. The Court does not shy away from activist rulings and has shown determination to challenge ruling majorities with populist leanings, yet, it has not faced any significant repercussions. Hence, the Court continues to perform its function as a check on other branches and contributes to preventing further backsliding of the Polish or Hungarian magnitude.

The case study of the Czech Constitutional Court and its comparison to the Hungarian and Polish cases allows us to formulate a few cautious conclusions. First of all, a sound institutional design, with a variety of actors who are differently constituted, contributes to shielding the Court from populist capture. Even though it contains some flaws, such as possible abuse of the (re)appointment procedure or the possibility of the ruling majority to amend the statutory regulation of the Court, these weak spots are tough to exploit. The Court is able to shield itself from any challenge mounted by amendments to the statutory law, such as limiting access to the Court or introducing an absurd quorum, by annulling such a law. Given the very broad access to the Court, it would hardly be a problem to 'find' a suitable petitioner. All the remaining court-curbing strategies would have a hard time overcoming the challenges posed by political fragmentation and the public support that the Court enjoys.

The fragmentation of the Czech political system makes it hard for any ruling Government or President to gain a strong enough position to mount a sustained attack on the Court. Bicameralism and supermajorities needed to change the Constitution prevent an overhaul of Court's powers via a constitutional revision. The appointment system requires the cooperation of the Czech President and the politically diverse Senate, which largely forestalls the establishment of a politically homogenous Court, fully cooperative with the Government and the lower chamber.

Presidents and Prime Ministers have occasionally verbally challenged the Court. However, these verbal challenges were rarely more than immediate opportunistic reactions to a particular judgement, and fizzled out very quickly. This is not purely accidental. The Czech political landscape's fairly competitive and fragmented nature makes it very difficult for the ruling powers to concentrate their efforts on the Court or the courts in general. In military terms, such a campaign would require a secure rear. But even Babiš's ANO 2011 party at its most dominant or President Zeman have always had the parliamentary opposition or the Senate to contend with, not even mentioning the notorious internal fragility of Czech coalition governments. These observations are in line with the existing literature on political fragmentation.[67]

Furthermore, the Czech technocratic populism of Andrej Babiš differs substantially from the ethnopopulism of Viktor Orbán or Jarosław Kaczyński. Hungarian and Polish versions of populism, with their significant nationalist emphasis and portrayal of various external enemies, has a higher mobilisation potential than general boilerplate about corruption and state-management by experts. The Czech Constitutional Court has not been subject to intense and sustained pressure of the Hungarian or Polish sort. This might be a case of self-censorship on the part of the Czech populist leaders, who have a certain respect for expert bodies. An assault on an independent court with a fairly deep reservoir of public support represents a risky endeavour that might alienate parts of their very diverse voter base.

Moreover, the Court is not a mere passive object in the political game but actively engages in supervising political competition. Its judgments have so far contributed to the preservation of a fragmented political system incapable of creating solid majorities and stable governments. The Court has managed to build on its reputation from the 1990s and has maintained an image as an independent expert legal institution. The Court has on several occasions dramatically intervened in the political competition while portraying its far-reaching judgments as a necessary exercise in its role as a guardian of fair political competition. The Court typically does not actively engage in a radical social transformation that would divide public opinion and polarise the Court's audiences. The close examination of the Czech Constitutional Court case offers a list of ingredients that, when appropriately combined, helps in building resistant constitutional courts, and hence also liberal democracy. We admit that it is fairly easy to present the Czech Constitutional Court as a resililient one, since it never came under an attack of the Polish or Hungarian kind. We also concede that we cannot predict with infallibility what would happen if such an attack would materialise in the future. But our argument is that for the reasons that we present in our article, such a scenario is much less likely to play out in Czechia than in Hungary or Poland. Resilience does not need to be understood only as an ability to withstand an actual attack; it can also be rooted in conditions that make an attack unlikely, especially when the Court itself contributes to such conditions.

Distinguishing between judicial activism in the separation of powers and political competition on the one hand and in human-rights-related sensitive issues on the other hand in relation to a court's resilience represents an important finding of this article. It nicely contributes to the recently renewed interest in John Hart Ely's *Democracy and Distrust*.[68] Although Ely's process-based theory turned out to be more influential in common law jurisdictions,[69] the Czech case shows that also continental jurisdictions might exercise the bravest judicial activism in the area of fair political competition, and not in rights review. Without even mentioning Ely, of course.

Notes

1. Elisabeth Bakke and Nick Sitter, 'The EU's Enfants Terribles: Democratic Backsliding in Central Europe since 2010', *Perspectives on Politics* 4, doi:10.1017/S1537592720001292.
2. Michael Carpenter, 'Slovakia and the Triumph of Nationalist Populism', *Communist and Post-Communist Studies* 30, no. 2 (1 June 1997): 205–19, doi:10.1016/S0967-067X (97)00005-6.

3. Katarína Šipulová and Hubert Smekal, 'Between Human Rights and Transitional Justice: The Dilemma of Constitutional Courts in Post-Communist Central Europe', *Europe-Asia Studies* 73, no. 1 (2 January 2021): 101–30, doi:10.1080/09668136.2020.1841739.

4. Bojan Bugarič and Tom Ginsburg, 'The Assault on Postcommunist Courts', *Journal of Democracy* 27, no. 3 (2016): 70, doi:10.1353/jod.2016.0047.

5. Tamir Moustafa, 'Law and Courts in Authoritarian Regimes', *Annual Review of Law and Social Science* 10, no. 1 (2014): 294–5, doi:10.1146/annurev-lawsocsci-110413-030532.

6. Kriszta Kovács and Kim Lane Scheppele, 'The Fragility of an Independent Judiciary: Lessons from Hungary and Poland—and the European Union', *Communist and Post-Communist Studies* 51, no. 3 (1 September 2018): 197–8, doi:10.1016/j.postcomstud.2018.07.005.

7. Aziz Huq, 'Democratic Erosion and the Courts: Comparative Perspectives', *New York University Law Review* 93 (2018): 22–7.

8. Huq, 27.

9. Michael Blauberger and R. Daniel Kelemen, 'Can Courts Rescue National Democracy? Judicial Safeguards against Democratic Backsliding in the EU', *Journal of European Public Policy* 24, no. 3 (9 March 2017): 321–36, doi:10.1080/13501763.2016.1229357.

10. Tomáš Langášek, *Ústavní soud Československé republiky a jeho osudy v letech 1920–1948* (Plzeň: Aleš Čeněk, 2011), 166–7.

11. Aziz Huq, 'Legal or Political Checks on Apex Criminality: An Essay on Constitutional Design', *UCLA Law Review* 65 (2018): 1530.

12. Mikhail Ivanovich Pastukhov, 'Features of Judicial Constitutional Control in the Republic of Belarus', *Studia politologiczne* 48 (2019): 38.

13. Jan Petrov, '(De-)judicialization of Politics in the Era of Populism: Lessons from Central and Eastern Europe', *The International Journal of Human Rights* (2021): 6; Renáta Uitz, 'Can You Tell When an Illiberal Democracy Is in the Making? An Appeal to Comparative Constitutional Scholarship from Hungary', *International Journal of Constitutional Law* 13, no. 1 (2015).

14. Petrov, 12–14.

15. Wojciech Sadurski, *Poland's Constitutional Breakdown* (Oxford: Oxford University Press 2019); Tomasz Tadeusz Koncewicz, 'The Capture of the Polish Constitutional Tribunal and Beyond: Of Institution(s), Fidelities and the Rule of Law in Flux', *Review of Central and East European Law* 43, no. 2 (2018). For examples of different court-packing tactics, see David Kosař and Katarína Šipulová, 'How to Fight Court-Packing?', *Constitutional Studies* 6, no. 1 (2020): 133–64.

16. Salvatore Caserta and Pola Cebulak, 'Resilience Techniques of International Courts in Times of Resistance to International Law', *International & Comparative Law Quarterly* 70 (2021): 745.

17. Zdeněk Kühn, 'The Czech Constitutional Court in Times of Populism from Judicial Activism to Judicial Self-Restraint', in *Populist Challenges to Constitutional Interpretation in Europe and Beyond*, eds. Fruzsina Gárdos-Orosz and Zoltán Szente (London: Routledge, 2021), 108.

18. Bugarič and Ginsburg, 69.

19. Pablo Castillo-Ortiz, 'The Illiberal Abuse of Constitutional Courts in Europe', *European Constitutional Law Review* 15, no. 1 (March 2019): 67–70, doi:10.1017/S1574019619000026.

20. Castillo-Ortiz, 70.

21. Diana Kapiszewski, Gordon Silverstein, and Robert A. Kagan, 'Conclusion: On Judicial Ships and Winds of Change', in *Consequential Courts: Judicial Roles in Global Perspective*, eds. Diana Kapiszewski, David Silverman, and Robert A. Kagan (New York, NY: Cambridge University Press, 2013), 399–401; Julio Ríos-Figueroa, 'Fragmentation of Power and the Emergence of an Effective Judiciary in Mexico, 1994–2002', *Latin American Politics and Society* 49 (2007); John Ferejohn, 'Judicializing Politics, Politicizing Law', *Law and Contemporary Problems* 65, no. 3 (2002): 55–60, doi:10.2307/1192402.

22. Arthur Dyevre, 'Unifying the Field of Comparative Judicial Politics: Towards a General Theory of Judicial Behaviour', *European Political Science Review* 2, no. 2 (2010): 317.

23. Diana Kapiszewski, Gordon Silverstein, and Robert A. Kagan, 'Conclusion: On Judicial Ships and Winds of Change', in *Consequential Courts: Judicial Roles in Global Perspective*, eds. Diana Kapiszewski, David Silverman, and Robert A. Kagan (New York, NY: Cambridge University Press, 2013), 403.

24. For example, the 2020 Bertelsmann Transformation Index puts Czechia ahead of Poland and Hungary both in the Political Transformation and the Governance index (https://www.bti-project.org/en/home.html?&d=G&cb=00000). The same applies for the 2021 Freedom House Index in both the Global Freedom and the Democracy Status (https://freedomhouse.org/explore-the-map?type=nit&year=2021).

25. Stanley groups all three countries under the label of 'backsliding democracies', although he admits that Czechia has performed better than Hungary and Poland (Ben Stanley, 'Backsliding Away? The Quality of Democracy in Central and Eastern Europe', *Journal of Contemporary European Research* 15, no. 4 (13 December 2019): 348–50, doi:10.30950/jcer.v15i4.1122).

26. Seán Hanley and Milada Anna Vachudova, 'Understanding the Illiberal Turn: Democratic Backsliding in the Czech Republic', *East European Politics* 34, no. 3 (3 July 2018): 277, doi:10.1080/21599165.2018.1493457.

27. Lenka Buštíková and Petra Guasti, 'The State as a Firm: Understanding the Autocratic Roots of Technocratic Populism', *East European Politics and Societies* 33, no. 2 (1 May 2019): 304, doi:10.1177/0888325418791723.

28. Vlastimil Havlík, 'Technocratic Populism and Political Illiberalism in Central Europe', *Problems of Post-Communism* 66, no. 6 (2 November 2019): 376, doi:10.1080/10758216.2019.1580590.

29. Czechia further differs from Poland and Hungary in the sequence of the concentration of power. While Babiš accumulated his economic and media power before entering politics, Orbán developed oligarchic networks only after (Hanley and Vachudova, 'Understanding the Illiberal Turn', 283–7).

30. Mattia Zulianello and Erik Gahner Larsen, 'Populist Parties in European Parliament Elections: A New Dataset on Left, Right and Valence Populism from 1979 to 2019', *Electoral Studies* 71 (1 June 2021): 102312, doi:10.1016/j.electstud.2021.102312.

31. Kopeček, Lubomír and Jan Petrov, 'From Parliament to Courtroom: Judicial Review of Legislation as a Political Tool in the Czech Republic', *East European Politics and Societies* 30, no. 1 (2016): 120–46.

32. Keenan D. Kmiec, 'The Origin and Current Meanings of "Judicial Activism"', *California Law Review* 92, no. 5 (October 2004): 1442.

33. Lino A. Graglia, 'It's Not Constitutionalism, It's Judicial Activism', *Harvard Journal of Law & Public Policy* 19, no. 2 (1996): 296.

34. See Kmiec, 1471.

35. Nathan J. Brown and Julian G. Waller, 'Constitutional Courts and Political Uncertainty: Constitutional Ruptures and the Rule of Judges', *International Journal of Constitutional Law* 14, no. 4 (1 October 2016): 829–30.

36. Marek Loužek, ed., *Soudcokracie v ČR: fikce, nebo realita?: sborník textů* (Praha: CEP – Centrum pro ekonomiku a politiku, 2006).

37. Judgement of the Czech Constitutional Court of 19 April 2011, Pl. ÚS 53/10.

38. IHNED.CZ, 'Nečas: Někteří členové Ústavního soudu jsou předpojatí', *IHNED.CZ*, 8 May 2011, https://domaci.ihned.cz/c1-51795570-necas-nekteri-clenove-ustavniho-soudu-jsou-predpojati.

39. For further details, see David Kosař and Ladislav Vyhnánek, 'The Constitutional Court of Czechia', in *Constitutional Adjudication: Institutions*, eds. Armin von Bogdandy, Peter Huber and Christoph Grabenwarter (Oxford: Oxford University Press, 2020), 119–79.

40. In this regard, we accept the argument put forward in Kühn, 95–108.

41. Judgement of the Czech Constitutional Court of 25 June 2002, Pl. ÚS 36/01.

42. Judgement of the Czech Constitutional Court of 10 September 2009, Pl. ÚS 27/09. See also Yaniv Roznai, 'Legisprudence Limitations on Constitutional Amendments? Reflections on

the Czech Constitutional Court's Declaration of Unconstitutional Constitutional Act', *ICL Journal* 8, no. 1 (2014): 29.

43. Idnes.cz, 'Respekt, či překročení pravomocí? Politiky verdikt soudu rozdělil', *Idnes.cz*, 10 September 2009, https://www.idnes.cz/zpravy/domaci/respekt-ci-prekroceni-pravomoci-politiky-verdikt-soudu-.

44. Judgment of the Czech Constitutional Court of 24 January 2001, Pl. ÚS 42/2000, *Grand Election Judgement.*

45. Zdeněk Kühn, 'Judicial Independence in Central-Eastern Europe: The Experience of the 1990s and 2000s', *The Lawyer Quarterly* 1, no. 1 (2011): 31–42.

46. These cases were analyzed in greater detail by David Kosař, *Perils of Judicial Self-Government in Transitional Societies* (New York: Cambridge University Press, 2016), 174–5.

47. See also David Kosař, Ladislav Vyhnánek, *The Constitution of Czechia* (London: Hart Publishing, 2021), 162.

48. Judgement of the Czech Constitutional Court of 2 February 2021, Pl.ÚS 44/17, *Grand Election Judgement II.*

49. Irozhlas.cz, 'Ústavní soud ztratil všechny zábrany. Otřásá důvěrou v politický systém, kritizoval Babiš' (3 February 2021) https://www.irozhlas.cz/zpravy-domov/andrej-babis-volebni-zakon-ustavni-soud-snemovni-parlamentni-volby-2021_2102031431_ako.

50. The Court has heard a couple of cases involving LGBTQ rights and has decided in a rather self-restrained and conservative manner. But bearing in mind the *Grand Election Judgment II*, this should not be attributed to any strategic deference to populist governments, but to the honest constitutional and ideological preferences of the current judges.

51. An interference with judicial independence occurred when the Chancellor of President Zeman contacted various judges and informed them about preferred outcomes of pending cases.

52. In other words, the Senate has no say in selecting the President and Vice Presidents of the Court. There is also no constitutional rule requiring e.g. gender, geographical, political or professional diversity and the Czech President thus enjoys unlimited discretion.

53. The same system works in Belarus, considered the last dictatorship in Europe, and hence a Member State of neither the European Union nor the Council of Europe.

54. See Jindřiška Syllová, 'Komora minimálních funkcí, nebo komora „odlišného ohledu"?' in *Dvacet let Senátu Parlamentu České republiky v souvislostech*, ed. Jan Kysela (Praha: Leges, 2016), 60.

55. Václav Havel was the President of Czechoslovakia (1989–1992) and during the drafting of the Czech Constitution, it was clear that he would become the first President of Czechia as well.

56. While Václav Havel and Miloš Zeman appointed all fifteen Justices, Václav Klaus (due to the death of the Chief Justice of the Havel Court in office and early resignations of two more judges, all three of which were replaced by Havel) 'inherited' three Havel appointees and appointed only twelve judges himself.

57. The Court has not been gender-diverse, though. The bench has been always dominated by men who has also held the positions of the Court Presidents.

58. One of them, Aleš Pejchal, was even rejected twice, which has not prevented him from becoming later the Czech judge at the European Court of Human Rights.

59. For further details of the transition between the Havel Court and the Klaus Court in 2003–2005, see Zdeněk Kühn and Jan Kysela, 'Nomination of Constitutional Justices in Post-Communist Countries: Trial, Error, Conflict in the Czech Republic', *European Constitutional Law Review* 2, no. 2 (June 2006): 194–205.

60. However, note that these three candidates included two reappointed judges from the Havel Court.

61. Stanislav Balík and Vít Hloušek, 'The Development and Transformation of the Czech Party System after 1989', *Acta politologica* 8, no. 2 (2016): 103–17.

62. Miloš Brunclík and Michal Kubát, 'The Czech Parliamentary Regime After 1989: Origins, Developments and Challenges', *Acta Politologica* 8, no. 2 (2016): 18.

63. Based on interpretation of Article 88(2) of the Czech Constitution, it is controversial whether the Court can annul a statute dealing with the procedure before the Court (see also the decision of the Constitutional Court of 10 December 2013, Pl. ÚS 23/12). But in the opinion of the authors, there is little doubt that the Court would annul a statute that would significantly hinder its role of a guardian of the constitutional order.

64. Centrum pro výzkum veřejného mínění, 'Časové řady vybraných otázek z výzkumu Naše společnost', https://cvvmapp.soc.cas.cz/#question31.

65. Irozhlas.cz, 'Ústavní soud ztratil všechny zábrany. Otřásá důvěrou v politický systém, kritizoval Babiš', (3 February 2021) https://www.irozhlas.cz/zpravy-domov/andrej-babis-volebni-zakon-ustavni-soud-snemovni-parlamentni-volby-2021_2102031431_ako.

66. Doplňující stanovisko soudkyně Ivetty Macejkovej k nálezu Ústavního soudu Slovenské republiky [The separate opinion of Judge Ivetta Macejková, the Slovak Constitutional Court], 31 May 2017, PL. ÚS 7/2017-159.

67. Hubert Smekal and Jaroslav Benák et al, *Mimoprávní vlivy na rozhodování českého Ústavního soudu* (Brno: Masarykova univerzita, 2021), 113–16.

68. John Hart Ely, *Democracy and Distrust: A Theory of Judidicial Review* (Cambridge, MA: Harvard University Press, 1980).

69. Rosalind Dixon and Michaela Hailbronner, 'Ely in the World: The Global Legacy of Democracy and Distrust Forty Years On', *International Journal of Constitutional Law* 19, no. 2 (1 April 2021): 3, doi:10.1093/icon/moab041.

70. Georg Vanberg, 'Legislative-Judicial Relations: A Game-Theoretic Approach to Constitutional Review', *American Journal of Political Science* 45, no. 2 (2001): 346–61. doi:10.2307/2669345.

71. Lee Epstein, Jack Knight, and Olga Shvetsova, 'The Role of Constitutional Courts in the Establishment and Maintenance of Democratic Systems of Government', *Law and Society Review* 35 (2001): 117–64.

72. Wojciech Sadurski, 'Judicial Review in Central and Eastern Europe: Rationales or Rationalizations', *Israel Law Review* 42 (2009): 503.

73. Jan Petrov, 'Unpacking the Partnership: Typology of Constitutional Courts' Roles in Implementation of the European Court of Human Rights' Case Law', *European Constitutional Law Review* 14, no. 3 (2018): 499–531. doi:10.1017/S1574019618000299.

74. Oscar Gakuo Mwangi, 'Judicial Activism, Populism and Counterterrorism Legislation in Kenya: Coalition for Reform and Democracy (CORD) & 2 Others v Republic of Kenya & 10; Others [2015]', *The International Journal of Human Rights*, doi:10.1080/13642987.2021.1887144.

75. Kálmán Pócza, Gábor Dobos, and Attila Gyulai, 'How to Measure the Strength of Judicial Decisions: A Methodological Framework', *German Law Journal* 18, no. 6 (2017): 1557–86. doi:10.1017/S2071832200022422.

76. Kosař and Šipulová 2020, 142.

77. Miklós Bankuti, Gábor Halmai, and Kim Lane Scheppele, 'Hungary's Illiberal Turn: Disabling the Constitution', *Journal of Democracy* 23, no. 3 (2012): 139–40, doi:10.1353/jod.2012.0054.

78. Aylin Aydin-Cakir, 'The Impact of Judicial Preferences and Political Context on Constitutional Court Decisions: Evidence from Turkey', *International Journal of Constitutional Law* 16, no. 4 (2018): 1101–20, doi:10.1093/icon/moy087

79. John Ferejohn and Pasquale Pasquino, 'Constitutional Courts as Deliberative Institutions: Towards an Institutional Theory of Constitutional Justice', in *Constitutional Justice: East and West*, ed. Wojciech Sadurski (Dordrecht: Kluwer, 2002), 21–36.

Disclosure statement

No potential conflict of interest was reported by the author(s).

Funding

This work was supported by the Czech Science Foundation (GACR) under grant number 17-10100S.

ORCID

Hubert Smekal http://orcid.org/0000-0001-7960-0559
Jaroslav Benák http://orcid.org/0000-0002-6981-7954
Ladislav Vyhnánek http://orcid.org/0000-0002-9761-5313

Judicial activism, populism and counterterrorism legislation in Kenya: coalition for Reform and democracy (CORD) & 2 others v Republic of Kenya & 10; others [2015]

Oscar Gakuo Mwangi ⓘ

ABSTRACT

This article examines the relationship between populism and judicial activism in Kenya's Security Laws (Amendment) Act, No 19 of 2014 High Court Case determined in 2015. The article defines populism as a political strategy rather than as a thin-ideology, and adopts majoritaianism and deference to elected branches, and judicial aggrandisement as indicators of judicial activism. The Act, which aims at, among others, augmenting counterterrorism, amended the provisions of 22 other security and security-related Acts of Parliament. The omnibus Act is an expression of penal populism. It is these amendments that precipitated the petition. The populism of both coalitions manifested itself in the issues raised for determination. Kenya's parliamentary opposition Coalition for Reform and Democracy, the key petitioner, challenged the constitutionality of the Act on issues of legislation and human rights. The governing coalition Jubilee defended the Act on issues of justiciability and national security. Though judicial activism was apparent in relation to judicial aggrandisement, and majoritarianism and deference, both coalition's populism, however, did not critically impact upon judicial decision making in the case. The implications for the integrity, independence and role of the judiciary in Kenya are offered in the conclusion.

Introduction

The judicialization of political and security matters in Kenya has been on the rise since the Jubilee political party was elected as the governing party in 2013. The rise in litigation of national security matters related to counterterrorism has largely been a function of populism. The formulation and implementation of counterterrorism related security policies, is often the domain of the executive and legislative branches of government in the country. However, counterterrorism issues are increasingly being adjudicated in courts of law. The jurisprudence on terrorism and counterterrorism matters continues to develop and cases that have been determined by judiciary explain the way in which it has interpreted the counterterrorism legislation in Kenya.[1] This article examines the relationship between judicial activism, populism counterterrorism legislation in Kenya with reference to the Security Law (Amendment Act) (SLAA) of 2014 case. The judgement of the case, Coalition for Reform and Democracy (CORD) & 2 others v Republic of Kenya & 10; others [2015] eKLR, was delivered on 23 February 2015 at the High Court in Nairobi, Kenya. The article is divided into four sections. The first section examines the conceptual relationship among judicial activism, populism and counterterrorism legislation so as to provide a framework that explains populism and judicial activism in the SLAA case. The second provides background information and litigation history of the case. The third section examines populist perceptions on SLAA as expressed in public statements by the leaders of the opposition and governing coalitions. The fourth discusses the relationship between populism and judicial activism in the case. The conclusion indicates the implications of populism for the integrity, independence and role of the judiciary in Kenya.

Judicial activism, populism and counterterrorism legislation

The concept of judicial activism embodies a number of different jurisprudential ideas. This is evident is the complex debates raised by scholars regarding the interpretation of the Constitution, scope of judicial review under separation of powers, the nature of a judicial holding, and the amount of dereference owed to different types of precedent.[2] Lindquist and Cross (2009) identify several correlated explanatory dimensions associated with judicial activism in academic and legal scholarship and group them into four general categories that can be used to measure the characteristics and utility of the concept. These are majoritarianism and deference to elected branches; precedential stability and legal fidelity; institutional aggrandisement, and; result-oriented judging or policy making.[3] The deference dimension generally refers to when courts choose not to defer the decisions made by other branches of government hence exercise control, not on behalf of the prevailing majority, but against it. According to Lindquist and Cross, deference to other branches of government is considered the most frequent criterion of judicial activism. The precedential stability dimension generally argues that overruling precedent is a judicial repeal hence constitutes judicial activism. The dimension specifies that, determining points in litigation according to precedent enhances stability and predictability in the rule of law, judicial independence and the integrity of the judicial process. The institutional aggrandisement dimension principally argues that the expansion of the courts legal authority to hear more cases and controversies gives them the power to decide which appeals they take for review, is a form of judicial activism. The result-oriented judging dimension generally refers to judicial activism as, when judges view the law as policy and decide to strike down legislation as unconstitutional, based on their personal policy preferences.[4] This article adopts the majoritarianism and deference to elected branches and institutional aggrandisement dimensions as indicators of judicial activism.

At the heart of these judicial activism dimensions is the liberal purposive interpretation of the Constitution. The purposive interpretation of the Constitution pays attention to the subjective-historical purpose and objective-modern purpose of the constitutional text. The essence of this interpretation is to understand how prevailing socio-political circumstances are influenced by historical circumstances. Hence both the subjective and objective elements ought to be simultaneously taken into account when determining the purposes of the constitution. This includes considering the values and principles that prevail at the time of the interpretation so as to synthesise and harmonise between past and present principles. However, more emphasis should be placed on the objective purposes so that the rules of interpretation as used by judges, enable the judiciary to fulfil its role of bridging the gap between law and society and protecting the constitution and democracy.[5] The subjective aspect allows room for judicial activism. In a democracy, courts believe that the democratic process is best way to correct a bad law. Activism is, therefore, a characteristic of the judicial function in democracies.[6] Judicial activism in a democratic setting should not, however, be seen as synonymous with judicial review, judicial restraint, and judicial independence. Judicial review of legislation is the subjection of the legislature to the rule of law. Aspects of judicial review can also apply to executive action whereby the executive's elective credentials are subject to the principle of the rule of law. A notable aspect of judicial review is when courts scrutinise legislation for its compliance with individual rights. The courts may, however, decide not to invalidate the law or moderate its application, because rights would otherwise be violated.[7] Judicial restraint refers to when courts adopt a cautious approach to the choices presented to them when adjudicating matters. The concept has three fundamental aspects. First, judges apply law, they do not make it. Second, judges defer to a great extent to decisions by other officials. Finally judges are highly hesitant to declare legislative or executive action unconstitutional, especially when such action is challenged as unconstitutional.[8] Central to the concept of judicial independence is that courts should not be subject to undue influence from the other branches of government, or from partisan interests.[9]

The concept of populism, like many other concepts in political science, is ambiguous. There are, however, two dominant interpretations of populism in political science literature. One pays attention to a passionate discourse and the other to expedient policies targeting the people so as to solicit their emotional rather than rational support in making choices.[10] Given this ambiguity, the concept of populism can, therefore, be derived from any of the appropriate theoretical approaches to the study of populism. The political science literature identifies three relevant distinct conceptual approaches used in comparative analyses on populism: ideational, political-strategic, and sociocultural approach. The ideational approach defines populism as a set of ideas that depicts society as divided between 'the pure people' versus 'the corrupt elite,' and that politics is about respecting popular sovereignty. This approach is useful for examining specific subtypes of populism. It is, however, not appropriate for developing a broader comparative populism-specific research agenda. The political-strategic approach defines populism as a political strategy employed by a charismatic leader who seeks to govern based on direct and unorganised mass support from her/his followers. The sociocultural approach regards populism as mythological style of politics used by leaders, who do not conform to norms, to establish links with certain sections of the electorate.[11] This article adopts the political-strategic approach.

The political-strategic approach, which adopts a minimalist definition, argues that populism is best conceptualised as a political strategy not a political style. Political style denotes the forms of political performance and emphasises populism's expressive aspects. This definition is broad hence prevents the clear delimitation of cases. By contrast, political strategy focuses on the methods and instruments of winning and exercising power. Political strategy is therefore better delimited than political style.[12] This approach emphasises that a personalistic leader seeks or exercises power based on direct support from large numbers of mainly unorganised followers. This relationship, between the leader and followers, usually bypasses established intermediary organisations and subordinates the followers to the leader's personal will. The leader wins extensive and intense support from the followers by claiming to represent those who are socially, economically and politically marginalised from national political life and by promising to liberate them from crises, threats, and enemies.[13] This political definition of populism recognises the flexibility and opportunism of populist leaders. The empirical value of the political-strategic approach is that its analysis deviates from pure nominalism and embraces conceptual pragmatism thereby explaining the diverse world of populist leaders and movements.[14] In relation to democracy, the approach argues that efforts by populists to dismantle democratic institutions and promote authoritarianism succeed in situations where institutions are relatively weak or characterised by severe crises. In situations where democracy-promoting institutions are relatively weak, populists can easily stifle democracy. Severe crises, such as terrorism, provide populist leaders who claim to contain such crises, opportunities to remove essential obstacles to authoritarian power concentration. Populist strategies aimed at stifling democracy are, however, unlikely to succeed if either one of these conditions is absent.[15]

In a democracy, populism impacts upon judicial decision making by judicializing politics. Judicialization of politics refers to the dependence on courts and judicial means for addressing controversial political issues, such as national security matters. Judicialization of politics, often endorsed by powerful political actors like populist leaders and political parties, is mainly driven by parochial interests.[16] Populist opposition leaders and political parties seek to judicialize politics through petitions and injunctions against government policies or resort to litigation in order to boost their popularity, irrespective of the actual outcome of litigation.[17] Populism creates 'significant risks to the rule of law through agenda-setting, policy impact, the shaping of discretionary decisions and convention-trashing'.[18] One way in which populism adversely affects the rule of law and democracy is by extending penal populism. Penal populism is defined as a major trend in democracies marked by a generalised need and call for enhanced security.[19] Penal populism is conservative and regressive and attempts to salvage the benevolent liberal penal system for what it perceives as the oppressed majority and harness it to their aspirations. In penal populist discourse, the rights referred to are usually the rights of the majority to safety and security, not the rights of the marginalised minorities adversely affected by penal policies. Penal populism also aims at gaining electoral popularity rather than crime reduction or promoting justice. Politicians often popularise and encourage the adoption of punitive laws and sentences not because legal measures reduce crime, but because such political leaders want to increase their chances of re-election.[20]

State-led coercive counterterrorism measures are a form of penal populism. They extend controls and create tougher criminal law and establish new structures devoted to counterterrorism. These measures include, bolstering police and prosecutorial power, decreasing the scope of judicial discretion and weakening the rule of law by using some of the methods used by terrorists themselves.[21] Though counterterrorism legislation is usually enforced against terrorist groups, the impact of the enforcement is, however, felt by religious, ethnic, and political minorities. There is an inclination on the part of the state to compromise their rights to compensate for enhanced security of the majority. The safety of the majority is, therefore, the ultimate law.[22] It is the responsibility of the judiciary, as the arbiter of counterterrorism laws, to balance the requirements of security with the responsibilities of democracy so as to protect basic liberties. Judges in a democratic setting are, arguably, protected from political influence hence from majoritarian prejudices, allowing them to act impartially, and protect minorities.[23] Courts should, however, be aware of the limitations of their own institutional competence, with respect to security matters. They should, therefore, not ignore the boundaries of legislative and executive competence in counterterrorism.[24] SLAA is, as discussed later, an expression of penal populism.

It is in the context of the foregoing conceptual arguments, this article examines the relationship between populism and judicial activism in the SLAA case. Though several issues were raised for determination in the petition, the article pays attention to those issues that are relevant for analysing majoritarianism and deference to elected branches and institutional aggrandisement as indicators of judicial activism. These issues were, the jurisdiction of the court in determining the case, and legislation of SLAA. The relationship between populism and jurisdiction of the court is analysed with regard to the doctrines of ripeness, avoidance and separation of powers. Justiciability doctrines, such as ripeness and avoidance, define the boundaries of law and adjudication hence limit access to the courts. The ripeness doctrine generally constraints courts from exercising jurisdiction over a case before a substantial controversy is raised as well as an actual and urgent threat of injury. The doctrine of avoidance generally requires courts to avoid constitutional interpretation and resolve cases on statutory grounds, or to avoid legislating from the bench. When courts interfere with the tripartite separation of government powers enshrined in the Constitution, this interference can regarded as judicial activism.[25] The relationship between populism and the enactment process is analysed with respect to role of parliament in national security, parliamentary standing orders, and the role of parliament in public participation. Kenya is a constitutional multiparty state and has a presidential system of government. Separation of powers is entrenched in Chapters 8, 9 and 10 of the country's Constitution, which pay attention to the legislature, executive and judiciary respectively. The national executive comprises the President, Deputy President and the rest of the cabinet. The parliament comprises the National Assembly and Senate. The judiciary has superior and subordinate courts. The superior courts are the Supreme Court, the Court of Appeal, the High Court and courts with the status of High Court that hear and determine disputes related to specific issues. Kenya's legal system is descended from the British Common Law System.[26]

Background and litigation history of SLAA case

Penal populism, as expressed in the formulation and implementation of counterterrorism laws, creates significant risks to the rule of law in a democracy. Consequently, the judiciary, as the arbiter of such laws, should strike a balance between the requirements of national security and democracy in a state. Striking such a balance at times necessitates judicial activism. Kenya experienced over 75 terrorist incidences between January and November 2014 that resulted in about 200 fatalities. More significantly is that 64 of the fatalities occurred within a week in late November the same year.[27] Consequently, the state enacted the Security Laws (Amendment) Act (SLAA), No 19 of 2014 to enhance national security. It received presidential assent on 19th December 2014. The SLAA came into force on 22nd December 2014.[28] It amended the provisions of 22 other Acts of Parliament concerned with matters of national security. These amendments are the ones that precipitated the petition. In their opening statements, the judges of the High Court pointed out that terrorism in Kenya had significantly compromised national and personal security, hence the pressing need for the state to adopt suitable measures to enhance national security and the security of its citizens. They stressed that, while it is the duty of the state to protect national security, the state, nonetheless, has the obligation not to take away the fundamental rights and freedoms guaranteed in the constitution of Kenya. The petition challenged the constitutionality of SLAA and requested the Court to determine, as discussed later, fundamental questions related to the legislation of SLAA and its contents.[29]

Several parties were involved in the case. The 1st petitioner was a coalition of opposition political parliamentary parties, the Coalition for Reform and Democracy (CORD). The 2nd petitioner was the Kenya National Commission of Human Rights (KNCHR), a constitutional commission. The 3rd petitioner was an advocate of the High Court who alleged a threat of violation of his constitutional rights and freedoms by SLAA. The respondent in the consolidated petition was principally the Attorney General (AG) of Kenya. For some unclear reason, CORD enjoined the state as a respondent in its petition. Pursuant to orders of the Court, the Director of Public Prosecutions (DPP) was enjoined as the 1st interested party. Also enjoined to the proceedings as the 2nd interested party was the governing coalition of political parties known as the Jubilee Coalition (Jubilee). Jubilee commanded a majority in the parliament of Kenya.[30] Four civil society organisations representing different interests were also allowed to participate in the proceedings as the 4th, 5th and 6th interested parties. The 7th interested party was the Terror Victims Support Initiative. Finally, the Court allowed the participation of two organisations as *amici curiae* or friends of the Court. The 1st *amicus curiae* was the Law Society of Kenya, a statutory body. The 2nd *amicus curiae* was the Commission on the Implementation of the Constitution, also a constitutional commission.[31] This article, however, focuses on CORD, Jubilee, the AG and the DPP petitions and responses, in the analysis of the relationship between judicial activism and populism in the SLAA case.

According to the judges, the basic facts precipitating the petition were largely undisputed. They pointed out that on 8th December, 2014 the Security Laws (Amendment) Bill 2014 was published in a special issue of the Kenya Gazette namely Supplement No. 163 (National Assembly Bill No. 309). The following day the Bill was introduced for the first reading in the National Assembly. Pursuant to Standing Order No.120 the publication period was reduced from 14 days to one day. Standing Order No. 120 pays attention to the publication process of a Bill.[32] Through an advertisement published on the 10th of December, 2014 in the *Daily Nation* and the *Standard* newspapers, the National Assembly specified the days for public participation would be the 10th, 11th and 15th December 2014. Members of the public were thereby invited to submit their views on the bill, either through written memoranda to the Clerk of the National Assembly or orally to the Administration and National Security Committee. The Committee was to sit on the prescribed days between 10.00am and 5.00pm. Despite the recommended dates, the Bill was tabled for the 2nd reading on 11th December, 2014. Notwithstanding objections raised in Parliament by the opposition regarding the prescribed period, the Speaker of the National Assembly ruled that public participation would continue after the 2nd reading. The petitioners complained that the process, discussed in detail later, was done contrary to the Standing Order No. 127. This Standing Order refers to the committal of Bills to committees and public participation.[33]

Consequently, CORD moved to court on 23rd December, 2014 seeking *ex-parte* conservatory relief to stay the operation of the Act. The Court directed that the application dated 23rd December, 2014 be served upon the respondents and set the *inter partes* hearing for 24th December, 2014. The hearing did not however, proceed as the Court granted to the DPP and other parties who had been enjoined to the proceedings time to file their responses. On 23rd December 2014, KNCHR filed its petition which was consolidated with the CORD petition a day later. On 29th December, 2014 the application for conservatory orders was duly heard by Justice Odunga. In his ruling on 2nd January 2015, the judge granted conservatory orders suspending the sections of the Act which had been challenged as constituting a threat or violation of the Constitution. Pursuant to Article 165(4) of the Constitution, which pays attention to the appointment of an uneven number of judges when a matter is a substantial question of law, the judge referred the consolidated petition to the Chief Justice for purposes of constituting a bench of an uneven number of judges to hear the petition. Consequently, a bench of 5 judges was constituted. On 21st January, 2015, the 3rd petitioner filed his petition which was consolidated with the CORD and KNCHR petitions. The petition was argued before the Court on the 28th, 29th and 30th of January 2015.[34]

Populism and SLAA

Political parties in Kenya are institutionally weak hence functionally ineffective as democratic and democracy-promoting institutions. Most parties adopt no coherent or sound ideology or doctrine on which to articulate interests, mobilise supporters and shape or structure public opinion. They also lack effective programmes aimed at achieving their objectives as evident in their poorly designed manifestos and constitutions. These problems are often compounded by poor leadership that appeals to sentiments based on parochial interests rather than the common good. Parties also do not have adequate financial resources to run them administratively on a daily basis, as well to enable them perform their political functions effectively during electoral and non-electoral periods. They also lack the requisite societal linkages to enable them to act as effective agents of socialisation and to integrate the political system.[35] It is in the context of these institutional weaknesses particularly those related to ideologies that this article opts to examine populism as a strategy of populist leaders and parties, rather than as a thin ideology.

The populism of Raila Odinga and Uhuru Kenyatta

The initial arguments for and against enactment of SLAA by Kenya's president and the leader of Jubilee, Uhuru Kenyatta and opposition CORD leader Raila Odinga respectively, were political strategies that can be defined as populism. Odinga's populist perceptions were contained in the statement he delivered on the proposed Security Laws (Amendment) Bill on 11 December 2014 prior to its enactment. Odinga began by arguing that Kenya was on the verge of regressing to the dark past when freedoms and rights in the country were curtailed. He requested Kenyans to remain alert and active as a 'regime hell bent on reinventing the past is rushing through our National Assembly an amendment Bill that if passed, takes us back to the 1980s, although its consequences could be much worse'.[36] Odinga compared the process legislating the Bill to the one of the afternoon of June 9 1982 when the ruling party, the Kenya African National Union (KANU) hurriedly officially made Kenya a single party state. He pointed out that whereas curtailing rights in the 1970s and 1980s was justified on grounds of enhancing national unity and development, in present-day Kenya, the excuse was 'war on terrorism'.[37] Odinga stated the opposition 'always said that something was afoot, that elements of security failures were induced to be used at appropriate time to roll back on the gains we have made'.[38] He also emphasised that the opposition had always suspected President Kenyatta and Deputy President William Ruto were uncomfortable with the Constitution and were looking for an excuse return Kenya to the repressive days of KANU hegemony. Hence for Odinga the 'single party era, with its abuses ... remain the model for President Kenyatta and his deputy'.[39] Odinga argued that the Bill was a major assault on democracy and fundamental rights and that it also presented a major abuse to established parliamentary procedures. It is, in the context of these populist views, that Odinga stressed, 'Kenyans must resist and CORD is prepared to lead the way. This is not the time for us to see ourselves as CORD or Jubilee supporters. This goes beyond party.' He insisted that Kenyans ought to have got tired of a country 'where leaders perpetuate wrong with impunity' and 'where our civil society is beholden to one side or the other', and also 'where even our Churches are silent and our people too afraid and too divided along ethnic and party lines to speak.' Odinga concluded by saying it was 'therefore be for us, all of us, to stop it and uproot it. We lie in ruins and it is an ideal place to stop and rethink'.[40] By expressing these populist perceptions, Odinga was laying the ground to convert the views into prudent populist strategies.

The populist views of President Kenyatta on SLAA were contained in the statement he delivered during a televised address to the nation after signing into law, the Security Laws (Amendment) Bill on 19 December 2014. Kenyatta began by emphasising the death of 64 Kenyans, due to terrorism, in late November 2014, propelled the executive branch of government to hold extensive consultations on the security crisis in the country. Consequently, as head of the executive branch, he constituted a team to undertake a comprehensive review of the security situation. Kenyatta received the team's report within a week. The review identified a number of gaps within Kenya's security laws as well as administrative challenges in the security sector. Hence the Security Laws (Amendment) Bill was drafted and hurriedly enacted.[41] Kenyatta highlighted that the SLAA dealt with, among others, 'emerging crimes that reinforce terrorism, including the phenomena of foreign fighters, radicalization and transnational and cross-border crimes.'[42] He argued that these crimes were increasingly assuming a 'degree of sophistication that calls for a radical approach.'[43] The SLAA, Kenyatta emphasised, also improved Kenya's capacity to detect, deter and disrupt any threats to national security, and that for the first time the country now had 'a law that focuses on prevention and disruption of threats.'[44] He insisted that, while aware of the lack of integrity and its role in accentuating vulnerability as well as compromising national security, SLAA set a higher threshold for any public and state officer charged with the responsibility of protecting Kenya and its people. Hence SLAA provided for heavy penalties for any security violation. Kenyatta, therefore, requested all Kenyans to support the law. Reiterating the need for enhanced security, he reminded Kenyans that SLAA was 'one instrument among the many measures that we need to put in place in order to guarantee our security. We must all remember that we are still at war and vulnerable to terror attacks.'[45] Kenyatta was emphatic about SLAA when he said 'Its intent is one; to protect the lives and property of all citizens.' [46] In the context of these populist views, this article argues that both the enactment of SLAA and its consequent petition, were political strategies of Kenyatta and Odinga respectively.

Judicial activism, populism and SLAA

The political-strategic approach to the study of populism, as discussed earlier, argues that political situations characterised by severe crises or weak democracy-protecting institutions, can provide populist state leaders opportunities to augment authoritarian policies. This also allows opportunities for opposition or other populist leaders to emerge and oppose such polices. The enactment of SLAA was an expression of penal populism hence political-legal opposition to it. The analysis of this article examines majoritarianism and deference to other branches of government, and institutional aggrandisement as mutually inclusive. The issues raised for determination, by CORD and Jubilee, in the context of these two indicators of judicial activism are perceived as expressions of populism. The issues primarily focused on jurisdiction of the Court in determining the case, legislation of the Act, and constitutionality of the Act's provisions with regard to the Bill of Rights. Majoritarianism, deference, and institutional aggrandisement are best examined in relation to the first two issues raise for determination by both parties. The determination of the third issue is not examined as it is does not fall within the article's scope and concept of judicial activism. This third issue was, arguably, a case of judicial review in that the Court declared certain provisions of SLAA that violated the bill of rights, unconstitutional. The relationship between populism and judicial activism is, therefore, examined in the context of jurisdiction of the Court in determining the SLAA case, and the enactment process of the Act.

With regard to the issues raised for determination, the Court was, first and foremost, required to determine whether an Act of Parliament is unconstitutional and also consider the objects, purpose and effect of the legislation. Several applicable constitutional principles guided the judges in determining these issues. The judges argued that it required an interpretation of various provisions of the Constitution and determination of whether there had been compliance or violation of the said constitutional provisions. The judges adopted a liberal purposive interpretation of the Constitution. They emphasised that by adopting a purposive interpretation, the principle that constitutional provisions must be read as an integrated whole, would guide the Court. The general presumption that every Act of Parliament is constitutional also guided the judges. As such, for the judges, the burden of proof lies on any person who alleges that an Act of Parliament is unconstitutional. The judges, however, emphasised that there can be no presumption of constitutionality with respect to legislation that limits fundamental rights. Most of the decisions were made according to precedent.[47] These general principles guided the judges in determining issues related to jurisdiction of the count and enactment of the Act.

Jurisdiction of the court

Expanding judicial institutional authority to hear cases and controversies is an indicator of judicial activism. This aggrandisement by the judicially can depose legislative or executive judgements in certain cases as justiciability doctrines limit access to the courts. Justiciability doctrines often present rather ambiguous standards hence judges differ in their interpretations of these constraints. Those who adopt a more liberal approach to the doctrines thereby allowing more litigants into court, might be considered more activist.[48] It is in the context of these arguments on institutional aggrandisement that this section examines the relationship between populism and jurisdiction of the court with regard to the doctrines on ripeness, avoidance, and separation of powers. The question of jurisdiction raised by Jubilee as a political party, and the AG together with the DPP representing the state on behalf of the Jubilee administration, was based on three aspects. First, the issues in dispute were not ripe for determination. Second, the Court should be guided by the doctrine of avoidance and should not deal with issues for which there is a different forum. Third, determining the issues would interfere with the doctrine of separation of powers as it would be akin to the Court entering a territory reserved by the Constitution for the Legislature.[49]

Doctrine of ripeness

The AG and the DPP argued the issues raised by CORD were not yet ripe for determination. The two state officers claimed that no person had appeared before the Court to claim that her/his or her rights had been violated as a result of the application of the impugned provisions of SLAA. Their contention was that for any perceived grievance to be justiciable, the context and circumstances underlying the controversy must be quantifiable in relation to the law. The state officers, therefore, emphasised that the challenge raised against SLAA was merely a time-consuming academic argument hence the petition be struck out summarily. According to the AG, the petitions were 'overloaded with unwarranted apprehension, speculation, suspicion and unfounded mistrust which had no basis in law'.[50] In response, CORD argued that the issues were justiciable by citing provisions of Article 22 of the Constitution, which provides that a party may petition the court alleging that 'a right or fundamental freedom in the Bill of Rights has been denied, violated or infringed, or is threatened.' CORD also cited Article 258, which allows a party to approach the Court claiming 'that this Constitution has been contravened, or is threatened with contravention'.[51].

In determining the issue of ripeness, the judges pointed out that the jurisdiction of the Court stems from Article 165 (3) of the Constitution, which determines, among others, when a right has been denied, violated, infringed or threatened, and whether any law is inconsistent with or in contravention of the Constitution. They also argued that Article 22 (1) of the Constitution grants every person the right to institute court proceedings claiming that a right or fundamental freedom in the Bill of Rights has been denied, violated or infringed, or is threatened. The judges agreed with the AG and the DPP that the Court should not engage in an academic or hypothetical exercise.[52] Having considered the clarity of the constitutional provisions related to the enforcement of Bill of Rights, the Court's jurisdiction to hear any question requiring constitutional interpretation, and the enforcement of the Constitution, the judges rendered controversy ripe and justiciable. The judges argued that: a party does not have to wait until a right or fundamental freedom has been violated, or for a violation of the Constitution to occur, before approaching the court. A party has a right to do so if there is a threat of violation or contravention of the Constitution. The judges argued that when a court is confronted with such alleged threats of violations, the circumstances of each case are relative and a court 'ought to differentiate between academic, theoretical claims and paranoid fears with real threat of constitutional violations'. The judges insisted that it is only clear and unambiguous threats to the basic design and architecture of the Constitution that a party seeking relief must prove, before the Court can intervene. In sum, the judges were satisfied that the petition raised issues that were justiciable and ripe for determination by the Court.[53] Hence Jubilee's position that the issues raised were not ripe for determination in defense of SLAA was populism.

Doctrine of avoidance

The DPP urged the Court to apply the doctrine of avoidance and restrain itself from dealing with the SLAA case. The state officer argued that the Court should not enter into a dispute if there were other fora in which the issues in dispute could be resolved. The DPP contended that the proper forum for the issues raised was a trial court, not the High Court. The trial court, he emphasised, would appropriately deal with the alleged violations by the impugned provisions of SLAA. Likewise the AG contended that some remedies prevail in the statutory rather than constitutional domain and, therefore, should not be determined in a constitutional petition like that of SLAA. The AG argued that remedies for the grievances, regarding statues of SLAA, could be found under the respective statutes. Hence the petitioners should only follow up with a constitutional petition if the application for that remedy was unsuccessful.[54] For Jubilee, this was akin to institutional aggrandisement because the High Court was usurping the role of trial courts. The fact that the judges had also declared that they would adopt a liberal interpretation of the constitution, allowing more litigants into the High Court indicates, arguably, judicial activism.

Addressing the issues raised, the judges emphasised the doctrine of constitutional avoidance requires courts to resolve disputes on a constitutional basis only when a remedy depends on the constitution. CORD had challenged the constitutionality of various provisions of diverse legislation which impact, on among other things, on constitutional guarantees in the Bill of Rights. Hence the judges argued it was not the mandate of trial courts to determine whether or not the amendments to various laws are constitutional. That constitutional mandate, the judges pointed out, is vested expressly in the High Court. To the judges, therefore, the doctrine of avoidance was not applicable in the SLAA case.[55] The issues raised by Jubilee in relation to the doctrine of avoidance were, therefore, evidence of populism.

Separation of powers

In its petition, Jubilee argued that by interfering with the law making powers of Parliament, the Court was disrespecting the doctrine of separation of powers. Jubilee emphasised that that Parliament has the powers to make changes to the laws as provided under Chapter 8 of the Constitution.[56] As such, Jubilee insisted the judiciary was interfering with the constitutional mandate of the legislature. On the question of separation of powers, the judges observed that the Court respects the principle of separation of powers clearly spelt out in Article 1 of Kenya's Constitution, which stipulates the respective mandates of the legislature, the executive, and the judiciary. The judges concurred with CORD's position on the mandates of these branches of government under separation of power. However, they emphasised the doctrine of separation of powers does not prevent the Court from examining the Acts of the legislature or the executive. The judges argued that judiciary has the constitutional authority to do so.[57] Jubilee's position on separation of powers in support of SLAA can, therefore, also be regarded as populism.

Enactment of SLAA

The circumstances under which a court chooses not to defer the decisions made by the legislative and executive branches of government is an indicator of judicial activism. This is perceived as an encroachment on legislative or executive authority. The court exercises control, not on behalf of the prevalent majority, but against it.[58] With regard to the foregoing arguments, this section examines the relationship between populism and judicial activism in the enactment of SLAA specifically on issues of the role of Parliament in national security matters, parliamentary standing orders, and public participation. CORD alleged that the enactment process of SLAA was totally flawed hence asked the Court to find the Act unconstitutional. The first of CORD's argument alleged that the Senate was not involved in the passage of SLAA. The opposition coalition hinged its argument on Article 110 (3) of the Constitution which required the Speakers of the Senate and the National Assembly to jointly resolve whether the Bill concerned counties and whether it was a special or ordinary bill. The second part of the argument contended that if the Court established Article 110 (3) did not apply given that the aforementioned issues had been jointly resolved by both speakers, then SLAA was invalid as it was not enacted in compliance with the requirements of Article 238 (2) of the Constitution. Article 238 (2) requires matters of national security be subject to the authority of Parliament.[59] This section confines itself to the second part of CORD's argument because the judges established that Article 110 (3) did not apply and more importantly is that the issues raised in part concerned national security matters. Courts have a tendency to defer national security matters, as discussed in the next section.

Parliament and national security

There are several institutional competency reasons as to why decisions made in the national security realm, for example counterterrorism, have attracted substantial deference from the courts.[60] The executive and legislative branches claim to have the expertise in combating terrorism. The legislature can exaggerate the effectiveness of its counterterrorism measures and claim that such measures are necessary to protect the rights of the victims and potential victims of terrorism. The executive can avoid account-ability by invoking secrecy when initiating and implementing counterterrorism laws.[61] Courts, therefore, operate under considerable limitations when adjudicating counterter-rorist laws. Courts ought to respect the competence and legitimacy of executive and leg-islature competence and in formulating and implementing security laws. Courts, however, have the expertise in reviewing such laws for compliance with human rights.[62] Since 9/11, however, courts in democracies have increasingly played a more vig-orous role in scrutinising counterterrorism laws with regard to human rights, despite cases of judicial deference in national security matters.[63] It is in the context of these argu-ments that this section examines SLAA, as an omnibus Act that amended the provisions of 22 other security and security-related Acts of Parliament. SLAA was initiated and enacted by the executive and legislative branches of government due to the terrorist crisis facing Kenya.

CORD's populist position on SLAA as an omnibus security law was evident when the opposition coalition argued that the Act's enactment process was not subjected to the leg-islature's competence in security matters. This particular, argument focused on insti-tutional competence not the contents of the Act. The opposition coalition argued that SLAA was invalid because the Parliament, as defined by the Constitution, was not involved in enacting a law concerning security matters. CORD alleged that Article 238 (2) (a) requires senate's involvement in all matters concerning national security. This argument was backed by the allegation that national security is subject to the authority of the Parliament since Article 93 (1) of the Constitution defines the Parliament as com-prising the National Assembly and Senate. CORD also alleged that provisions of Article 96 stipulate the role of the Senate in representing and protecting the interests of counties and their governments. Hence these interests must necessarily involve issues of security. In essence, CORD was, arguably, requesting the Court to determine the legislature's com-petence in national security matters. In response, the AG maintained that according to Article 259 (3) which specifies how provisions of the Constitution are construed, Article 238(2) (a) has to be read together with specific provisions Articles 95 which give the national assembly oversight roles of state organs and approvals of declarations of war and extensions of states of emergency. The AG argued that Article 96 of the Con-stitution does not provide Senate the role of approving declarations of war and exten-sions of states of emergency.[64]

Regarding the issue of national security, the judges were required to determine whether national security matters are exclusively vested on the National Assembly or both the National Assembly and the Senate and in what circumstances. By doing so, the judges cited the relevant provisions of Articles 238, 95, and 240 of the Constitution that specify the role of the National Assembly in security matters.[65] The judges also examined the limit of the Parliament in security matters as stipulated in the provisions of aforementioned Articles and found no provision that obligates the National Assembly to legislate on security matters in consultation with the Senate. They argued that Article 238(2) (a) is not such a provision. Hence, according to the judges, Article 238(2) (a) was not violated by the National Assembly in the passage of SLAA.[66] Though the decision was based on constitutional procedures, the issue, as one that focused on the legislature and national security matters, did not, arguably, attract judicial dereference. The decision was

Parliamentary standing orders

Parliamentary standing orders are written rules that regulate the proceedings of the house. The issue raised by CORD on SLAA and parliamentary standing orders was also a manifestation of populism. The opposition coalition disparaged the Jubilee dominated legislature, by, arguably, requested the court to determine the national assembly's competence in implementing its standing orders. CORD challenged the enactment of SLAA, arguing that the process was marred by breaches of the standing orders of the National Assembly. The opposition coalition requested the court to scrutinise the conduct of the National Assembly with regard to its standing orders. CORD alleged that the entire process was characterised by fracas whereby strangers, including security personnel and other staff, participated in voting. Hence this was a breach of the constitution and standing orders. CORD also alleged that the Hansard of the National Assembly was doctored hence not authentic. The AG countered that there was no breach of standing orders and that despite the chaos, debate proceeded on the Bill, and a vote took place. The AG emphasised that the passage of and presidential assent to SLAA was evidence of that fact.[67]

On the issue of parliamentary standing orders, the Court was required to determine if it had the jurisdiction to interrogate parliamentary procedures, particularly whether the National Assembly breached its own standing orders. Article 124(1) of the Constitution grants parliament the powers to establish committees and standing orders for 'orderly conduct of its proceedings, including the proceedings of its committees'.[68] Based on precedent, and provisions of Article 124, the judges argued that the Court has jurisdiction to intervene where there has been a failure to abide by provisions of standing orders. The judges emphasised that, depending on the specific circumstances of each case, the Court, however, must exercise restraint and only intervene in appropriate instances.[69] In the process of determining the issues raised, the judges pointed out that they received conflicting evidence between the Hansard and a ten-minute video clip of the day's events on the alleged fracas and confusion during the passage of SLAA. While evidence was presented of the chaotic scenes in the House during debate on the Bill, no evidence was presented of the allegation that strangers participated in the proceedings and voting. Article 124 (3) of the Constitution anticipates such an eventuality as it provides that: 'The proceedings of either House are not invalid just because of … The presence or participation of any person not entitled to be present at, or to participate in, the proceedings of the House'.[70] The judges argued the alleged doctoring of Hansard was serious and unfortunate as it was not in any way, either authenticated or corroborated. Their view was that neither the video evidence nor submissions on the inauthenticity of the Hansard could supersede the fact that, as an official record, the Hansard cannot be disregarded by the court without strong evidence to the contrary. The video clip did not irrefutably demonstrate that the chaotic scenes in the House occurred during the debate and voting. The Court, guided by evidence placed before it, did not use the ten minute clip, whose source was never disclosed, as uncontested evidence of mayhem and chaos that extremely hence adversely affected the vote on SLAA. The Hansard indicated that although there was disorder in the National Assembly, SLAA was passed and eventually assented by the President. Hence the judges found that there was no clear, blatant disregard of the standing orders of the National Assembly.[71] As such CORD's allegations, in opposition to SLAA, that the National Assembly disregarded its own standing order was a case of populism. In this issue, the decision of the court did not interfere with that of the legislature, which represents the prevalent majority, but supported it.

Parliament and public participation

The parliament, as a representative of the people, can be described as an agent of public participation. The decision by CORD to challenge the constitutionality of SLAA on the basis of insufficient public participation prior to its enactment was also a populist strategy. It was also meant to discredit SLAA by demonstrating the incompetency of the Jubilee dominated legislature as an effective agent of public participation. It was, arguably, a populist strategy in that CORD was also requesting the judiciary to question whether the legislature had the institutional competence to implement its constitutional role of enhancing popular sovereignty. The opposition coalition argued that Article 1 of the Constitution provides the sacrosanct source of the constitutional doctrine of public participation entrenched in the principle of sovereignty of the people. In addition, CORD indicated that Article 2 considers direct and indirect exercise of sovereignty by the people through elected representatives. CORD also emphasised that the right of public participation is further enshrined in Article 10 of the Constitution. In the context of these arguments CORD emphasised the mode of advertisement in the *Daily Nation* and *The Standard* newspapers of December 10, 2014 did provide a suitable avenue for public participation. The opposition coalition argued that the advertisement was made one day prior to a consultative meeting with the Administration and National Committee of the National Assembly hence no adequate and proper circulation of the notice or the Bill itself. CORD also argued that public participation on the Bill was limited only to Nairobi County, out of the 47 counties of Kenya. As such, compared to advertising in local community radio or other such media, there was no nation-wide civic education targeting the majority of Kenyans, who would be affected by the Bill's limitations of rights.[72] The AG contended that there was sufficient public participation prior to the enactment of SLAA. The AG maintained that the widely circulated published notice in the local dailies required written memoranda to be submitted within five days of the date of the notice. The notice also informed the public that the Administration and National Security Committee would sit for three full days in order to receive oral submissions. To the AG, the circumstances that required urgent legislative responses and short timetables justified the passage of SLAA in response to the loss of lives and property caused by the escalation of insecurity in the country.[73]

In determining the question of public participation, the judges examined the National Assembly notice inviting the public to make submissions on the Bill with regard to Article 118 (1) (b) which stipulates parliamentary procedures and roles in the context of public access and participation, and Standing Order 127 (3) of the National Assembly which specifies the departmental committee to which a Bill is committed facilitates, public participation on the Bill through appropriate mechanisms that include, '(a) inviting submission of memoranda; (b) holding public hearings; (c) consulting relevant stakeholders in a sector; and (d) consulting experts on technical subjects'.[74] The invitation notice allowed the submission of views, representations, sending mail or making hand-deliveries to the Office of the Clerk of the National Assembly. The submissions indicated date and time submitted. The notice also indicated that dates, times and the venue the Committee would be sitting to conduct public hearings on the Bill. According to the judges, a number of persons and organisations engaged the National Assembly on the Bill, within the stipulated public participation period. The memoranda of the Administration and National Security Committee on the Security Laws (Amendment) Bill, 2014 indicated that a total of 46 stakeholders gave their input on the Bill. Some of the organisations were also parties to the petition.[75]

Given the urgency prompted by the security crises, the judges were satisfied that the National Assembly acted reasonably in the manner in which it facilitated public participation on SLAA. They underscored that the parties, which participated and gave their representations during the legislative process of SLAA, represented the various and diverse interests of Kenyans. The parties were also undoubtedly well versed with the contents and controversies of SLAA. While acknowledging that an opportunity could have been availed for greater public participation, the judges noted it would be too much to insist and expect that every Kenyan's view ought to have been considered prior to the passage of SLAA. In any case, the judges emphasised, the members of the National Assembly constitutionally also represent the people of Kenya. The judges argued that SLAA was, therefore, not unconstitutional on account of lack of public participation. Hence '*a fortiori*, the Presidential assent cannot be faulted as the process leading to the same was in our view within the ambit of the law'.[76] Likewise, CORD's allegation that the National Assembly did not provide opportunities for adequate public participation, was an act of populism. The decision of the judges that the enactment of SLAA was constitutional on the basis of adequate public participation, is, arguably a case of judicial restraint.

Conclusion

Aspects of judicial review, judicial restraint, and judicial activism were apparent in the SLAA case. Judicial review was evident, though not examined in this article, when provisions of SLAA were declared unconstitutional for violating the Bill of Rights. Judicial restraint manifested itself when the Court determined issues related to the enactment process. Features of judicial activism were, arguably, apparent in relation to institutional aggrandisement once the Court decided to adopt a liberal purposive interpretation of the constitution particularly with justiciability doctrines and declared that it had the jurisdiction to determine the case. Aspects of judicial activism were, in the context of majoritarianism and deference, arguably, manifest after the Court decided to determine issues related to the enactment process of SLAA. By determining such issues, the Court can be perceived as encroaching on legislative or executive authority hence competence in legislating an omnibus security law.

The populism of CORD and Jubilee, however, did not impact upon judicial decision making in the SLAA case. The judgment raised important issues regarding the way in which populism impacts upon judicial decision-making on counterterrorism legislation, and the implications for the integrity, independence and the role of the judiciary in

Kenya. Taking into account the populism of both political coalitions, the judges emphasised that their decision had implications on, judicial restraint, and subsequently judicial independence in the country. The judges argued that while the High Court had wide constitutional hence legitimate interpretative powers, it must be hesitant to interfere with the legislative process except in the clearest of cases. The judges cited the words of a senior counsel, which stated:

> ... the High Court should not be turned into an alternative forum where *losers in Parliamentary debates rush to assert revenge on their adversaries*. It would render parliamentary business impossible if the *deliberate disruption of legislative proceedings by a member or members unhappy with decisions of the speaker was to lead to invalidation of legislation by the courts*. In saying so, we maintain that the doors of the courts shall remain open and *deserving litigants will always obtain relief from the fountain of justice* (emphasis added).[77]

The above quote, arguably, indicates the Court's decision was not influenced by populism or any other partisan interests. Populism did not allow the judges to interfere with the legislative process of SLAA. CORD was judicializing politics having been unable to have its way in the legislature albeit having raised substantial issues on the constitutionality of SLAA.

The judges also insisted that whereas they have found no wrong-doing on the part of both speakers of the Parliament, it was incumbent upon the speakers to 'ensure that their constitutional and Standing Order obligations are undertaken to the highest standards. The respect and dignity of the two Houses can hardly be maintained if the Chambers are turned into anything other than hallowed legislative temples.' The judges were emphatic, that despite the fact that the role of the legislature is inherently political, populism should not adversely affect its legislative procedures hence institutional competence.[78] With regard to judicial independence in the country, the judges concluded by saying

> Let this judgment therefore send a strong message to the Parties and the World; the Rule of Law is thriving in Kenya and its Courts shall stand strong; fearless in the exposition of the law; bold in interpreting the Constitution and firm in upholding the judicial oath.[79]

This was also an indicator that the courts would not be subjected to undue influence from the other branches of government as well as from partisan interests such as populism.

Notes

1. See Brian Kimari and Melissa Mungai, 'Case Digest. Decisions of Kenyan Courts on Terrorism', Centre for Human Rights and Policy Studies, Nairobi, May 2020.
2. Keenan Kmiec, 'The Origin and Current Meanings of "Judicial Activism"', *California Law Review* 92 (2004): 1476.
3. Stefanie Lindquist and Frank Cross, *Measuring Judicial Activism* (Oxford: Oxford University Press, 2009), 32.
4. Lindquist and Cross, *Measuring Judicial Activism*, 33–40.
5. Aharon Barak, 'On Society, Law and Judging', *Tulsa Law Review* 47, no. 2 (2011): 305–8.
6. Michael Kirby, 'Judicial Activism: Power Without Responsibility? No, Appropriate Activism Conforming to Duty', *Melbourne University Law Review* 30 (2006): 592; Clint Bolick, 'The Role of the Judiciary', *Cato's Letter* 16, no. 2 (2018): 3–4.
7. Jeremy Waldron, 'The Core of the Case Against Judicial Review', *The Yale Review Journal* 115 (2006): 1348–55.

8. Aileen Kavanagh, 'Judicial Restraint in the Pursuit of Justice', *The University of Toronto Law Journal* 60, no. 1 (2010): 24–5; Richard A. Posner, 'The Rise and Fall of Judicial Restraint', *California Law Review* 100, no. 3 (2012): 520–1.
9. Mia Stuart, 'Independence of the Judiciary', *Oxford Constitutional Law*, March 2019, 2.
10. Cas Mudde, 'The Populist Zeitgeist', *Government and Opposition* 39, no. 4 (2004): 542–3.
11. Cas Mudde and Christobal Rovira Kaltwasser, 'Studying Populism in Comparative Perspective: Reflections of the Contemporary and Future Research Agenda', *Comparative Political Studies* 51, no. 13 (2018): 1668–72.
12. Kurt Weyland, 'Clarifying a Contested Concept: Populism in the Study of Latin American Politics', *Comparative Politics* 34, no. 1 (2001): 12.
13. Ibid., 14.
14. Ibid., 18–19.
15. Kurt Weyland, 'Populism's Threat to Democracy: Comparative Lessons for the United States', *Perspectives on Politics* 18, no. 2 (2020): 390.
16. Ran Hirschl, 'The Judicialization of Politics', in *The Oxford Handbook of Political Science*, ed. Robert Goodin (Oxford: Oxford University Press, 2013), 1–5.
17. Ibid., 17.
18. Nicola Lacey, 'Populism and the Rule of Law', LSE Working Paper 28, January 2019, 20.
19. John Pratt, *Penal Populism* (London: Routledge, 2007), 3–10; Marie Clark, 'Penal Populism in New Zealand', *Punishment & Society* 7, no. 3 (2005): 304.
20. Pratt, *Penal Populism*, 3; Clark, 'Penal Populism in New Zealand', 304.
21. Vincent Seron and Sophie Andre, '30 Measures Against Terrorism: Penal Populism Between Expected Efficiency and Potential Collateral Damage', in *Counterterrorism in Belgium: Key Challenges and Policy Options*, ed. Thomas Renard (Brussels: Egmont Institute, 2016), 16; Seron and Andre, '30 Measures Against Terrorism', 16; Lacey, 'Populism and the Rule of Law', 18.
22. Shylashri Shankar, 'Judicial Restraint in an Era of Terrorism: Prevention of Terrorism Cases and Minorities in India', *Socio-Legal Review* 11, no. 1 (2015): 104–5.
23. Shankar, 'Judicial Restraint in an Era of Terrorism', 105.
24. Kent Roach, 'Judicial Review of the State's Anti-Terrorism Activities: The Post 9/11 Experience and Normative Justifications for Judicial Review', *Indian Journal of Constitutional Law* 3 (2009): 166–7; Lacey, 'Populism and the Rule of Law', 18.
25. Ariel L. Bendor, 'Are There Any Limits to Justiciability? The Jurisprudential and Constitutional Controversy in Light of the Israeli and American Experience', *Indiana International & Comparative Law Review* 7, no. 2 (1997): 312, Lindquist and Cross, *Measuring Judicial Activism*, 26, 38.
26. Republic of Kenya, *The Constitution of Kenya, 2010, Kenya Gazette Supplement* No.55, Special Issue, 27th August, 2010 (Nairobi: Government Printer, 2010), 63–113.
27. Uhuru Kenyatta, Statement by President Uhuru Kenyatta During a Televised Address to the Nation After Signing into Law the Security Laws (Amendment) Bill 2014, 19th December, 2014, 1.; National Consortium for the Study of Terrorism and Responses to Terrorism (NCSRT). 2018. *Global Terrorism Data Base, Kenya*. https://www.start.umd.edu/gtd (accessed November 30, 2019)
28. Republic of Kenya, *The Security Laws (Amendment) Act, 2014. Kenya Gazette Supplement*, Acts, 2014. 22nd December 2014. (Nairobi: Government Printer, 2014).
29. National Council for Law Reporting (NCLR), *Coalition for Reform and Democracy (CORD) & 2 others v Republic of Kenya & 10 others [2015]* (Nairobi: NCLR, 2015), 32.
30. NCLR, *Coalition for Reform and Democracy*, 32–3.
31. Ibid., 33.
32. NCLR, *Coalition for Reform and Democracy*, 33–4; Republic of Kenya, Parliament: *The National Assembly Standing Orders*, 4th ed. (Nairobi: Government Printer, 2018), 105.
33. Ibid., 33–4; Kenya, *The National Assembly Standing Orders*, 108.
34. NCLR, *Coalition for Reform and Democracy*, 34–5.

35. Oscar G. Mwangi, 'Political Corruption, Party Financing and Democracy in Kenya', *The Journal of Modern African Studies* 46, no. 2 (2008): 269.
36. Raila Odinga, 'Statement on the Proposed Security Amendment Bill', December 11, 2014.
37. Ibid.
38. Ibid.
39. Ibid.
40. Ibid.
41. Uhuru Kenyatta, Statement by President Uhuru Kenyatta During a Televised Address to the Nation After Signing into Law the Security Laws (Amendment) Bill 2014, 19th December, 2014.
42. Ibid.
43. Ibid.
44. Ibid.
45. Ibid.
46. Ibid.
47. NCLR, *Coalition for Reform and Democracy*, 47–8.
48. Lindquist and Cross, *Measuring Judicial Activism*, 37–8.
49. NCLR, *Coalition for Reform and Democracy*, 48.
50. Ibid., 49.
51. Ibid., 49.
52. Ibid., 50.
53. Ibid., 51–2.
54. Ibid., 52.
55. Ibid., 52.
56. NCLR, *Coalition for Reform and Democracy*, 52.
57. Ibid., 53–4.
58. Lindquist and Cross, *Measuring Judicial Activism*, 33.
59. NCLR, *Coalition for Reform and Democracy*, 55.
60. Aileen Kavanagh, 'Constitutionalism, Counterterrorism, and the Courts: Changes in the British Constitutional Landscape', *I*CON9* 9, no. 1 (2011): 177–8.
61. Roach, 'Judicial Review', 140–1.
62. Kavanagh, 'Constitutionalism, Counterterrorism', 180.
63. Roach, 'Judicial Review', 155.
64. NCLR, *Coalition for Reform and Democracy*, 57.
65. Ibid., 59.
66. Ibid., 59.
67. Ibid., 59–60.
68. Kenya, *The Constitution of Kenya*, 77.
69. NCLR, *Coalition for Reform and Democracy*, 61–3.
70. Ibid., 63–4.
71. Ibid., 63–4.
72. Ibid., 64–5.
73. Ibid., 65.
74. Kenya, *The Constitution of Kenya*, 75; Republic of Kenya, Parliament: *The National Assembly Standing Orders*, 108–9; NCLR, *Coalition for Reform and Democracy*, 65.
75. NCLR, *Coalition for Reform and Democracy*, 68–9.
76. Ibid., 68–9.
77. Ibid., 116.
78. Ibid., 117.
79. Ibid., 117.

Disclosure statement

No potential conflict of interest was reported by the author(s).

ORCID

Oscar Gakuo Mwangi http://orcid.org/0000-0002-3559-5900

Pandemic and community's sense of justice through *suo motu* in India

Tarun Arora

ABSTRACT

An ideal citizen centric society wedded to the democratic governance always keeps its laws in motion to build an egalitarian and just order. Aesthetic virtue of law lies in the realisation of justice and the creation of an egalitarian order. Against this backdrop, the present paper aims to examine the approach of the Supreme Court of India (SCI) towards COVID-19 Pandemic through suo motu proceedings from various perspectives of jurisprudence and constitutionalism. The government claimed to have strived intensively with full vigour but the response due tolack of preparedness and intense gravity of the catastrophe, the efforts of the government appeared negligible. It warranted prompt revisit of priorities which compelled the SCI to intervene and evaluate the legitimacy of the executive action. Furthermore, it impelled to examine the role of the SCI in responding to the community's sense of justice and humanising justice. The paper presents the solution to the paradox generated out of the inherent friction between constitutional authority of judicial review and resistance of judicial review of executive actions by a populist government. The scope of the discussion has primarily been confined to Orders of the SCI in suo motu hearings and examined accordingly.

The relationship between law and justice is dynamic and indispensable. An ideal citizen-centric civilised and progressive State wedded to democratic governance always keeps its laws *in motion* to build an egalitarian and just order. Such laws possess organic contents, resilience and adaptability to the variable socio-politic forces. Simultaneously, these laws preserve their basic structure intact and stick to their axis of the welfare of their subjects. The Universal Declaration of Human Rights (UDHR) places all member States under an obligation to recognise inherent dignity and worth of human person equally, promote social progress and better standards of life in larger freedom. The Declaration further encapsulates the responsibility of the State to establish such an atmosphere where human being can enjoy their inalienable freedoms without any fear and want. Accordingly, the preamble to the Constitution of India enshrines justice as a first promise to be administered by the State and enumerates obligations of the State through fundamental rights and directive principles. The State has to protect right to life, personal liberty,

---

Supplemental data for this article can be accessed at https://doi.org/10.1080/13642987.2021.2010048.

livelihoods, education, privacy, medical assistance, freedom of speech and expression, religion and prevention of misinfodemics etc.

The COVID-19 threw unprecedented challenges before the government, as the individuals were stripped of their inalienable rights, lives were endangered and personal liberties even for basic needs were downsized. The government claimed to have strived intensively with full vigour but the response and efforts of the government appeared negligible due to lack of preparedness and intense gravity of the catastrophe. The impact was unprecedentedly and so forceful that it arrested each individual on the earth in the grip of fear. The majority of the individuals living on this earth were placed under house arrest except for medical professionals, security forces, police personnel and essential service providers. Even the judicial officers performed their duty to administer justice either from the homes or chambers through the online mechanism and in rarest of rare cases from Courts with strict guidelines. Despite these measures, several judges of the SCI, as well as other forums, could not escape themselves from the grip of COVID-19. Snatching the individuals from the hold of the parental institute of State under *Parents Patriae*, COVID-19 pushed every individual under the sense of fear warranting revisit, reconfigure and respond judiciously and cautiously to the adversities. Little attention and meagre investment in the health sector added to the quantum of loss and resulted in questions on the accountability of the government.

To quote Dushyant Dave, ' … Parliament is in recess. The judiciary is in state of coma. Consequently, the executive has a free hand in the functioning or malfunctioning of the nation'. He expressed his empathy over the silence of two powerful organs – the Parliament and the judiciary on the suffering of hundreds of millions of citizens. His satire that the government of India and the Prime Minister are trying to do something good for the country uncovers a lack of inter-ministerial coordination.[1]

It impelled to examine the role of the SCI in responding to the **community's sense of justice** *and* humanising justice. The analysis of the role of the SCI can be carried out in the context of procedural as well as substantial aspects of justice. The SCI reflected its commitment to the cause of justice by taking *suo motu* notice to address the demands of time to switch over to online and video conferencing mode for hearings and extending limitations. *Suo motu* notices of the matters concerning violation of human rights have been pioneered by the SCI even in the past by liberally interpreting Article 32 of the Constitution along with Article 42. The SCI has taken around 13 matters into notice since January 2020 out of which 10 were concerning COVID-19. But on the flip side, the SCI appeared evasive, as observed by Dushyant Dave, to address the sufferings of farmers, downtrodden and poor migrant workers during COVID-19.

Dean Roscoe Pound observed that 'Law must be stable, yet it cannot stand still'. The views of Pound carry thorough ramifications in the context of governance. Though one can draw *the prima facie* impression out of this observation regarding inherent contradictions yet it is a real truth. A legal system has to gear its movement towards the goal of justice to maintain its sanctity which can be preserved only if it is consistent with a reasonable amount of flexibility. The faith of the subjects can be preserved by reducing its rigidity and unreceptiveness to changes. However, it must also be taken into account that frequent changes may also result in surfacing the scepticism and undermine the sanctity for the law. Authority of law and legal institution sustains with accountability. Aesthetic virtue of law lies in the accountability, realisation of justice and the creation of an egalitarian order. It necessitates the predominance of legal spirit instead of cosmetic virtues of law. Pre-dominance of legal spirit can prevail on a synthesis of the absence of arbitrary powers, accountable and responsive governance treating all individuals equally without any discrimination on extra-constitutional grounds. Consistency in objectivity and accountability implies antithesis of arbitrariness. The minimum amount of consistency in legal order and its norms is a prerequisite for sustaining the faith of the people.

In the context of the judicial organ and their role to maintain the faith of the people in law, the judges are empowered to administer justice according to law. However, the judges are also human beings and may not be immune to fallible human instincts. Such vulnerabilities and temptations may result in incorrect decisions setting wrong precedents in the administration of justice. Therefore, Pound underscored the need for some degree of normative guidance in the form of black and white content of the law, the doctrine of *stare decisis*, canons of conduct, rule of equity etc.[2] These concepts were also discussed in the Roman legal system as *jus civile* and *ius honorarium*. Rule of equity or *ius honorarium* affords the room for relaxing the rigour of civil law by engrafting exceptions through the judicial process. Such equitable decisions may not have their roots in codified laws or a plethora of precedents but the conscience of a judge.[3] For the maintenance of peace in a society and ensuring the supremacy of law, it must be infused with the spirit of justice as the law is merely an instrument of justice. Justice is and ought to be the end of government. It is a prerequisite of civil society. It has been and will be pursued until it is obtained, or until liberty is lost in the pursuit.[4]

Every legal system must at times find the peculiarly hard case that cries aloud for relief, the case which no judge could decide according to rule without putting an intolerable strain on his conscience.[5] In such circumstances, the judge has to ride a judicial vehicle namely 'individual equity' to dispense justice. It is a tool with the judges to inject flexibility to bring out the inertia of black and white content of law and stretch it within the bounds of justice without being destructive of the normative system. Therefore, the laws around the world equip judges with the tools of equity to effectuate legitimate innovations in the body of law itself. The Constitution of India empowers the judges of the higher courts with wide powers. This scope of this paper is confined only to the power of the Supreme Court of India (SCI) under Article 142 read with Article 32 and other provisions of the Constitution *to do complete justice*. Article 142 encapsulates extra-ordinary powers of the SCI 'to pass such decree or order as may be necessary for doing complete justice between the parties'. This power has been conferred upon the SCI to ensure that no injustice is caused by the rigour of the law. It confers jurisdiction for dealing with an extraordinary situation in the larger interest of the administration of justice and preventing any manifest injustice from being done.[6] However, such kind of power should be exercised in exceptional circumstances for furthering the ends of justice and not casually or mechanically.[7] In *Supreme Court Bar Association v. Union of India and Another*,[8] the SCI explained the nature of power to do complete justice under Article 142 as a corrective measure. It is meant to give preference to equity over law to ensure that no injustice is caused. The purpose of this power was also explained in the matter of *Zahira Habibullah Sheikh & Anr. v. State of Gujarat*[9] as under:

> The purpose of Article 142 is to do effective, real and substantial justice, coextensive and commensurate with the needs of justice in a given case to meet any exigency that may arise.

Against this backdrop, the present paper aims to examine the approach of the SCI towards the COVID-19 Pandemic through *suo motu* proceedings from various perspectives of jurisprudence and constitutionalism.

The catastrophe needed to be faced together and interdependently by all the organs of the governments. The SCI exercised its discretion by taking *suo motu* notice under Article 142 to extend the period of limitation and adhere to the online administration of justice. However, it showed judicial self-restraint to intervene in the matters of response to the pandemic by the Executive till March 2021 in the context of substantive rights. The SCI supported the decision of the government in matters concerning migrant labourers or access to essential supplies and services during the pandemic, imposition or relaxation of lock-down measures. Several instances of dismissing Public Interest Litigations (PILs) during the pandemic such as protests against citizenship laws, farmers, different kinds of celebration events, religious tourism, holding of elections etc. afford the room for analysing judicial approach. At some of the quarters, the SCI was expected to move the wheel of justice as a guardian of the fundamental rights of the people yet it preferred to be a silent spectator and exercise restraint. On the pretext of affording reasonable freedom to the executive to respond as per its wisdom, it restrained itself and did not blow the judicial whistle when needed during the tenure of former Chief Justice S.A. Bobde. The judiciary was found on the lowest ebb by discouraging petitions under Article 32.[10] But a day before his retirement when India was blatantly hit by the second wave of COVID-19, several High Courts bounced back and came heavy-handedly on the government to protect the lives of citizens.[11] The HC of Delhi convened late-night hearings to monitor the supply of oxygen at the hospital to save patients' lives. The very next morning, the SCI treated the application of Vedanta Ltd. praying for reopening its oxygen plant to manufacture oxygen as a *suo motu* petition concerning COVID-19 and passed an extraordinary order.[12] This sudden change in the stance of SCI raised the eyebrows of constitutionally literate people.

This proactive instance of the SCI resulted in the origin of two schools of thought – one which views it as negative interference while the other opined it as an accountable and much-awaited deliberative approach. India has subscribed to the parliamentary form of government like the U.K. It was reasoned that government is a democratically elected government and enjoys a majority in the Parliament. It was stated that the Council of Ministers is responsible and answerable only to the House of the People. No institute, however supreme in its domain, is above the Constitution and the People. None can, therefore, cast itself in the role of a conscience keeper of the nation or of a superior which can call the duly elected government to order. Judges were advised not to be a substitute for those in government or the opposition. It was emphatically asserted that no doubt, the independence of the judiciary is important, but so is the independence of the Parliament, the Election Commission and other institutions. The populist government can be held accountable to the supreme masters – the people.

The supporters of this school observed that the SCI, known as the sheet anchor of democracy and justice, has lost its proverbial cool, remarked derogatory, admonished the Election Commission and the government. It was further mentioned that the *obiter dicta* of the courts released negativity from the bench and guided several high courts to admonish democratically elected governments.[13]

The supporters of the other school of thought were of the view that taking *suo motu* cognisance to review executive action by the SCI, shown a ray of hope to the millions to get some reparative and restorative justice. Through these orders, the SCI introduced inclusive and democratic measures to meet the challenges posed by the pandemic.

It reminded an important observation made by Upendra Baxi in his masterwork *Indian Supreme Court and Politics,* to quote:

> ... is sensitive to the claims of other major institutions of the national government and plays politics of accommodation to the extent possible by 'skillfully managing shifts in the management of the distribution of power.[14]

This observation fits in the present context as the impression given due to judicial evasiveness on the pretext of policy matter and purely of executive domain while basic tenets of social contract theory – freedom from fear and freedom from want were endangered. The approach of the SCI during the pandemic to give free play to the executive turned Baxi's observations as a classic. He pointed out that psycho-dynamics of these different pulls and pressures actuates the court to play politics – politics of power, of accommodation, of survival, of establishment, of aspiration and innovation, of order, of substantive justice, politics for or against the people depending upon the socio-political context and constraints in which it has to operate. He cautioned that whenever it plays politics and more so politics of opposition in the context of a one-party state, it is inevitably drawn into the vortex of controversy.

An attempt has been made to find out the solution to the paradox generated out of the inherent friction between the constitutional authority of judicial review and resistance of judicial review of executive actions by a populist government. The objectives of the present paper have been divided into two heads:

(1) General Objectives:
   (i) To identify the need for distinguishing inter-relationship between judicial review and separation of powers during ordinary and extraordinary circumstances;
   (ii) The examine the judicial approach towards aspects of the administration of procedural justice and substantive justice during a pandemic;
(2) Specific Objectives:
   (i) To critically evaluate the use and misuse of a judicial tool of *suo motu* to respond to the community's sense of justice;
   (ii) To revisit the psychodynamics of judicial pull and political push back in the context of the pandemic.

1. Material and method

For the study, primary documents and secondary sources of information have been gathered. In primary documents such as various orders of the Supreme Court, High Courts and some notifications issued by various Ministries and Departments available on government websites have been used as primary documents of information. The scope of the discussion has primarily been confined to following judgments or Orders of the SCI in *suo motu* hearings. These *suo motu* hearings have been mainly divided into two parts – procedural justice and substantive justice. There are around ten *suo motu* hearings by the SCI till 30th June 2021. Part I deals with procedural aspects of the administration of justice elaborating judicial approach towards access to justice through online mode and extending limitation period. In part II, three landmark *suo motu* hearings dealing with different aspects of substantive justice covering the right to access to the vaccine, examination of national vaccine policy, rights of the prisoners and migrant workers highlighting the performance of the State have been covered.

SN	Aspects of Administration of Justice	Title of Judgment
1	Procedural justice	
	(a) Access to Justice	*In Re. Guidelines for Court Functioning Through Video Conferencing During COVID 19 Pandemic*[15]
	(b) Extension of Limitation Period	*In Re. Cognizance for Extension of Limitation*[16]
2	Substantive justice	
	(a) Pandemic management, right to health, and distribution of essential supplies and services	*In Re. Distribution of Essential Supplies and Services During Pandemic*[17]
	(b) Prison Administration	*In Re. Contagion of COVID-19 Virus in Prisons*[18]
	(c) Migrant Labourers	*In Re. Problems and Miseries of Migrant Labourers*[19]

A cursory reference of other relevant hearings has also been given at the relevant places. In secondary data, the articles in the journals and newspapers concerning social contract theory, law, governance, pandemic etc. have been collected and analyzed. To examine the content of the judgments, jurisprudential principles thereunder and *ratio decidendi*, Critical Discourse Analysis (CDA) has been applied to examine the role of the SCI in democratising the constitutional philosophy of justice. The analysis also deconstructs paradigm shifts from judicial self-restraint to realise the community's sense of justice in the light of Bodenheimer's backward pull forward push theory.

2. Results/case analysis

This section presents an examination of the inter-relationship between the concepts of State, Law and Justice. The performance of the judicial organ of the State has been examined on the yardstick of its commitment to the tenets of the social contract in modern perspectives, rule of law and enforcing the right to constitutional remedies. The SCI has been adequately equipped with various constitutional tools to keep the guarantees given under the Constitution intact and dispense justice. During the last seven decades of the commencement of the Constitution, the SCI has opened its doors for making justice within the access of the millions of downtrodden, illiterate and backward people by inventing the tool of PIL,[20] Spot Visit[21] and exercising epistolary jurisdiction.[22] The fertile language of Article 32[23] (providing for constitutional remedies) read with Article 142[24] (to do complete justice) has been interpreted progressively to make governance and justice inclusive. It recognised a variety of rights within the framework of the right to life guaranteed under Article 21 of the Constitution in the light of preambular goals of justice, equality, the dignity of individual etc.[25] The tools of interpretation of statutes such as the rule of purposive construction, harmonious construction and liberal interpretation have been used extensively by the SCI.[26] Recent attempts of the SCI by taking *suo motu* notice of miseries of the people suffering due to COVID-19 pandemic, leakage points in the pandemic response policy and administration of justice during restrictions of movement etc. have been analyzed in forthcoming discussion.

2.1. Procedural justice

Since a nationwide lockdown was imposed on 22 March 2020 and mobility of the individuals was not allowed. Under Section 144 of Cr.P.C., prohibitory orders were passed by the District Magistrate as directed by the Ministry of Home Affairs. The directions also contained punitive provisions under Section 188 of Indian Penal Code, 1860 and Sections 51-60 of Disaster Management Act, 2005 for violation of containment measures. Except for the health department, goods transport and police mechanism, the whole governance including the administration of justice by courts came at a standstill. Thus, the SCI took *suo motu* notice to revisit its mechanism as under:

2.1.1. Access to justice (In Re. Guidelines for court functioning through video conferencing during COVID 19 pandemic[27])

The SCI, to co-operate in the implementation of the preventive steps for containing the spread of infection scaled-down traditional method of hearings. To ensure the safety of the stakeholders, it directed to avoid the need for physical presence in hearings and to continue administration of justice.[28] Reiterating its constitutional responsibility to ensure delivery of justice, it laid down guidelines to avoid congregation during court hearings. Acknowledging the contribution of modern technology to enhance the quality and effectiveness of the administration of justice, it acknowledged the limited infrastructure.[29] The SCI did not ignore the litigants having any access to videoconferencing facilities. It directed all the high courts to formulate their Standard Operative Procedures (SoPs) given the peculiar circumstances prevailing within their jurisdiction. For urgent hearings, the High Courts were directed to adhere to video conferencing mode. The Bench accorded free charter to the High Courts to use any application which works within their jurisdiction. In this way, the pandemic provided an opportunity to the Courts to adapt to digital modes of working and institutionalise a hybrid model of working which provides further room for investigation and studies.[30]

2.1.2. Extension of limitation period (In Re. Cognizance for extension of limitation[31])

The approach of the SCI regarding the limitation period can be discussed with the help of the following timeline:

(i) On 23 March 2020, the SCI showed its sensitivity towards the challenges being faced by the litigants in filing their petitions, applications, suits, appeals and all other proceedings because of the COVID-19 and lockdown. Taking the ground situation into account, the SC directed to extend the limitation period, whether prescribed as condonable or not under the general law or special laws, till further order to be passed. This power was exercised by the SCI u/a 142 r/w 141. This order was binding order within the meaning of Art. 141 on all courts/ tribunals and authorities.

(ii) On 10 July 2020, this proceeding was not only a *suo motu* but also to entertain different applications wherein directions were sought from the court to extend the time where time is an essence to perform a particular act and that may or already have expired during the lockdown.

Like – under *Section 29-A of Arbitration and Conciliation Act, 1996,* it specifies the fixed time to do certain acts i.e. making arbitral award within a time frame. Section 23(4) of this Act provides for 6 months for the completion of the statement of claim and defence which was extended by the Court.

Further, *Section 12-A of the Commercial Courts Act, 2015* – stipulates time for completing the process of compulsory pre-litigation, mediation and settlement. This given time limit was extended for 45 days by the SCI from the day of lifting the lockdown. Similarly, the service of notices, summons and exchange of pleadings or documents in each legal proceeding in the prescribed time limit was not possible during the period of lockdown. In this regard, the mode of delivery was replaced from physical delivery to virtual delivery through messaging services, email, FAX, WhatsApp, telegram and signal etc.

The next point of consideration in this matter was regarding the validity of a cheque under the *Negotiable Instruments Act, 1881.* The Court clarified that the Act does not deal with the period of validity of a cheque. Rather it is a matter dealt with under Section 35 of *the Banking Regulation Act, 1949* – therefore, the SCI left the matter to be decided by the RBI as an Expert and Autonomous Institution.

(iii) 8 March 2021, the SCI observed that in calculating any period of limitation for any suit, appeal, application or proceeding, the period from 15 March 2020 till 14 March 2021 shall stand excluded. Where any balance period of limitation remaining on 15 March 2020 was in existence, it shall be available from 15 March 2021.

Where a limitation period was expired b/w 15 March 2020–14 March 2021, it is extended by 90 days from 15 March 2021. The period of 15 March 2020 to 14 March 2021 was excluded from all proceedings whether under Arbitration Act, Commercial Courts Act or N.I. Act and other laws to extend limitation not only for instituting suits, application or other time-bound issues.

2.2. Substantive justice

A civilised society is always under a constant obligation to ensure the growth of its individual along with the protection of lives and liberties, for the existence and development of society itself depends upon the same. The linkage between human rights and civilised society is inextricable. The efforts made by the SCI through suo motu proceedings to respond to the sense of justice can be taken as a mirror of civility. These efforts can be elaborated as under:

2.2.1. Prison administration (In Re. Contagion of COVID 19 virus in prisons[32])

On 13 March 2020, the attention of the SCI was drawn towards prison with the news of infection of 107 inmates who were tested positive. Taking *Suo Motu* notice of the over-crowding prisons (more than four lakhs prisoners in 1339 prisons) in the country on 16 March 2020, the SCI directed all respective agencies involved in prison administration to suggest immediate measures to be adopted for the medical assistance to the inmates and juveniles in the Remand Homes.[33] On 23 March 2020, the Court directed States/UTs to constitute High Powered Committees to classify prisoners and undertrials who can be released on parole or an interim bail. It illustrated the guiding principle of considering the quantum of punishment for convicted and undertrials for the alleged offence. Large numbers of prisoners were released on interim bail and parole on the recommendation of High Power Committees. 90% of the released prisoners reported back in February–March 2021. Later, because of the second wave of COVID-19, the SCI re-took cognisance of the prison administration on 7 May 2021 along with different applications. Mr Colin Gonsalves, appearing on the behalf of one of the applicants submitted to release all those prisoners who have been released last year on regular bail. Besides, the inmates who have been granted parole last year should be granted parole for further 90 days. He further requested the Court to direct all High Powered Committees to put all orders on the website of the National Legal Services Authority (NALSA).

Given the grim situation, the Attorney General also submitted to decongest the prisons and requested for relaxation of handcuffing of the prisoners during the outbreak of the COVID-19 as it may result in the spread of infection.

The SCI after entertaining the above submissions observed that prison decongestion is a matter concerning the health and right to life of both the prisoners and the administration. It demands effective and timely synchronisation between consideration of criminal justice administration, health impacts and rights of the accused. While proper management of the pandemic was viewed as a matter of utmost concern and significance of the response of the prison administration towards pandemic was underlined by the Court. Therefore, shouldering the responsibility to control and limit the authorities from arresting the accused, the Court reiterated the guidelines for arrest in *Arnesh Kumar* v. *State of Bihar*[34] for the guidance of implementing mechanism. It directed all the States/UTs to adopt guidelines to consider the release of prisoners. It took note of the states that have not constituted High Powered Committees and directed them to constitute immediately after accepting all the submissions of Mr Colin Gonsalves. Moving a step ahead for those who had not to be released either on parole or bail, the SCI directed the prison authorities to be considerate towards arranging testing, treatment, maintaining hygiene and sanitation within the prison walls.

2.2.2. Pandemic management, right to health, and distribution of essential supplies and services (In Re: distribution of essential supplies and service during pandemic[35])

This matter requires micro-level analysis of the approach of the SCI as in this matter the government resisted judicial intervention and claimed its freedom under the garb of the doctrine of separation of powers. The SCI directed the government to provide comprehensive details of the executive policies on vaccination, hospital beds, oxygen cylinders and other issues concerning COVID-19 Pandemic Response through *suo motu* proceedings which can be presented as under:

2.2.2.1. Background. India reasonably controlled to save lives during the 'first wave of COVID-19' despite the unprecedented challenges faced by the health department and health workers due to unpreparedness for responding to the disaster. Till December 2020, the death toll and infection rate was comparatively lower than many advanced countries of the world. However, the laxity on the part of the people as well as different governmental organs pushed the COVID-19 containment measures and safety precautions were blown out in the air. In many states, the COVID-19 wards and response units were discontinued. The State governments and regulatory agencies of different sectors such as banking, education, and insurance were resuming their operations in new normal. But the sudden rise in the number of COVID-19 positive cases during February–March 2021 swayed the whole of India. The period also witnessed high staked elections for the legislative assemblies in the five states and local bodies in the two states. After elections, due to ongoing tussle between the Union Government and the States, the UoI unilaterally made a press statement that the State Governments would procure COVID vaccines directly from the manufacturers from 1st May as per the Liberalised Pricing and Accelerated National COVID-19 Vaccine Strategy.[36] It reasoned that policy has been framed according to the constitutional scheme. The Seventh Schedule of the Constitution places health as a subject in State list.[37] Additionally, various reports of media presented a dismal state of affairs pressing government health and other infrastructure under rigorous test. News regarding the shortage of oxygen, vaccine, hospital beds were reported in the public domain, which compelled the SCI to take *suo motu* cognisance of the management of COVID-19 by the Union of India and States. The SCI initiated the proceedings on 22 April 2021 and passed an extraordinary order to the government to file a comprehensive affidavit concerning vaccination policy, supply of essential drugs, medical oxygen, medical infrastructure, augmentation of healthcare workforces and challenges being faced by them on 30 April 2021.

2.2.2.2. Submission on behalf of the UoI. The UoI submitted an affidavit on 9 May 2021 in which it pleaded that unnecessary judicial intervention is in contradiction of the principle of separation of powers.[38] It claimed that the government needs the discretion to frame its policy in the public interest and its wisdom should be trusted.

It contended that the present policy is consistent with Articles 14 and 21 of the Constitution. It keeps room for free play in the joints to deal with pandemics of such intensity. It did not warrant any judicial examination.[39]

It was further contended that executive policies should be brought under judicial review only if these appear arbitrary. In matters of a grave emergency, where the inputs of medical and scientific experts are required, the judiciary should not intervene.[40]

Any over-zealous judicial intervention, though well-intentioned, may result in unwarranted results on account of lack of expertise. Such a situation may place the executive with little room to explore innovative solutions.[41]

The UoI submitted that the discussion between the government and foreign vaccine manufacturers were ongoing at political and diplomatic levels to ensure the proper supply of vaccines. As per its vaccination policy, it would complete the vaccination drive by the end of December 2021. In an affidavit, it was denied that the policy would promote competition among States/UTs. It was further submitted that the individuals above 45 years could continue to get vaccinated at a facility through *on-site registration* without previous booking through CoWIN.

2.2.2.3. Concerns by **Amici.** The *Amici* submitted the foreign vaccine manufacturers were generally not receptive and not entertaining the States or UT governments. The foreign manufacturers expressed their limitations to deal only with the federal government on account of their corporate policies. Hitherto, the UoI implemented Universal Immunisation Programme which authorised it to procure and distribute to the States/UTs. The programme was run successfully under the single procurement model which was being followed by other nations for ensuring fast and effective administration of vaccines against COVID 19. The *Amici* submitted that the Liberalised Vaccine Policy allowed the vaccine manufacturers to implement differential procurement prices for the UoI for vaccinating persons above 45 years of age and for the State/UT Governments and private hospitals for vaccinating the persons between 18 and 44 years of age. Such a policy may impose an unreasonable burden on persons between 18 and 44 years of age particularly those belonging to poor socio-economic classes.

The *Amici* presented that due to Liberalised Vaccine Policy, the vaccine manufacturers were placed in dominating position to fix their prices and create their monopoly. The States were not enjoying a unique position as the UoI being a single buyer to negotiate under the single procurement model.

It was further contended by the *Amici* that certain public health is a subject under Entry 6 of List II (State List) of the Seventh Schedule of the Constitution. Nonetheless, Entry 81 of List I of (Union List) deals with inter-state migration and inter-state quarantine, and Entry 29 of List III (Concurrent List) provides for prevention of extension from one State to another of infectious or contagious diseases. Therefore, such a policy may create constitutional disequilibrium. Besides, the policy did not provide any clarity on the ground of *pro-rata* allotment of the doses to each state. It could specify either population or state-wise situation of pandemic or number of morbidities between 18-44 years of age be taken into consideration. In case, such a *pro-rata* had to be decided by the manufacturer, which would not meet the test of reasonableness under Article 14 of the Constitution.

Pointing out the silence of the policy regarding UoI's role in vaccine distribution or redistribution, the *Amici* highlighted various loopholes such as the absence of any measures for prioritising persons with co-morbidities, persons with disabilities or other illnesses, caregivers for elderly and sick, teachers and others in the age group of 18–44 years, digitally illiterate people, crematorium workers etc. The claim of the UoI to complete vaccination by December 2021 was also countered by the *Amici* as there was a huge gap between the projected population and projected vaccine production. The data was not matching on the issue that how 100 crore persons would be vaccinated in 200 crore doses with the proposed procurement policy and projected rate of production by the manufacturers. It was highlighted that two vaccine manufacturers were able to produce less than 10 crore doses per month while the approximate population between 18 and 44 years of age was 59 crore requiring 122 crore doses. Even if proposed doses of Sputnik i.e. 15–20 crore are procured, this group of the population can be vaccinated probably in 12 months.[42]

Apart from the above, the concern was raised by the *Amici* regarding COVID appropriate behaviour, decent burial and creation of infrastructure for the electric crematoriums and a protocol for the cremation of dead bodies.

2.2.2.4. Judgment. The Court divided Liberalised Vaccination Policy into three parts namely vaccine distribution between different age groups, vaccine procurement and augmentation of the vaccine available in India. The Court examined each clause of the policy to underline the grey areas. The clause of Liberalised Vaccination Policy for paid vaccination by the State/UTs and private hospitals for the persons between 18-44 years was held as lacking reasonable differentia and in contradiction of Article 14. The Court observed the policy as *prima facie* arbitrary and irrational. The cognisance of the multi procurement model and response to the floated tenders was also taken up by the Court. It accepted the submissions of the *Amici* that the Central Government representing the second most populous country would certainly be better placed to negotiate the prices for higher quantities. The Court underscored ambiguities and lack of clarity regarding the distribution of vaccines among the States. It suggested clearing the ambiguities in the policy concerning distribution on the logical ground of the stage of the pandemic in a particular state, healthcare infrastructure, literacy rate, age and overall health condition of its population etc. for *pro-rata* supply. It directed to reframe the policy by addressing the above loopholes making it inclusive and filing another affidavit after compliance.

2.2.3. Migrant workers (In Re. Problems and miseries of migrant labourers[43])

On the issues of migrant workers, initially on 31 March 2020, the SCI recorded the statement of the Solicitor General on behalf of the UoI. It was stated by Solicitor General:

> Mass migration has stopped and all the migrant workers who were on the road had been shifted to relief camps/shelter homes set up at various points in each State/UT.

The Court rather expressed its concern on fake news causing distress and panic resulting in migration. It directed the media to publish the official version of developments, made available by the government in the form of a daily bulletin. The Court relying on the face value of the statement of the government declined to entertain the matter and decided not to interfere with the decisions taken by the government on 21 April 2020. It observed that the current migrant crisis cannot be prevented and there is nothing much that the court and the government can do to prevent workers from walking back to their native places. The issue of migrant workers was highlighted in print and electronic media.[44]

In between, various petitions were filed by some social activists Harsh Mandar, Aruna Roy, Swami Agnivesh and many others which were clubbed by the SCI with taking *suo motu* cognisance of a letter written by Mahua Mitra and disposed on 21 April 2020.[45] These petitions were filed on the issue of starvation, food, ration, shelter and minimum wages. It was submitted by the interveners and public-spirited persons that despite governmental measures, thousands of labourers still lack access to basic amenities. However, the Court appeared convinced with the submissions of the government that various measures were already in place to address the issues of migrant workers including a helpline number where people could report issues concerning implementation at the ground level.

Later on, the Full Bench of the Supreme Court took *suo motu* cognisance of the matter *In Re. Problems and Miseries of Migrant Labourers*[46] on 26 May 2020. However, the Court referred to its orders dated 9 June 2020 to remind States/UTs to maintain a record of all such migrant workers. The order of 9 June 2020 contained directions on taking necessary steps for running the relief camps, shelter camps, attending to the needs of food and water of the migrants, attending to the requirement of transportation of migrant workers to their native places. The SCI mentioned that it took note of the matters raised by intervenors in their applications concerning shortcomings and lapses in the implementing of policies referred in affidavits, and directed the States/ UTs to strictly vigil and supervise. Later the proceedings of *suo motu* were clubbed with intervenor's application in 2021 praying for a direction to distribute dry ration to migrant workers, facilitating their transport either by road or by train to their native places and with a request to direct for running of a community kitchen for migrant labourers for service two meals a day. Various issues concerning scope of National Food Security Act, 2013, lack of ration card for availing the benefit of the 'one nation one ration card', coverage of Rural and Urban population under National Food Security Act, 2013, Inter-State Migrant Workmen (Regulation of Employment and Conditions of Service) Act, 1979, the issue of registration of unorganised workers etc. were raised for the consideration of the Court. It expressed its concern over the failure of the Union Ministry of Labour and Employment for not being alive to concerns of migrant workers.[47] Therefore, it directed various states to provide dry rations to migrant workers under *Atma Nirbhar Bharat* Scheme or any other scheme w.e.f. from May 2021. It further directed that while distributing dry ration, the officials should not insist on an identity card for those migrant labourers who do not possess them for the time being and give ration based on self-declaration made by the dejected migrants. The order of the Court also sought the establishment of Grievance Redressal Mechanism including a helpline for deprived migrant workers and governments to make details of all social and food security schemes public.

Discussion

(i) Regarding *suo motu* on functioning through video conferencing, the SCI was sensitive enough about the digital illiteracy and probable obstacles which could arise during a hearing. It directed the respective authorities to maintain a helpline for any complaint regarding the quality or audibility of the feed. At different stages of judicial proceedings – trial, arguments etc., all the courts were given special guidelines with adequate room to the High Court for playing between the joints and filling the normative vacuum if any. Many teething problems were faced by the judges as well as lawyers while switching over to the online model of proceedings, but these were initial hiccups. Though in context of the SCI's order on Migrant Workers in March – April 2020 is said to be misconstrued to poor audio connectivity yet the initiative of the SCI is worth appreciation.

(ii) On the issue of extending the limitation period due to extra-ordinary circumstances prevailing, the SCI showed its compassion towards litigants by extending the limitation period from time to time. Another important aspect was that the GoI was directed by the Court while formulating guidelines for regulated movement to be considerate about time-bound applications for legal purposes, educational and job-related requirements along with essential goods and services. The orders of the SCI discussed above reflect the sensitivity of the Court towards the hardships faced by litigants as well as applicants in different spheres of life.

Besides, it is worth mentioning here that while extending the time limit for filing various cases or the proceedings where the time was an essence, it took care not to intrude in technical areas demanding expertise knowledge. To dispose of the application by an intervenor regarding extending the validity of cheque clubbed with *suo motu* proceedings, the SCI left the matter for consideration of the Reserve Bank of India.

(iii) On the matter concerning the safety of prisoners from COVID-19, the SCI was considerate and sympathetic enough wherein the government/s complied with the directions. It ingrained the seeds of humanising justice in prison jurisprudence. Not only towards undertrials or convicted inmates who could be and were released on regular bails and parole, but also the interests of inmates serving life imprisonment and convicts of other serious crimes were taken into consideration with a humanitarian approach. It would not be irrelevant to refer here the travesty of justice in the context of denial of medical bail to Stan Swamy – 84 old priest suffering from Parkinson who died due to post COVID complications. The Court was found at its weakest and most deferential to the wish of the executive as he was in custody in case of terrorism and national security.[48]

(iv) During May–June 2021 while reviewing vaccine policy as presented on affidavit, the observations of the Court in the judgment depicted fact scepticism and raised concern on the legitimacy of the policy due to gaps in the policy. Being a guarantor and guardian of the fundamental rights, the Court was candid towards the rights of the vulnerable population and sought inputs on progress in procurement.

The Court rejected the contention of the Solicitor General to restrain itself from reviewing the executive policy by adhering to the doctrine of separation of powers. The Court reasonably explained that separation of powers is a part of the basic structure of the Constitution. It accepted that the policymaking is and has been beyond doubt within the executive domain. It accepted its limitation being a non-representative organ but at the same time also underlined that the executive is democratically accountable for its actions as it is enjoying access to resources useful in the framing of policies.

Firm on exercising its jurisdiction to carry out the judicial review, it observed emphatically that our Constitution does not envisage courts to be silent spectators when constitutional rights of the citizens are infringed by the executive policies. It made it clear that judicial review is equally a part of the basic structure and equips the court to examine the constitutional legitimacy of the policy of the executive.

(v) On issues concerning migrant labourers, though the SCI responded to the community's sense of justice a bit late yet it cannot be ignored that during the first wave, it exercised judicial self-restraint which appeared like an abdication of its courageous role as a *sentinel on the qui vive*.

While dismissing PILs on issues concerning migrants, the Court even recorded that there is no migrant on the roads merely based on a statement by the government. The negative vibes from the Bench were unbecoming of the Constitutional repository of faith presiding over the Bench, to quote, 'If they are being provided meals, then why do they need money for meals?' The intervenor represented that 'they do not just need food in the shelter homes .... We need to give them money to send to their families back home. They (family members) are not in shelter homes'.[49] Though it was not *suo motu* wherein the Intervenor brought it to the notice of the Court that quality of the food supplied at the shelter homes was not up to the Mark and it was inedible. It was shocking to hear from the Court 'we are not experts. We do not intend to interfere with what the government is doing without knowing what it is all about .... We do not plan to supplant the wisdom of the government with our wisdom. We are not experts in health or management. We will ask the government to create a helpline'. It simply excused not to take a better policy decision and said that we don't want to interfere in government decisions for the next 10–15 days. This SCI went on the back foot while it was expected at such a crucial time to join hands with the government to take corrective measures. There had been alternatives with the Court to appoint *Amicus Curiae* or submit time-bound ATR etc. Even the SCI just paid lip service by directing states/ UTs on inter-state migrant issues falling within the domain of concurrent list to prepare data, employment details and so on. Such cosmetic services did not bring any positive outcome or redressal of miseries. It is only on 30 June, after the retirement of former Chief Justice of India, whose most of the judgments during the first wave of COVID-19 depicted his conformist nature downgrading SCI mere as an agency to collect affidavits and build paper castles.

The upshot of the aforesaid discussion is that doctrine of separation of powers is merely a principle of law and evolved to rule out the possibility of tyranny by the concentration of all powers in a single organ. It did not mean that the doctrine has made any constitutional organ irrelevant when the constitutional guarantees are endangered. This view finds its support from Baxi's work that 'it is better for the court to face controversy rather than irrelevance'. Baxi already cautioned that the moment judiciary will assert its relevance, it will have to face criticism. It happened when it was stated by supporters of majoritarianism that the courts reached new levels of overreach in the form of *suo motu* notice developments – becoming both the petitioner and the judge on the pretext of the pandemic. Nonetheless, the SCI corrected its course of action by taking *suo motu* notice and responding reasonably to the community's sense of justice. It has to be understood in the sense of accountability of organs not of authority as alleged by referring to the parliamentary form of government of the U.K. Simultaneously, it cannot be ignored that the Indian Parliament is not as supreme as British Parliament and it is itself a creation of the Constitution. Therefore, it has no existence beyond and outside the Constitution.

The Constitution implies that all these institutions have a sacrosanct responsibility to protect the life, liberty and property of ' ... we the people of India'. Cicero justified the existence of sovereign power in *government* to preserve the existence of liberties.

Constitutionally speaking, sovereignty lies in the people of India. The functioning of the last seven decades of the Constitution reflects that the interest of the people of India is brushed aside in wake of politics of accommodation, power tussle, self-assertion and self-projection by those in power.[50] Ideally speaking, paramount importance must be given to preserve and protect the interests of the people instead of false interpretation of certain principles. The institution which takes care of the interests of the people would certainly prevail over the other and pass the test of the performance of constitutional responsibility. The lives and the liberties have to be accorded the highest place instead of disguising or twisting the legal principles by colourable interpretation. The extra-ordinary circumstances required commitment to the interests of people not to the powers or their doctrines. To quote Martin Luthar King:

> Power without love is reckless and abusive, and love without power is sentimental and anaemic. Power at its best is love implementing the demands of justice, and justice at its best is power, correcting everything that stands against love.[51]

If the above words of illustrious vision are reproduced by substituting a word 'love' by 'law', it implies the essence of the relationship between law and justice. The power game is always tempting. If the executive has been vested with the power over the purse and policymaking, at the same time, it is also entrusted to serve the people and be accountable for its deeds. It cannot claim immunity to judicial review and is allowed to play hide and seek with people. If any attempt is made by the executive to give a go-bye, the same must be stopped firmly and effectively. All organs should owe their allegiance to the people of India and the Constitution. Similarly, the judges should also owe their allegiance to the same instead of letting the SCI fall from grace due to the individualisation of justice. When the judiciary acts above partisanship, it should be appreciated instead of labelling it as an opposition. The SCI fell from grace by being a conformist and exponent of the government's submissions and referring to various legislations and policies on paper in the distribution of food, shelter and transportation to the migrant labourers. Here the question in such a grim situation was not the existence of policies on paper but the ground. Relying on face value was a blunder committed by the SCI. However, immediately after the retirement of the former Chief Justice of India, the SCI was joined by the different High Courts in damage control exercises. Exercising dialogic jurisprudence, it bound itself by a deliberative approach and minutely dissected vaccine policy, red-flagged the defects which could further aggravate inequities. This is where the approach depicted through the SCI's *suo motu* proceedings in May 2020 on migrant issues, in May 2021 on vaccine policy and in June 2020 on migrant issues differs. The same Court now termed government response towards migrants as unpardonable and directed to submit the compliance report by 31 July 2021.[52] Even, in hearing a PIL on the issue of Compensation for COVID Deaths to kin, the SSCI expressed its displeasure over the approach of NDMA and UoI and directed compliance within six weeks.[53] On 16 July, the SCI took *suo motu* notice of *Kanwar Yatra* and underlined that 'the health of the citizenry of India and their right life are paramount. All other sentiments, albeit religious, are subservient to this most basic fundamental right'.[54] The seeds of differentiation lie in the individualisation of justice, which has been referred to by Mahatma Gandhi in the beginning as 'conscience of the court'. It is the judicial system itself that has to bring about reform and constant repair from within in such quandaries.[55] This damage control exercise of the SCI underscores a judicial renaissance to make space for resurgent constitutionalism indicating the space between absolutism, positivism and anarchy.[56] Justice N.V.Ramana, the present Chief Justice of India observed that the judiciary should have complete freedom to apply checks on governmental power and action. It cannot be controlled, directly or indirectly, by the legislature or the executive or else the Rule of Law would become illusory. He also cautioned the judges that they should not be flowed away by the emotional sentiments based on public opinion or social media etc. They must be cautious as the noise now a day is amplified which may not be reflective of what is right and what the majority believes in. Opportunities to make one incapable of distinguishing between right and wrong, good and bad, real and fake have increased due to new media tools. He urged that the judges should work independently and withstand all external aids and pressures. While there is a lot of discussion about the pressure from executives, it is also imperative to start a discourse as to how social media trends can affect the institutions. Striking the balance between his appeal to be careful about false narratives built by the social media, he acknowledged that the judges should not completely alienate themselves from what is happening on the ground level. They cannot stay in 'ivory towers' and decide questions that pertain to social issues. Therefore, they should perform their duty without fear or favour, affection or ill-will, applies the law equally to all governmental and non-governmental entities.[57]

To sum up, in such extraordinary circumstances, the courts should rise above the limitations of constitutional politics and strive to ensure constitutional morality. No doubt, the executive is needed to be given free hand to respond to the COVID-19 catastrophe, yet it was not expected from the Court to fold its hand and turn its back towards citizens in the name of judicial self-restraint or separation of powers. As pointed out by Dushyant Dave, only the Prime Minister was working while the Parliament was in recess, the government despite in majority seems to have lost its moral footing to claim the shelter of separation of powers.[58] Justice K. Iyer quotes pascal:

> Justice without power is inefficient; power without justice is tyranny. Justice without power is opposed because there are always wicked men. Power without justice is soon questioned. Justice and power must, therefore, must be brought together, so that whatever is just may be powerful and whatever is powerful may be just.[59]

Therefore, those in power must appreciate that the great powers comes not alone but with a sense of great responsibility buckled with accountability. The judges should not forget the advisory of Justice Brewer (1898) that the life and character of justices should be the objects of constant watchfulness by all and its judgments subject to freest criticism.[60] To pay tribute to legendary Justice Krishna Iyer who always responded to the community's sense of justice and humanise the notion of justice exercising individual equity, it would be apt to quote him:

> A judge is a social scientist in his role as a constitutional invigilator and fails functionally if he forgets this dimension in his complex duties.[61]

On the other hand, the courts should certainly restrain themselves from interfering in the matters of the purely executive domain but when the matters directly or indirectly affect the constitutionally guaranteed fundamental rights, it must certainly blow the judicial whistle. The ultimate lesson taught by COVID-19 Pandemic is that humanity is more important than the glory of power, politics and anything else in this universe. The SCI has performed its obligation of being responsive and accountable by exercising its *suo motu* jurisdiction to ensure rule of law even during the pandemic. Though earlier it exercised its restraint on the pretext of separation of powers yet when basic rights of the people were at stake, it viewed itself accountable and exercised its authority.

Notes

1. Dushyant Dave, 'Missing Parliament and the Judiciary in the COVID Crisis', *Indian Express*, April 18, 2020, 7.
2. Roscoe Pound, *Jurisprudence – Vol. II* (St. Paul: West Publishing Co., 1959), 352–74.
3. O' Donoghue, 'The Law Beyond the Law', *American Journal of Jurisprudence* 18 (1973): 150.
4. James Madison, *The Federalist* (Middletown, CT: Wesleyan University Press, 1961), 352, see also, Roscoe Pound, 'The Causes of Popular Dissatisfaction with the Administration of Justice', *Baylor Law Review* 8 (1956): 1, 9; Anthony D' Amato, 'Rethinking Legal Education,' *MARQ. L. REV.* 74 (1990): 1, 35; Peter L. Davis, 'Why not a Justice School? On the Role of Justice in Legal Education and the Construction of a Pedagogy of Justice,' *Hamline Law Review* 30 (2007): 514.
5. H.G. Hanbury, *Modern Equity* (London: Stevens, 1957), 4.
6. B.S. Chauhan, 'Courts and Its Endeavour to Do Complete Justice', http://nja.nic.in/17%20Complete%20Justice.pdf (accessed July 17, 2021).
7. http://www.nja.nic.in/17%20Complete%20Justice.pdf (accessed May 17, 2021).
8. AIR 1998 SC 1895.
9. AIR 2004 SC 3467.
10. In an extra-judicial interview during the first wave of COVID-19, he stated that 'executive knows best, the courts should refrain from interfering'. Gautam Bhatia, 'Mouse under the Throne: The Judicial Legacy of Sharad A. Bobde', April 24, 2021, https://thewire.in/law/mouse-under-the-throne-the-judicial-legacy-of-sharad-a-bobde (accessed July 17, 2021); See also https://thewire.in/law/supreme-court-siddique-kappan-arrest-article-32 (accessed July 17, 2021).
11. https://www.indiatoday.in/india/story/state-duty-protect-right-to-life-bombay-hc-on-oxygen-shortage-goa-1801932-2021-05-13 (accessed July 17, 2021); https://www.indiatoday.in/law/story/maharashtra-aurangabad-patients-oxygen-shortage-bombay-high-court-1805292-2021-05-21 (accessed July 17, 2021); https://indianexpress.com/article/india (accessed July 17, 2021); https://www.thehindu.com/news/cities/Delhi/hc-asks-centre-why-it-should-not-face-contempt-for-failing-to-supply-oxygen-to-delhiasordered/article34481630.ece#:~:text=The%20Delhi%20High%20Court%20Tuesday,Court%20told%20the%20central%20government (accessed July 17, 2021); https://timesofindia.indiatimes.com/india/oxygen-supply-to-national-capital-sc-stays-delhi-high-courts-contempt-notice-against-centre/articleshow/82403793.cms (accessed July 17, 2021); https://www.hindustantimes.com/cities/delhi-news/like-an-ostrich-delhi-high-court-s-contempt-notice-to-centre-on-oxygen-supply-101620134390033.html (accessed July 17, 2021); https://indianexpress.com/article/india/eci-responsible-for-spreading-COVID-19-says-madras-hc-7289824/ (accessed July 17, 2021).
12. W.P. (Civil) No. 3/2021.
13. Subash C. Kashyap, 'Why the Judiciary must Step Back', *Hindustan Times*, May 17, 2021.
14. Upendra Baxi, *The Indian Supreme Court and Politics* (Lucknow: Eastern Book Company 1979), i–iii.
15. WP. (Civil) No. 5/2020.
16. W.P. (Civil) No. 3/2020.
17. W.P. (Civil) No. 3/2021.

18. W.P. (Civil) No. 1/2020.

19. W.P. (Civil) No. 6/2020 clubbed with *Bandhua Mukti Morcha* v. *Union of India and Ors.* W.P.(C) No. 916 of 2020 (29 Jun. 2021).

20. *Mumabi Kamgar Sabha* v. *M/s. Abdulbhai Faizullabhai and Others* 1976 (3) SCC 832; *Fertilizer Corporation Kamgar Union* v. *Union of India* AIR 1981 SC 344; *S.P. Gupta* v. *Union of India* AIR 1982 SC 149; *Hussainara Khatoon* v. *State of Bihar* AIR 1979 SC 1369, *M.C.Mehta* v. *Union of India* AIR 1987 SC 965; *Parmanand Katara* v. *Union of India* AIR 1989 SC 2039.

21. *Ratlam Municipality* v. *Vardichand* AIR 1980 SC 1622; *Rural Litigation and Entitlement Kendra* v. *State of U.P.* AIR 1985 SC 652; *Narmada Bachao Andolan* v. *Union of India and Others* AIR 2000 SC 3753.

22. Epistolary Jurisdiction *Ms Veena Sethi* v. *State of Bihar* 1982 (2) SCC 583; *Citizens for Democracy through its President* v. *State of Assam and Others* 1995 KHC 486, 1995 (3) SCC 743.

23. The Constitution of India, Article 32. Remedies for enforcement of rights conferred by this Part-

    (1) The right to move the Supreme Court by appropriate proceedings for the enforcement of the rights conferred by this Part is guaranteed;

    (2) The Supreme Court shall have power to issue directions or orders or writs, including writs in the nature of habeas corpus, mandamus, prohibition, quo warranto and certiorari, whichever may be appropriate, for the enforcement of any of the rights conferred by this Part;

    (3) Without prejudice to the powers conferred on the Supreme Court by clause (1) and (2), Parliament may by law empower any other court to exercise within the local limits of its jurisdiction all or any of the powers exercisable by the Supreme Court under clause (2);

    (4) The right guaranteed by this article shall not be suspended except as otherwise provided for by this Constitution.

24. The Constitution of India, Article 142. Enforcement of decrees and orders of Supreme Court and unless as to discovery, etc. (1) The Supreme Court in the exercise of its jurisdiction may pass such decree or make such order as is necessary for doing complete justice in any cause or matter pending before it, and any decree so passed or orders so made shall be enforceable throughout the territory of India in such manner as may be prescribed by or under any law made by Parliament and, until provision in that behalf is so made, in such manner as the President may by order prescribe.

25. *Kharak Singh* v. *State of U.P.* AIR 1963 SC 1295; *Sunil Batra* v. *Delhi Administration* AIR 1978 SC 1674; *Samantha* v. *State of A.P.* AIR 1997 SC 3297; *Akhtari Bi* v. *State of U.P.* AIR 2001 SC 1528; *Francis Coarlie Mullin* v. *U.T. of Delhi* AIR 1981 SC 746; *People 's Union for Democratic Rights* v. *Union of India* AIR 1982 SC 1473; *Bandhua Mukti Morcha* v. *Union of India* AIR 1984 SC 802, *Olega Tellis* v. *Bombay Municipal Corporation* AIR 1986 SC 180; *Virender Gaur* v. *State of Haryana* (1995) 2 SCC 577; *Consumer Education and Research Centre* v. *Union of India* AIR 1995 SC 922; *Parmanand Katara* v. *Union of India* AIR 1989 SC 2039; *Mr X* v. *Hospital Z* AIR 1999 SC 495; *Maneka Gandhi* v. *Union of India* AIR 1978 SC 597; *Joginder Kumar* v. *State of U.P.* AIR 1994 SC 1349; *M.H. Hoskot* v. *Union of India* AIR 1978 SC 1548; *Justice K.S. Puttaswami* v. *Union of India* C.W.P. 494/2012; *Navtej Singh Johar* v. *Union of India* AIR 2018 SC 4321.

26. *Navtej Singh Johar* v. *Union of India* AIR 2018 SC 4321.

27. WP. (Civil) No. 5/2020.

28. Krishnadas Rajagopal, 'Coronavirus-Restrictions on Court Hearings Lawful, Says Supreme Court', https://www.thehindu.com/news/national/coronavirus-restrictions-on-court-hearings-lawful-says-supreme-court/article31274285.ece (accessed May 17, 2021).

29. Ibid., Paras 3 and 4.

30. https://dakshindia.org/wp-content/uploads/2021/01/Laywer-Survey_06.pdf (accessed May 17, 2021).

31. Ibid.

32. W.P. (Civil) No. 1/2020.

33. Ibid.
34. *Arnesh Kumar* v. *State of Bihar* (2014) 8 SCC 273.
35. W.P. (Civil) No. 3/2021.
36. *The Hindu*, April 19, 2021.
37. V.K. Paul, Member, Niti Ayog, *Hindustan Times*, May 27, 2021, https://www.hindustantimes.com/india-news/health-is-a-state-subject-centre-defends-vaccine-strategy-in-7-points-101622105429701.html; Krishan Reddy, Union Minister of State for Home Affairs, May 31, 2021, https://www.thehindu.com/news/cities/Hyderabad/healthcare-is-state-subject-says-kishan-reddy/article34693266.ece.
38. W.P. (Civil) No. 1/2020, para 13 (i).
39. Ibid., para 13 (ii).
40. Ibid., para 13 (iv).
41. Ibid., para 13 (v).
42. Ibid., para 8–11.
43. W.P. (Civil) No. 6/2020.
44. 'The Failure of Supreme Court to Rescue the Migrant Workers', Countercurrents, https://countercurrents.org/2020/05/the-failure-of-supreme-court-to-rescue-the-migrant-workers/ (accessed July 20, 2021).
45. *Swami Agnivesh and Another* v. *Union of India* decided on April 20, 2020; *Aruna Roy and Anr.* v. *Union of India*, decided on April 8, 2020 – Both *available at* https://www.barandbench.com/columns/homecoming-the-worst-migrant-crisis-of-the-nation (accessed July 20, 2021).
46. W.P.(C) No. 6/2020.
47. https://www.barandbench.com/news/litigation/suo-motu-migrant-crisis-supreme-court-directs-implement-one-nation-one-ration-scheme (accessed July 17, 2021) and it was clubbed with *Bandhua Mukti Morcha* v. *Union of India and Others* W.P. (C) No. 916/2020.
48. Payoshi Roy, 'The Injustice to Stan Swamy', *Indian Express*, May 27, 2021, 9. Ricardo Da Silva, 'Father Stan Swamy has Died of COVID-19, still in the Custody of the Indian Government', https://www.americamagazine.org/politics-society/2021/07/05/stan-swamy-jesuit-dies-COVID-india-240982 (accessed July 5, 2021).
49. https://www.telegraphindia.com/india/if-meals-are-given-why-do-they-require-wages-supreme-courts-query-during-coronavirus-lockdown/cid/1762977 (accessed July 17, 2021).
50. B.S. Nirwan, 'Parliament versus Judiciary', in *Relations in Working of Legislature, Executive and Judiciary – An Introspection and Prospective Vision*, ed. J.K. Chauhan (Faridabad: ALA, 2007), 26.
51. Martin Luther King, Jr., 'Where Do We Go From Here?' Annual Report Delivered at the 11th Convention of the Southern Christian Leadership Conference, August 16, Atlanta, GA, 1967, http://www-personal.umich.edu/~gMarchkus/MLK_WhereDoWeGo.pdf (accessed July 27, 2021).
52. *Indian Express*, 'Govt. Migrant response "unpardonable", Says SC, sets deadline for ration plan- court seeks central portal for migrants, tell states to supply dry rations, set up community kitchen', June 30, 2021, 1.
53. *Indian Express*, 'NDMA failed in its Duty: Bench-SC: Kin of COVID Victims entitled to relief, so frame guidelines', June 30, 2021.
54. *Indian Express*, 'Reconsider even symbolic Kanwar Yatra, health important: SC to UP', 17 July 17, 2021, 1.
55. Upendra Baxi, 'Rekindling Our Institutions; Any Reform of the Judicial System will have to Come from Within the Court', *Indian Express*, July 16. 2018.
56. Upendra Baxi, 'A Constitutional Renaissance: SC's Delhi Verdict Affirms: Constant Repair and Renewal of Constitutionalism is the Prime Function of Adjudication', *Indian Express*, July 16, 2018.
57. N.V. Ramana, 'Rule of Law vs Rule by Law', *Indian Express*, July 2, 2021, 9.
58. Dushyant Dave, 'Missing Parliament and the Judiciary in the COVID Crisis', April 18, 2020, 9.

59. K. Iyer, *Justice at Crossroads* (New Delhi: Deep and Deep Publications, 2019), 17.
60. Balram K. Gupta, 'Judicial Review or Confrontation', in *Relations in Working of Legislature, Executive and Judiciary – An Introspection and Prospective Vision*, ed. ed. J.K. Chauhan (Faridabad: ALA, 2007), 11.
61. *State of Karnataka* v. *Shri Ranganath Reddy and Anr.* (1977) 4 SCC 471.

Disclosure statement

No potential conflict of interest was reported by the author(s).

Abortion, same-sex marriage, and gender identity during the Pink Tide: Venezuela compared to Latin American trends

Victor Molina

ABSTRACT

During the so-called Pink Tide (1998–2018), in which a surge of left-wing governments assumed power in Latin America, the region significantly expanded guarantees of equality and non-discrimination. In that period, six Latin American countries took steps to decriminalise abortion, eight recognised equal marriage, and twelve recognised the right to gender identity and a name change procedure for trans people. Nevertheless, in Venezuela, where the Pink Tide started, the authorities resisted all efforts to advance abortion decriminalisation or promote human rights related to sexual orientation and gender identity, even though Venezuela's leaders have associated themselves with the principles and values of social justice. A comparative analysis between the performance of Venezuela and other Latin American countries, and the findings of several interviews with Venezuelan human rights defenders, show a lack of chavismo's political will, rooted in populism and militarism, to support the participation processes that allow legislative advocacy and judicial activism to advance human rights related to abortion, same-sex marriage, and gender identity. Although Venezuelan authorities proposed alternatives to private property and social assistance programmes, they perpetuated heteropatriarchy by ignoring critical components of the agendas of sexual, reproductive, and gender identity rights defenders, prioritising electoral calculations and relations with religious movements.

Introduction

The election of Lieutenant Colonel Hugo Chávez in 1998 in Venezuela initiated Latin America's Pink Tide, an unprecedented surge of left-wing leaders who assumed power in twelve of the eighteen countries in the region, embracing a narrative on egalitarianism and equality.[1] Emphasising his poor background, Chávez's focus was on sovereignty and rejecting neoliberalism. He also coined the term 'twenty-first-century socialism' to define his type of government.[2] Chávez's electoral triumph was followed by the election of many other leftist-identified leaders, such as Luiz Inácio Lula da Silva in Brazil (2003–2011) and

Evo Morales in Bolivia (2006–2019). Twenty years later, the Pink Tide ended. By 2018, the left only governed seven of the many Pink Tide countries.[3]

After almost two decades of left-wing governments in Latin America, many scholars expected advances in abortion decriminalisation, same-sex marriage, and gender identity.[4] Nonetheless, it produced mixed results regarding these human rights demands. Based on twenty years of Pink Tide policies, this paper analyses how and why several Pink Tide countries did or did not take crucial steps favouring abortion decriminalisation and sexual orientation and gender identity (SOGI) rights. Unlike institutionalised partisan-left governments and movement-left governments, such as Uruguay and Chile, populist-left governments, such as Venezuela and Nicaragua, did not perceive feminists and diversity movements as potentially valuable allies. Moreover, leaders in Venezuela and Nicaragua prioritised their relations with Catholic or Evangelical religious leaders.[5] Hence, they continued to promote traditional gender roles and heteronormativity[6] and rejected or reversed abortion decriminalisation.[7]

Following the election of several new left-wing governments in the region in recent years, such as Gabriel Boric in Chile and Xiomara Castro in Honduras, Latin America is at the gates of a second Pink Tide.[8] The concept of 'democratic socialism' is also gaining political influence in countries like the United States, and 'Socialist Millennials' are mobilising both against poverty and for a sustainable environment.[9] Some scholars have also called for reclaiming the populist left as the only way for the left to be successful electorally.[10] This argument does not reflect the fact that populist-left governments may not deliver the social changes desired by many activist groups.[11] They also do not consider the fundamental role of grassroots movements[12] to achieve such change.

Sexual, reproductive, and gender identity rights affect how people live, their health, well-being, and their risk of premature death.[13] For example, given that 4.7–13.2% of maternal deaths can be attributed to unsafe abortion,[14] public policy focused on girls, women, and birthing people's rights is a matter of life and death. Additionally, restrictions on abortion disproportionately affect girls and women living in poverty because their demands for access to safe abortion services are more commonly unheard due to a lack of adequate legal representation.[15] Social security is not extended to same-sex partners in countries that do not authorise same-sex civil unions or marriage. Therefore, when LGBT people enjoy fewer legal rights, it negatively influences their access to health care.[16] Recognising gender identity is also necessary to ensure access to the most basic services. A lack of documents that match an individual's gender identity leads to travel limitations, humiliation, bullying, and LGBT-targeted violence.[17]

This paper aims to analyse how a populist-left government, the Chávez-Maduro rule in Venezuela, did not embrace crucial elements of the feminist and the diversity agenda even though this government was a leader in the Pink Tide. This paper focuses on the government's failure to advance abortion decriminalisation, same-sex marriage, and gender identity recognition. Literature, legal instruments, official communications, press content, and NGO reports were reviewed to examine this issue. Additionally, I conducted a quantitative analysis based on the World Bank statistics through 2018.[18] I also conducted semi-structured interviews with five Venezuelan human rights defenders who tried to promote abortion decriminalisation, same-sex marriage, and gender identity recognition during the Pink Tide. The University of Minnesota's Institutional Review Board waived the requirement for approval to conduct such interviews because the participants joined in their role as experts.

The paper is organised as follows. First, I describe the human rights law related to sexual, reproductive, and gender identity rights and advances in other Latin American nations. Next, I explore the authorities' defiance in Venezuela regarding these topics. Finally, as a gay, queer Venezuelan human rights defender with over 14 years of experience in the field, I assess the consequences of trusting chavismo as an ally of social justice without considering sexual minorities, trans people, women, girls, and birthing people' rights, and the enjoyment of the right to participate in public affairs in the sexual, reproductive, and gender identity rights context.

Conceptual framework and limitations

To understand the scope and significance of abortion decriminalisation and SOGI rights, I conducted a literature review of academic articles, international human rights law, and reports published in the last twenty years, focusing on Latin America. In this section, I define the most important terms.

Abortion, commonly understood as a process or procedure that ends a pregnancy, 'is the removal of pregnancy tissue, products of conception, or the foetus and placenta from the uterus'.[19] There are two types of abortion: at home pill-induced abortions and in-clinic abortions.[20] Although some sources differentiate the term 'abortion' from 'termination of pregnancy' based on different criteria, such as local legal frameworks or gestational progress, I use the term abortion to refer to all processes that deliberately interrupt a pregnancy by medical or surgical means.

The sexual orientation and gender identity (SOGI) literature, the feminist literature, and literature focused on stakeholders' participation in public affairs are semantically different and sometimes incompatible. For instance, in feminist literature, authors often refer to the right to access abortion as 'women's right to decide'. In SOGI literature, authors sometimes use terms such as 'female assigned at birth' – less sensitive to intersex people – and people with a uterus. Instead, I use 'girls, women, and birthing people's right to decide' to ensure that all stakeholders, including trans men and queer people, are appropriately included. Using 'girls' is also essential to avoid an adult-centric approach that can make the harsh reality of the many girl victims of rape in Latin America usually forced to become mothers[21] invisible.

Since I am only analysing the advances in Latin America in terms of same-sex marriage and recognition of gender identity in 'male' or 'female' terms, it is logical to only refer to lesbian, gay, bisexual, trans (LGBT) people in this paper. It is a significant limitation since there are many traditional non-Euro-American queerness identities in the region. 'Travestis'[22] 'vestidas', 'pintadas', 'mujercitos',[23] 'maricas',[24] or 'muxes'[25] do not necessarily identify in terms of the 'male' and 'female' binary and have been systematically overlooked by authorities, social movements, and political activism during the Pink Tide.[26] This paper uses the term 'trans', which has been used in the United Nations and human rights documents to refer to a person who identifies with a different gender than the one assigned at birth.[27]

Feminists and SOGI movements challenge heteropatriarchy, a social system that promotes traditional gender norms and heterosexuality as the norm. In the historical context of Latin America, heterosexuality is a phenomenon perpetuated by the States, either deliberately or due to their inaction, institutionalising men's social, political, and economic power over women and queer people, focusing public policy only on heterosexual relationships.[28] Among the many demands that such efforts might contemplate, I only focus on three of them that I consider relatively easy to measure. Even narrower, I only analyse the legal framework that regulates these demands. I use this strategy to complete a comparative analysis of the political will of the Pink Tide governments regarding gender and sexuality.

Abortion, same-sex marriage, and gender identity in human rights law

I consider gender, sexuality, and participation within human rights frame of this paper because feminists and SOGI movements – as actors that challenged heteropatriarchy – built coalitions to address their linked demands in Latin America before and during the Pink Tide.[29] Similarly, the advances in SOGI rights and abortion decriminalisation achieved during the Pink Tide suggest that there is a correlation. Authoritative human rights bodies increasingly recognise these questions as implicating human rights.

To respect gender equality following the Convention on the Elimination of All Forms of Discrimination against Women, States parties, including Venezuela, should legalise abortion to fully respect the autonomy of girls, women, and birthing people.[30] Extensive international doctrine demands abortion decriminalisation.[31] By the beginning of the Pink Tide, at least 122 observations on ninety-three countries by United Nations treaty bodies had established that abortion criminalisation jeopardises the enjoyment of human rights.[32]

The Inter-American Court of Human Rights has confirmed that gender identity for trans people must be recognised, and marriage must be equally extended to same-sex couples.[33] The Court's Advisory Opinion OC-24/17 on Gender Identity, and Equality and Non-Discrimination of Same-Sex Couples of 2017, 'Concerning the Right of Change of Name and Gender Identity, and Rights Derived from a Relationship between Same-Sex Couples'[34] (33) is binding for all American States, whether they are party to the American Convention or not.[35] Although Venezuela denounced the Convention in 2012 under Hugo Chávez, this Advisory Opinion remains binding for the country. Renouncing the Convention does not affect Venezuela's obligations related to the minimum protection threshold through the Charter of the Organization of the American States, in this case, the principle of non-discrimination that remains under the Inter-American Commission.[36]

Sexual, reproductive, and gender identity rights defenders in Latin America have consistently demanded abortion decriminalisation and SOGI rights before and during the Pink Tide.[37] Consulting and listening to these rights holders are part of the human right to political participation.[38] The right to participation in public affairs, both in electoral and non-electoral contexts, is recognised in Article 21 of the Universal Declaration of Human Rights, the International Covenant on Civil and Political Rights, and the International Covenant on Economic, Social and Cultural Rights.[39] Stakeholders' active, free, and meaningful participation is central to effective government decision-making.[40] Authorities must widely understand, accept, and routinely realise participation in decision-making processes with particular attention given to individuals and groups that are marginalised or have experienced discrimination,[41] such as girls and women, and LGBT people.

Advances in Latin America

To analyse abortion criminalisation and LGBT rights in Venezuela, it is essential to consider the international framework of human rights and the progress in terms of sexual, reproductive, and gender identity rights in the surrounding countries.[42]

During the Pink Tide, Latin America made progress towards legally recognising sexual, reproductive, and identity rights. Twelve countries advanced in recognising gender identity for trans people, eight countries advanced in equal marriage,[43] and six countries advanced abortion decriminalisation.[44] Except for Mexico and Colombia, presidents associated with the left governed all these countries, and leftist political parties resurged in legislative, State, and municipal elections with no exception.[45]

In this regional context, advances in abortion decriminalisation, same-sex marriage, and gender identity appeared to be correlated. All the countries that took steps in favour of decriminalising abortion during the Pink Tide also recognised same-sex marriage, and all the countries that recognised same-sex marriage recognised the gender identity of trans people – except for Cuba, which already had a comprehensive legal framework guaranteeing girls, women, and birthing people's right to decide before the Pink Tide.[46] Table 1 lists the advances for the twelve Latin American countries.

Venezuela, Paraguay, Dominican Republic, El Salvador, Guatemala, and Nicaragua do not appear in Table 1 because none of these Latin American countries took steps toward abortion decriminalisation or recognised same-sex marriage and gender identity during the Pink Tide.

Recognition of gender identity for trans people

Most Latin American countries took steps toward recognise gender identity during the Pink Tide. The 486 million people living in those countries, accounted for 76.5% of

Table 1. Advances in abortion decriminalisation, same-sex legal union or marriage, and gender identity recognition in Latin America, 2006–2019.

	Steps towards abortion decriminalisation	Same-sex marriage	Gender recognition for trans people
Argentina	2012	2010	2012
Brazil	2012	2013	2018
Bolivia			2016
Chile	2017	2015	2019
Colombia	2006	2016	2015
Costa Rica		2014	2018
Cuba	(1965)		2008(*) (**)
Ecuador		2019	2016
Mexico	2007*	2009*	2014, 2019
Panama			2006(*), 2016
Peru			2016(**)
Uruguay	2012	2013	2009(**), 2018

* First in Mexico City, followed by some other States.
(*) Requires gender-affirming surgery.
(**) Judicial procedures are required.

the total population of Latin America and the Caribbean. In addition, most Latin American countries that recognised the identity of trans people did so before many Western countries, such as Canada.[47]

In 2006, Panama became the first Latin American country to recognise gender identity for trans people[48] during the Pink Tide. Thirteen years later, by the end of this period, most countries in the region had approved laws, regulations, and procedures to recognise gender identity. In almost all cases, they were approved by legislative initiative. Specifically, Argentina, Bolivia, Chile, and Uruguay enacted specific laws for the trans population. Costa Rica, Ecuador, Mexico, and Panama reformed their civil or family codes.[49] In Cuba, the executive power established gender identity recognition.[50]

In Colombia, gender identity recognition resulted from participation between the judicial and executive powers. A Constitutional Court ruling was the precedent for a decree published by the Republic President.[51] In Peru and Brazil, recognition of gender identity for trans people came through the Constitutional Court[52] and the Supreme Court.[53] At the heart of this judicial activism was interpreting the purpose[54] of the Colombian, Peruvian, and Brazilian constitutions through the lens of the socio-economic context of the Pink Tide to expand constitutional guarantees of non-discrimination toward trans people.

Some legal frameworks aimed to recognise gender identity for trans people in Latin America during the Pink Tide but did not meet the minimum human rights standards established by the Inter-American Court of Human Rights. The Inter-American Court of Human Rights established that States must make efforts to facilitate a legal change of identity for trans people through administrative processes. These administrative processes must be expedited and based solely on the free and informed consent of the applicants.[55] To allow a legal name and gender change for trans people, however, Cuba and Panamá required gender-affirming surgery or gender-confirmation surgery,[56] which refers to procedures such as facial surgery, top surgery, or bottom surgery to help a person transition to their self-identified gender. Most people who decide to undergo gender-affirmation or gender-confirmation surgeries report improved quality of life.[57] Nevertheless, trans people, for different reasons such as lack of money, poor health, or subjectivities in the ways they display gender, might not be able to or may not wish to transform their bodies to physically match social normativity.[58] Additionally, genitalia modification and gonads removal may involve permanent sterilisation. Forced sterilisation of trans people has been actively challenged as a human rights violation since trans people should be able to make decisions regarding their bodies and whether they want to reproduce without unwanted interference from the State.[59]

Cuba and Peru also failed to comply with regional standards because both countries required trans people to undergo judicial processes before their self-perceived identity was recognised.[60] In the case of Peru, it was complicated for trans people to win such trials because they were pathologising – judges often maintained the position that LGBT people were 'diseased' –, procedurally complicated, emotionally draining, expensive for the petitioners, and unlikely to be declared admissible.[61]

In short, Latin America mostly came to recognise the identity of trans people during the Pink Tide through different legal and legislative pathways. Furthermore, with some exceptions, Latin American countries established non-pathologising processes to access a name and gender change in legal documents.

Same-sex marriage

Although most Latin American countries did not approve same-sex marriage, by the end of the Pink Tide, most of the region's population could access this right, constituting 474 million people, 74% of the total population of Latin America and the Caribbean – because the countries that recognised same-sex marriage have a considerable population weight, such as Brazil, Colombia, and Argentina. Most Latin American countries that recognised same-sex union and equal marriage did so before many Western countries, including the United States at the federal level.[62]

In 2008, Argentina became the first Latin American country to recognise same-sex legal unions and, two years later, they recognised same-sex marriage, providing same-sex couples with the same legal protections guaranteed to heterosexual couples. It included the right to adoption without restrictions.[63] Eleven years later, by the end of the Pink Tide, eight countries in the region had approved laws, regulations, and procedures toward the progressive realisation of the right of same-sex couples to form a family.[64]

Argentina's Parliament passed the New Equal Marriage Act in 2010,[65] emphasising the due uniformity of the right to marriage between people of the same sex and between people of different sexes. The Argentinian civil society preferred the term 'equal marriage' over same-sex marriage. This terminology was later used during the Pink Tide in the rest of Latin America to create a new legal language and advocate for LGBT rights. In Uruguay, legislative initiatives recognised equal marriage in 2013.[66]

The case of Mexico is unique because of its federal system of government. From 2009 to 2010, a legislative initiative modified the constitution to allow same-sex marriage, but the conditions under which the right to marriage between people of the same sex can be accessed vary according to each State.[67] By the end of the Pink Tide, 16 Mexican states and Mexico City approved same-sex marriage and adoption with no restrictions. In the rest of the 32 states, same-sex marriage is possible but requires additional judicial processes that heterosexual couples do not need to carry out.[68]

Like Argentina and Uruguay, Brazil and Colombia nationally approved same-sex marriage and adoption with no restrictions, meeting the human rights standards. This recognition came through the courts in these countries. Ecuador, Chile, and Costa Rica approved same-sex marriage through the courts but did not permit same-sex couples to adopt.[69]

In short, through different legal and legislative pathways, Latin America mostly came to recognise same-sex marriage during the Pink Tide. Furthermore, with some exceptions, Latin American countries that recognised same-sex marriage allowed same-sex couples to adopt.

Abortion decriminalisation

Before the Pink Tide, most Latin American countries had taken legal steps toward allowing abortion when necessary to save the girls, women, or birthing people's lives in case of mortal danger – only Chile, Dominican Republic, and El Salvador stipulated no exceptions for criminal sanctions regarding abortion.[70] Argentina became one of the first countries in the world to decriminalise abortion when performed after rape in 1922, followed by Brazil, Mexico, and Uruguay in the 1930s.[71] The region, however, did not advance any further actions to decriminalise abortion during the subsequent decades,[72] and by the beginning of the twenty-first century, it was the most regressive in the world regarding abortion.[73] The Pink Tide period finally broke this stalemate.

A sentence by the Colombian Constitutional Court modified the criminal code of Colombia in 2006, decriminalising abortion under three circumstances: danger to the life or health of the girl, woman, or birthing person; severe malformation of the foetus that makes their life unviable; and if pregnancy was the result of rape or incest.[74] Similarly, in 2012, the Supreme Court of Argentina determined that applying the provisions of the 1922 Penal Code concerning abortion resulting from rape, girls, women, or birthing people did not need a judicial resolution to access an abortion procedure but only an affidavit.[75] This judgment was an important step to eliminate barriers to access to abortion in Argentina since the judicial procedures that were previously required could be long and cumbersome, and could ultimately compromise the girls, women, and birthing people's right to decide when pregnancy resulted from rape.[76] Brazil also enhanced abortion decriminalisation through the Supreme Court during the Pink Tide, enabling girls, women, and birthing people to decide whether to terminate anencephalic pregnancies in 2012, without criminal charges.[77]

Legislative initiatives were the way to move towards the decriminalisation of abortion on demand in Mexico City and Uruguay during the Pink Tide, granting girls, women, and birthing people the right to decide during the gestation first trimester regardless of the circumstances, even if conditions applied, such as obligatory counselling and required waiting periods.[78] Mexico City approved a reform to the penal code in 2007,[79] and Uruguay changed its abortion law in 2012.[80] Similarly, a legislative initiative in 2017 decriminalised abortion in Chile under three circumstances: the threat to the girl, woman, or birthing people's life, rape, and fatal foetal deformity, which replaced the previous complete ban.[81]

By the end of the Pink Tide, six Latin American countries had made significant legal advances toward decriminalising abortion. These countries had a population of 347 million people, representing 54% of Latin America and the Caribbean's population in 2018. These advances took place equally through legislative initiative and judicial activism.

Explaining Venezuela's lack of progress

From 1999 to the end of the Pink Tide, Venezuela was ruled by Lieutenant Colonel Hugo Chávez (1999–2013) or his designated successor, Nicolás Maduro (2013-present). This political phenomenon is called 'chavismo'. Even though many authors consider it the most successful reincarnation of the Venezuelan left in its entire history,[82] Venezuela remained one of the countries where abortion was most restricted.[83] In addition, the authorities resisted all efforts to recognise same-sex marriage or gender identity.[84]

To understand why Venezuela stayed behind on abortion decriminalisation and SOGI rights during the Latin American Pink Tide, I interviewed five prominent Venezuelan sexual, reproductive, and gender identity rights defenders in the country. It was a diverse group of cisgenders and trans, heterosexual, gay, lesbian, and bisexual people from different country regions. In addition to their role at the national level, these experts have participated in relevant international or regional human rights forums, such as the Universal Periodic Review at the Human Rights Council, hearings at the Inter-American Commission on Human Rights, or the United Nations world population conferences. A draft of this paper was shared with the participants to ensure that the findings fit the reality of the events and dynamics they described.

When preparing the questionnaires and interpreting the results, I used the conceptual framework proposed by Merike Blofield and Christina Ewig related to the role that the different types of leftist governments in Latin America have played in facilitating or hindering the work of feminist activists. There are four parts to this case study. First, I tested Blofield and Ewig's finding that 'populist left' governments, such as Venezuelan chavismo,[85] where personalist leadership did not feel constrained by institutional rules. It gave feminists, and, by extension, activists in favour of diversity, fewer opportunities to influence policy.[86] Going deeper, I analysed three synergies between elements of the chavismo populist set: (1) the lack of separation of powers and militarism, diminishing judicial independence; (2) the personal positionality of the leaders and religion, which is an important variable to consider according to Blofield and Ewig's and other authors, such as Mala Htun and Elisabeth Jay Friedman; and (3) clues about Venezuelan government tokenism regarding human rights, and the lack of strength of feminism and SOGI movements in Venezuela. I will discuss each of these elements below.

Personalist leadership gave sexual, reproductive, and gender identity rights defenders fewer opportunities to influence policy

According to the sexual, reproductive, and gender identity rights defenders interviewed for this paper, neither Hugo Chávez nor Nicolás Maduro provided adequate space for stakeholders to debate SOGI rights and abortion decriminalisation. These findings are consistent with the literature on the power dynamics of chavismo during the Pink Tide. Top-down governmental decision-making hindered pluralism and active participation of grassroots movements promoting sexual and gender rights[87] regardless of the official Venezuelan narrative in favour of participatory democracy.[88]

The personalist leadership of Hugo Chávez is profoundly linked to the way he entered the public scene in 1992 as one of the mid-level officer leaders of a failed military coup. Chávez failed to achieve his Caracas objectives and requested a television appearance to advise his colleagues to put down their arms. This brief television appearance[89] created a new popular hero[90] against the governments of that time that had implemented neoliberal adjustments without popular support.[91] Given Venezuela's historic dependence on oil exports – over 90% of total along the second half of the twentieth century – the abrupt global decline in oil prices from the 1980s through the 1990s undermined the country's economic foundation.[92] Between 1990 and 1997, per capita income fell from US$5,192 to US$2,858, and Venezuela's human development index dropped from 0.8210 to 0.7046. Public spending contracted from 37% of the gross domestic product in 1982 to 16% in 1998.[93] Chávez's electoral victory later in 1998, premised on vague principles, can be parsed as an opportunistic appropriation of the current political void.[94] Although he criticised the Latin American 'savage capitalism' during his first electoral campaign, he did not refer to socialism except in ambiguous terms.[95] Starting in 2005, however, his government soon underwent a steadily increasing revision process of the previous forms of private property emblematised by his advocacy for a 'Socialism of the Twenty-first Century'.[96] His narrative focused on his person as a central element of the public policies of his government,[97] implying that he was the channel through which the people manifested their concerns and desires.[98]

Early in Chávez's rule, the process of preparing the Constitution of the Bolivarian Republic of Venezuela in 1999 allowed meaningful participation from diverse sectors of Venezuelan society.[99] The debate removed the 'protection of the child from the moment of conception', as established in the previous constitution.[100] This amendment was an important step to open the door to a future civil code reform regarding abortion. However, the new constitutional legal language, which was a product of an initial consensus that left room for interpretation, did not translate into the necessary successive reforms to decriminalise abortion since chavismo's authorities did not take steps to create subsequent consultation spaces with feminists. Debates on abortion decriminalisation, with fewer participants and shorter duration, took place at three points: in 2004, when a Penal Code reform was attempted; in 2007, during a constitutional reform; and in 2010, before a new initiative to reform the Penal Code. These debates were not successful in decriminalising abortion or advancing change.[101] The Venezuelan Penal Code, enacted in 1915, prohibiting abortion except to save the life of the 'woman in labour', persisted in force.[102]

Regarding same-sex marriage, the new constitution resulted in a setback by expressly establishing marriage protection as a union 'between a man and a woman'[103] due to pressure from religious sectors of the extreme right. The constitutional commission rejected a proposal to establish that marriage was not limited to heterosexual couples amid laughter and ridicule from some commission members in a way that was not transparent or respectful of previously established constitutional commission's procedures.[104] It should be noted that elected candidates chosen by Hugo Chávez occupied 121 of the 131 seats of the National Constituent Assembly in charge of elaborating the new constitution. They included Chávez's wife, brother, five former ministers of his cabinet, and several retired officials, comrades-in-arms in the 1992 coup.[105] Later, President Chávez gave his opinion on same-sex marriage in Venezuela in statements offered to the Italian TV Show Le Lene, indicating that same-sex marriage was simply not well accepted in the country.[106] Gender identity for trans people was not even discussed during the elaboration of the new constitution, explained the experts.

Shortly after the proclamation of the new constitution, there were complaints regarding the poor implementation of its constitutional principle of popular participation. Numerous Enabling Laws were introduced via presidential decrees, rather than representative processes, in education, finance, and public administration.[107] Chávez created parallel institutions alongside the traditional welfare state apparatus, such as in health, education, food distribution, housing,[108] and unionisation.[109] These programmes, which were planned and sponsored by the state bureaucracy, were orchestrated from above. They were enlarged, dissolved, or replaced quickly as Chávez laid out some new proposals in response to the crisis.[110]

Lack of separation of powers and militarism

Given the leading roles of judicial and legislative power in Latin America during the Pink Tide in advancing SOGI rights and the decriminalisation of abortion, it is worth asking if Chávez and Maduro, as leaders of the executive power, were responsible for the lack of progress in these matters in Venezuela. In this sense, it is essential to consider the power of chavismo over the Venezuelan institutions.

Throughout more than thirteen years as president of Venezuela, charismatic Hugo Chávez[111] carried out a series of reforms to strengthen his executive power, and thus successfully placed himself in a position of effective political hegemony.[112] For instance, after approving the new constitution that increased centralisation and established a one-chamber Congress, the presidential period was extended from five to six years. A subsequent constitutional reform Chávez supported introduced the possibility of indefinite re-elections.[113] This political system with a higher concentration of power in the presidential figure would be inherited by his designated successor, Nicolás Maduro.[114] The legislative power in Venezuela was also primarily dominated by representatives of the chavismo political parties throughout most of the Pink Tide.[115]

During chavismo legislative hegemony, Venezuelan National Assembly shelved the petitions for laws and reforms of the criminal code in favour of abortion decriminalisation[116] and same-sex marriage.[117] Venezuelan sexual, reproductive, and gender identity rights defenders interviewed for this paper, who were directly involved in petitions for abortion decriminalisation, explained that representatives of the National Assembly initially showed ignorance of the abortion situation in the country, thinking that it was allowed. After advocacy conversations, these representatives acknowledged their understanding of the legitimacy of abortion decriminalisation. However, they privately stated that they did not want to bring the issue up for debate because they feared a possible negative impact on elections, especially the presidential election.

Advocates who turned to Venezuelan courts to protect their rights were also stymied. Venezuelan sexual, reproductive, and gender identity rights defenders interviewed for this paper, who were directly involved in petitions for same-sex marriage and gender identity recognition before the Supreme Court of Justice of Venezuela, suggested a lack of independence between the courts and the national chavismo government to the detriment of the development of SOGI rights. These experts pointed out that prominent judges privately recognised the legitimacy of sexual, reproductive, and gender identity rights petitions but admitted that without an 'order from above', they were not authorised to move forward. Instead, the proposed that organisations promoting such rights should discreetly directly advocate with the high authorities instead. For example, although the Supreme Court innovated during the Pink Tide in favour of vulnerable groups, such as providing additional protections against child prostitution,[118] the Supreme Court declared inadmissible requests to extend the figure of marriage to same-sex couples, ruling that the National Assembly should legislate in this regard.[119] The lack of judicial independence described is consistent with the United Nations High Commissioner for Human Rights' report regarding its independent international fact-finding mission on the Venezuelan justice system. This report highlighted the legal reforms and political interference, which contributed to the deterioration of judicial system independence in Venezuela since 1999, including regular threats of dismissal or pressure to request early retirement and resignation of independent judges.[120]

According to the interviewed Venezuelan sexual, reproductive, and gender identity rights defenders, the logic of institutions at the service of high authorities was related to the militaristic logic of chavismo that promoted a strict top-down line of command. The military had had a long history of involvement in Venezuelan politics,[121] but, during the Pink Tide, Venezuela had even more active or retired national armed forces officers in the courts and the public administration.[122] Additionally, even if the military had a celebrated egalitarian tradition because of the social mobility it offered for young men from poorer sectors,[123] this militarist culture was openly contrary to gender and sexual orientation diversity. For instance, Venezuela's Military Code of Justice punished same-sex conduct by service personnel for 'sexual acts against nature' with prison and dismissal under a chapter called 'on cowardice and other crimes against military decorum'.[124] This directive made Venezuela one of the few countries in the region to criminalise same-sex conduct.[125] At least one reported conviction occurred in 2013 during the Pink Tide, but the law had wider consequences since it was used to harass gay and lesbian service personnel.[126]

Regarding gender identity for trans people, Venezuela went backwards during the Pink Tide instead of moving forward like most Latin American countries did. Venezuela shifted from being the first Latin American country to recognise a name and gender change for trans people in 1974[127] to a country that rejected all such requests after 1999. According to the interviewed Venezuelan expert on gender identity for trans people, before the Pink Tide, more than 150 trans people changed their name and gender in their documents in Venezuela after undergoing gender-affirming surgeries – top surgery for trans men and bottom surgery for trans women. It was a pathologising procedure before the courts,[128] but at least it was an option for some individuals and an innovative step towards the progressive realisation of the right to recognition of identity for trans people. Since 1999, however, the new courts dominated by chavismo positioned themselves entirely against even those limited opportunities to protect gender identity recognition for trans people. In 1999, career judges in all judicial circuits were removed and replaced by other judges without safeguards to ensure their transparent, merit-based, and non-political selection.[129] From then on, all requests for name and gender changes in legal documents by trans people were rejected because such changes were contrary to 'the law', without specifying exactly which law, explained the expert.

Given the absolute rejection of all requests, advocacy groups demanded a law from the legislative branch to clarify the right to a name and gender change for trans people. According to the interviewed Venezuelan expert on gender identity for trans people, chavismo representatives, who made up an absolute majority in the National Assembly, rejected the proposal, arguing that such a law could facilitate same-sex marriage. Instead, the National Assembly introduced a reform in the Organic Law of Civil Registry allowing only name changes, with no legal option for gender changes.[130] Even so, the civil registry, also controlled by officials appointed by chavismo, interpreted this reform so that trans people could never benefit from it.[131] The civil registry only allowed name changes if a person with male genitalia, who had been given a woman's socially accepted name at birth, wanted to change their name to a man's socially accepted name; or if a person with female genitalia, who had been given a man's socially accepted name at birth, wanted to change their name to a woman's socially accepted name.[132]

Religion, tokenism regarding human rights, and lack of strength of feminism and SOGI movements

The chavismo populist, personalistic, and militaristic leadership did not provide spaces for effective participation of sexual, reproductive, and gender identity rights defenders. However, these leadership characteristics may not exclusively explain Venezuela's lack of progress in favour of abortion decriminalisation, same-sex marriage, and gender identity. The interviewed sexual, reproductive, and gender identity rights defenders consistently mentioned additional factors. The most common factors they mentioned were the role of religious movements in Venezuelan politics during the Pink Tide, weak commitment to human rights from the chavismo high command, weak feminist organisations, and weak movements in favour of diversity.

While Chávez was president of Venezuela, he expressed an open positionality as a religious follower. Christian invocations appeared in almost all his speeches, and he often carried a crucifix in his hands, which he held up and kissed at prominent public appearances.[133] Nicolás Maduro declared himself a Christian.[134] Following Hugo Chávez's death in 2013, he referred to him as 'the Christ of the poor'.[135] It is challenging to know to what extent Chávez's or Maduro's believes shaped their personal views on abortion, same-sex marriage, and gender identity. The interviewed sexual, reproductive, and gender identity rights defenders agreed, however, the close relations between chavismo and the evangelical Christian churches, including the participation of members of the Pentecostal church as representatives of the National Assembly and high-ranking judges, played a significant role in hindering the development of SOGI rights, and girls, women, and birthing people's right to decide.

A weak commitment to human rights on the part of the chavismo's high command was also consistently mentioned by the interviewed sexual, reproductive, and gender identity rights defenders. These assertions were also consistent with the government's actions, such as the withdrawal of Venezuela from the Inter-American Court of Human Rights jurisdiction,[136] and Venezuela's abstention – with Belarus and Iran – at the creation of the United Nations Human Rights Council.[137] Amnesty International has also reported alleged crimes against humanity perpetrated by the chavismo authorities since 2014.[138] Independent experts from the International Criminal Court continue to investigate this possibility as of the writing of this paper.[139] Underscoring this lack of commitment to universally recognised human rights, some experts interviewed for this paper pointed out that crucial government leaders involved in the ideological machinery of chavismo asserted that 'homosexuality' was nothing more than a 'bourgeois deviation'.

Finally, the interviewed sexual, reproductive, and gender identity rights defenders consistently pointed out the weakness of feminist organisations and movements favouring diversity in Venezuela. Among other challenges, the experts described a disconnection with public opinion, lack of resources, persecution by the authorities, and lack of international support by sectors of the international human rights community. This lack of support was especially true for regional actors with global influence who refused to believe that there was a possibility that chavismo systematically violated LGBT rights. In this sense, the experts highlighted the remarkable effectiveness of puppet organisations created by chavismo propaganda[140] to position a narrative in which the Venezuelan authorities were champions in promoting social justice, regardless of the facts in the field.[141] These assertions are consistent with my fourteen years of professional experience promoting human rights, focusing on Venezuela and international solidarity.

Conclusions

Despite the widespread legal advances favouring abortion decriminalisation, same-sex marriage, and gender identity in Latin America during the Pink Tide, Venezuela did not take steps forward on these protections. On the contrary, the country stepped back from these protections. Although the Venezuelan government identified with the left, the lack of adequate spaces provided by Venezuelan authorities for the political participation of rights holders in decision-making prevented sexual, reproductive, and gender identity rights defenders from positioning critical elements of their agendas.

Several Venezuelan sexual, reproductive, and gender identity rights defenders agreed that the militaristic nature of chavismo translated into top-down decision-making during the Pink Tide. These experts also agreed that the official discourse of chavismo in favour of participatory democracy was not genuine. Electoral calculations carried greater weight than legitimate requests from grassroots movements regarding girls, women, and birthing people's right to decide, and regarding SOGI rights. The central government's control over the judiciary and legislature restricted the ability of institutions to protect these rights.

These findings have important implications for evaluating the potential outcomes of leftist governments in the past and the future. The Venezuelan case has shown that leftist governments' responses to critical social issues may not be uniform, depending on different variables. Further research could explore the role of religion within chavismo and the potential negative attitudes of leadership against human rights as factors that impede advances in favour of abortion decriminalisation, same-sex marriage, and gender identity. The weakness of the feminist movements and the organisations that worked on rights related to SOGI is also another factor to be considered in future studies. For instance, work is needed to explore whether and to what extent it resulted from internal challenges, pressure produced by chavismo, or a lack of support from some sectors of the international human rights community.

Notes

1. Kendall D. Funk, Magda Hinojosa, and Jennifer M. Piscopo, 'Still Left Behind: Gender, Political Parties, and Latin America's Pink Tide', *Social Politics* 24, no. 4 (2017): 399.
2. Barry Cannon, *Hugo Chávez and the Bolivarian Revolution* (Manchester: Manchester University Press, 2009), 67.
3. Omar Alejandro Bravo, *Las nuevas derechas* (Cali: Universidad ICESI, 2020).
4. Elisabeth Jay Friedman, *Seeking Rights from the Left* (Durham and London: Duke University Press, 2019), 9.
5. Merike Blofield and Christina Ewig, 'The Left Turn and Abortion Politics in Latin America', *Social Politics* 24, no. 4 (2017): 501.

6. Friedman, *Seeking Rights from the Left*.
7. Blofield and Ewig, 'The Left Turn and Abortion Politics in Latin America', 481.
8. Chris Arsenault, 'How Left-wing Forces are Regaining Ground in Latin America', *Al Jazeera*, December 14, 2021, https://www.aljazeera.com/features/2021/12/14/how-left-wing-forces-are-regaining-ground-in-latin-america (accessed April 10, 2022).
9. Albena Azmanova, *How Fighting Precarity Can Achieve Radical Change Without Crisis or Utopia* (New York: Columbia University Press, 2020), 197.
10. Cannon, *Hugo Chávez and the Bolivarian Revolution*, 4.
11. Albena Azmanova, 'Crisis? Capitalism is Doing Very Well. How is Critical Theory?' *Constellations* 21, no. 3 (2014): 351.
12. Paulo Freire, *Pedagogy of the Oppressed 30th Anniversary Edition* (London: Bloomsbury Academic & Professional, 2014), 65.
13. World Health Organization, *Closing the gap in a generation* (Geneva: United Nations, 2008).
14. World Health Organization, *Abortion. Key facts* (Geneva: United Nations, 2021).
15. Ximena Casas, 'How Latin American Women Can Keep Fighting for Abortion Rights and Win', *Human Rights Watch*, November 1, 2021, https://www.hrw.org/news/2021/11/01/how-latin-american-women-can-keep-fighting-abortion-rights-and-win# (accessed April 10, 2022).
16. Monica Malta and others, 'Sexual and Gender Minorities Rights in Latin America and the Caribbean: A Multi-country Evaluation', *BMC International Health and Human Rights* 19, no. 1 (2019): 2.
17. Malta and others, 'Sexual and Gender Minorities Rights in Latin America and the Caribbean'.
18. World Bank, *World Bank Open Data*, https://data.worldbank.org/ (accessed April 10, 2022).
19. Harvard Health Publishing, *Abortion (Termination of Pregnancy). What is it?*, January 9, 2019. https://www.health.harvard.edu/medical-tests-and-procedures/abortion-termination-of-pregnancy-a-to-z (accessed April 10, 2022).
20. Planned Parenthood Federation of America Inc, *Aborto*, https://www.plannedparenthood.org/es/temas-de-salud/aborto (accessed April 10, 2022).
21. NiñasNoMadres, *Son niñas no madres*, https://www.ninasnomadres.org/ (accessed April 10, 2022).
22. The International Lesbian, Gay, Bisexual, Trans and Intersex Association, *Trans Legal Mapping Report* (Geveva: ILGA World, 2020), 23.
23. Thomas J. Billard and Sam Nesfield, *(Re)making "Transgender" Identities in Global Media and Popular Culture* of *Trans Lives in a Globalizing World: Rights, Identities and Politics*, ed. J. Michael Ryan (London and New York: Routledge, 2020), 73.
24. Juan Pablo Sutherland, *Nación marica* (Santiago de Chile: Ripio Ediciones, 2009), 20.
25. Human Rights Council, *Protection Against Violence and Discrimination Based on Sexual Orientation and Gender Identity* (Geneva: United Nations, 2018), 3.
26. Maja Horn, 'Queer Dominican Moves in the Interstices of Colonial Legacies and Global Impulses of Development', in *Sexual Rights and Global Governance*, ed. Amy Lind (London: Routledge, 2010), 169.
27. Human Rights Council, *Protection Against Violence and Discrimination Based on Sexual Orientation and Gender Identity*, 3.
28. Elisabeth Jay Friedman, *Seeking Rights from the Left*, 11.
29. Ibid., 11–3.
30. CEDAW & CRPD Committees, *Guaranteeing Sexual and Reproductive Health and Rights for All Women, in Particular Women with Disabilities* (Geneva: United Nations, 2018).
31. The Office of the High Commissioner for Human Rights, *Information Series on Sexual and Reproductive Health and Rights. Abortion* (Geneva: United Nations, 2020).
32. Human Rights Watch, *International Human Rights Law and Abortion in Latin America* (New York: Human Rights Watch, 2005), 4.

33. Jorge Contesse, 'The Inter-American Court of Human Rights' Advisory Opinion on Gender Identity and Same-Sex Marriage', *The American Society of International Law* 22, no. 9 (2018).
34. *Gender Identity, and Equality and Non-Discrimination of Same-Sex Couples*, OC-24/17 Inter-American Court of Human Rights, 2017.
35. Jorge Contesse, 'Sexual Orientation and Gender Identity in Inter-American Human Rights Law', *North Carolina Journal of International Law* 44, no. 2 (2019): 381–2.
36. *La denuncia de la Convención Americana sobre Derechos Humanos y de la Carta de la Organización de los Estados Americanos y sus efectos sobre las obligaciones estatales en materia de derechos humanos*, OC-26/20 Corte Interamericana de Derechos Humanos, 2020.
37. Mala Htun, *Sex and the State: Abortion, Divorce, and the Family under Latin American Dictatorships and Democracies* (Cambridge: Cambridge University Press, 2003). Javier Corrales, *The Politics of Sexuality in Latin America: A Reader on Lesbian, Gay, Bisexual, and Transgender Rights* (Pittsburgh: University of Pittsburgh, 2010).
38. Nicholas McMurry, 'Applying Human Rights to Enable Participation', *The International Journal of Human Rights* 23, no. 7 (2019): 1063.
39. Victor Molina, 'Guidelines for States on Effective Implementation of the Right to Participate in Public Affairs', *Humphrey Public Affairs Review Volume* 8, no. 1 (2022): 58.
40. Sherry R. Arnstein, 'A Ladder of Citizen Participation' *JAIP* 35, no. 4 (1969).
41. Office of the High Commissioner for Human Rights, *Draft Guidelines for States on the Effective Implementation of the Right to Participate in Public Affairs* (Geneva: United Nations, 2018).
42. Kathryn Sikkink, *Evidence for Hope. Making Human Rights Work in the 21st Century* (Princeton: Princeton University Press, 2017).
43. Malta and others, *Sexual and Gender Minorities Rights in Latin America and the Caribbean*.
44. Blofield and Ewig, 'The Left Turn and Abortion Politics in Latin America'.
45. Bravo, *Las nuevas derechas*.
46. María Cecilia Santa Espinosa and others, 'Maternal and Child Health Care in Cuba: Achievements and Challenges', *Panamá Salud Pública* 42, special edition (2018): 2.
47. *An Act to amend the Canadian Human Rights Act and the Criminal Code*, BILL C-16 Forty-second Parliament, 2017.
48. Nery Chaves García y Bárbara Ester, 'Los derechos LGBTI+ en América Latina', June 28, 2021, *Centro Estratégico Latinoamericano de Geopolítica*, https://www.celag.org/los-derechos-lgbti-en-america-latina/#:~:text=En%202006%2C%20Panam%C3%A1%20fue%20el,la%20privacidad%20del%20propio%20hogar (accessed April 10, 2022).
49. Betilde Muñoz Pogossian, 'Democracia y Derechos de las Personas LGBTI en América Latina', *Revista derecho electoral* 30, no. 2 (2020): 101–2.
50. Yarlenis Ileinis Mestre Malfrán and João Manuel de Oliveira, 'Un abordaje interseccional de la ciudadanía trans en Cuba', *Revista Psicología Política* 20, no. 48 (2020): 450.
51. Pogossian, *Democracia y Derechos de las Personas LGBTI en América Latina*, 102.
52. *Sentencia del Tribunal Constitucional*, 06040-2015-PA/TC Tribunal Constitucional, 2016.
53. Joyceane Bezerra de Menezes and Ana Paola de Castro e Lins, 'Identidade de gênero e transexualidade no direito brasileiro', *Revista Brasileira de Direito Civil* 17, no. 2 (2018).
54. Oscar G. Mwangi, 'Judicial Activism, Populism and Counterterrorism Legislation in Kenya: Coalition for Reform and Democracy (CORD) & 2 others v Republic of Kenya & 10; Others [2015]', *The International Journal of Human Rights* (2021): 2–3. doi:10.1080/13642987.2021.1887144.
55. *Gender Identity, and Equality and Non-Discrimination of Same-Sex Couples*, 57–63.
56. Malta and others, *Sexual and Gender Minorities Rights in Latin America and the Caribbean*, 7–8.
57. Cleveland Clinic, 'Gender Affirmation (Confirmation) or Sex Reassignment Surgery', *Cleveland Clinic*, https://my.clevelandclinic.org/health/treatments/21526-gender-affirmation-confirmation-or-sex-reassignment-surgery (accessed April 10, 2022).

58. Ana Cristina Marques, *Displaying Trans (In)visibilities* of *Trans Lives in a Global(izing) World*, ed. Michael Ryan (London and New York: Routledge, 2019), 22.
59. Katherine T. Hsiao, *Fertility Preservation Options for Transgender and Trans Masculine Patients Planning Hysterectomy* of *Gender Confirmation Surgery*, ed. Loren S. Schechter (Cham: Springer Nature Switzerland, 2020), 115.
60. Malta and others, *Sexual and Gender Minorities Rights in Latin America and the Caribbean*, 8–9.
61. William Homer Fernández Espinoza, 'El proceso de cambio de nombre y de reconocimiento de la identidad de género: propuestas para una reforma judicial y legislativa', *Revista Oficial del Poder Judicial* 13, no. 15 (2021): 185.
62. *Obergefell et al. v. Hodges, Director, Ohio Department of Health, et al.*, 14–556 Supreme Court of the United States, 2015.
63. Darrel Montero, 'Attitudes Toward Same-Gender Adoption and Parenting: An Analysis of Surveys from 16 Countries', *Advances in Social Work* 15, no. 2 (2014): 448.
64. Malta and others, *Sexual and Gender Minorities Rights in Latin America and the Caribbean*, 7–9.
65. Milagros Belgrano Rawson, 'Ley de matrimonio igualitario y ley de matrimonio igualitario y aborto en Argentina: notas sobre to en Argentina: notas sobre una revolución incompleta', *Estudos Feministas, Florianópolis* 20, no. 1 (2012): 173.
66. Felipe Arocena and Sebastián Aguiar, 'Tres leyes innovadoras en Uruguay Aborto, matrimonio homosexual y regulación de la marihuana', *Revista de Ciencias Sociales* 30, no. 40 (2017): 42.
67. María P. Fernández-Cuevasa and Denitza López-Téllez, 'Equal Marriage in Mexico: Normative Evolution', *DIVULGARE* 12, no. 1 (2019): 24–30.
68. Malta and others, *Sexual and Gender Minorities Rights in Latin America and the Caribbean*, 12.
69. Ibid.
70. Human Rights Watch, *International Human Rights Law and Abortion in Latin America*, 4.
71. Htun, *Sex and the State*, 143.
72. Ibid., 142.
73. Human Rights Watch, *International Human Rights Law and Abortion in Latin America*, 1–2.
74. Iván Darío Garzón Vallejo, 'La despenalización del aborto en algunos casos y bajo ciertos supuestos', *Facultad de Derecho y Ciencias Políticas* 36, no. 106 (2007): 187.
75. María Gabriela Irrazábal, 'La religión en las decisiones sobre aborto no punible en la Argentina', *Estudios Feministas, Florianópolis* 23, no. 3 (2015): 743.
76. Irrazábal, 'La religión en las decisiones sobre aborto no punible en la Argentina'.
77. Rebecca Cook and Marta Rodríguez de Assis Machado, 'Constitutionalizing Abortion in Brazil', *Revista de Investigações Constitucionais, Curitiba* 5, no. 3 (2018): 185–6.
78. Blofield and Ewig, 'The Left Turn and Abortion Politics in Latin America', 489.
79. Marta Lamas, 'La despenalización del aborto en México', *Nueva Sociedad* no. 220 (2009): 154.
80. Shelly Makleff and others, 'Experience Obtaining Legal Abortion in Uruguay: Knowledge, Attitudes, and Stigma among Abortion Clients', *BMC Women's Health* 19, no. 155 (2019).
81. Blofield and Ewig, 'The Left Turn and Abortion Politics in Latin America', 495.
82. Jesús Puerta, *Los rasgos de la cultura política chavista* of *Chavismo genealogía de una pasión política*, eds. Alba Carosio, Indhira Libertad Rodríguez, and Leonardo Bracamonte (Buenos Aires and Caracas: CLACSO and Fundación Centro de Estudios Latinoamericanos Rómulo Gallegos, 2017), 95.
83. Magdymar León Torrealba, 'Temas centrales en el debate sobre el aborto en Venezuela y argumentos teóricos para su despenalización', *Revista venezolana de estudios de la mujer* 17, no. 39 (2012): 169.
84. Malta and others, *Sexual and Gender Minorities Rights in Latin America and the Caribbean*, 10.

85. Blofield and Ewig, 'The Left Turn and Abortion Politics in Latin America', 487.
86. Ibid., 482.
87. Ibid., 502.
88. Omar Hurtado Rayugsen, *El chavismo, una historia of Chavismo genealogía de una pasión política*, eds. Alba Carosio, Indhira Libertad Rodríguez, and Leonardo Bracamonte (Buenos Aires and Caracas: CLACSO and Fundación Centro de Estudios Latinoamericanos Rómulo Gallegos, 2017), 69.
89. Hugo Chávez, 'Hugo Chávez: El 4 de febrero de 199[2] recogió el anhelo de millones', *YouTube*, February 4, 1992, https://youtu.be/xzzgtKspZGw (accessed April 10, 2022).
90. Cannon, *Hugo Chávez and the Bolivarian Revolution*, 55.
91. Michael Bray, 'El Estado Somos Todos, El Pueblo Soy Yo?', *Theory & Event* 17, no. 1 (2014): 2.
92. Cannon, *Hugo Chávez and the Bolivarian Revolution*, 35–6.
93. Ibid.
94. Bray, 'El Estado Somos Todos, El Pueblo Soy Yo?'
95. Omar Hurtado Rayugsen, *El chavismo, una historia of Chavismo genealogía de una pasión política*, eds. Alba Carosio, Indhira Libertad Rodríguez, and Leonardo Bracamonte (Buenos Aires and Caracas: CLACSO and Fundación Centro de Estudios Latinoamericanos Rómulo Gallegos, 2017).
96. Bray, 'El Estado Somos Todos, El Pueblo Soy Yo?', 3.
97. Hugo Chávez, 'Chávez por siempre: ¡Chávez ya no soy yo, yo soy un pueblo que se hizo rebelde, que se hizo libre!', *YouTube*, November 16, 2006, https://youtu.be/x4_hYQc8WME (accessed April 10, 2022).
98. *El pueblo soy yo*. Directed by Enrique Krauze and Carlos Oteyza. Caracas, Venezuela, and Mexico City: Producciones Eugenia, 2018.
99. Torrealba, 'Temas centrales en el debate sobre el aborto en Venezuela y argumentos teóricos para su despenalización', 170.
100. *Constitución de la República de Venezuela*, § 74 Congreso de la República, 1961.
101. Torrealba, 'Temas centrales en el debate sobre el aborto en Venezuela y argumentos teóricos para su despenalización', 171–3.
102. Ibid., 169.
103. *Constitución de la República Bolivariana de Venezuela*, § 77 Asamblea Nacional Constitu-yente, 1999.
104. Unión Afirmativa de Venezuela, 'Chávez no ve bien el matrimonio gay', *Fundación Reflejos de Venezuela*, November 29, 2009, https://www.fundacionreflejosdevenezuela.com/hagamos-un-hecho/chavez-no-ve-bien-el-matrimonio-gay/ (accessed April 10, 2022).
105. REUTERS, 'Así consiguió Chávez "refundar" Venezuela', *Diario El Mundo*, December 16, 1999, https://www.elmundo.es/elmundo/1999/diciembre/16/internacional/chavez.html (accessed April 10, 2022).
106. Unión Afirmativa de Venezuela, *Chávez no ve bien el matrimonio gay*.
107. Cannon, *Hugo Chávez and the Bolivarian Revolution*, 62.
108. Bray, 'El Estado Somos Todos, El Pueblo Soy Yo?'3.
109. Human Rights Council, *Situation of Human Rights and Technical Assistance in the Bolivar-ian Republic of Venezuela* (Geneva: United Nations, 2021), 4.
110. Bray, 'El Estado Somos Todos, El Pueblo Soy Yo?' 3.
111. Blofield and Ewig, 'The Left Turn and Abortion Politics in Latin America', 497.
112. Cannon, *Hugo Chávez and the Bolivarian Revolution*, 61–5.
113. Ibid.
114. Maye Primera, 'Hugo Chávez nombra sucesor: "Elijan a Nicolás Maduro como presidente"', *El País*, December 9, 2012, https://elpais.com/internacional/2012/12/09/actualidad/1355022539_272029.html (accessed April 10, 2022).
115. BBC Mundo, '6 preguntas para entender el proceso de elección de la Asamblea Constitu-yente en Venezuela y sus posibles consecuencias', *BBC*, May 24, 2017, https://www.bbc.com/mundo/noticias-america-latina-40023863 (accessed April 10, 2022).

116. Torrealba, 'Temas centrales en el debate sobre el aborto en Venezuela y argumentos teóricos para su despenalización', 172.
117. A.C. Venezuela Igualitaria, 'Coalición de movimientos LGBTI y de DDHH nos unimos para denunciar al Estado, sus Instituciones y Partidos Políticos', *Venezuela Igualitaria*, June 30, 2020, https://www.venezuelaigualitaria.org/2020/06/comunicado-coalicion-de-movimientos.html (accessed April 10, 2022).
118. Sonja C. Grover, *The Torture of Children During Armed Conflicts* (Berlin: Springer, 2014), 23.
119. *Sentencia 190-08*, Exp. 03-2630 Tribunal Supremo de Justicia, 2008.
120. Human Rights Council, *Report of the Independent International Fact-Finding Mission on the Bolivarian Republic of Venezuela* (Geneva: United Nations, 2021), 4–5.
121. Cannon, *Hugo Chávez and the Bolivarian Revolution*, 55.
122. José Antonio Rivas Leone, 'Precariedad jurídica y militarismo en Venezuela 2000–2012', *Provincia* 26, no. 2 (2011): 73.
123. Cannon, *Hugo Chávez and the Bolivarian Revolution*, 56.
124. *Código orgánico de justicia militar*, § 6 El Congreso de la República de Venezuela, 1998.
125. Cristian González Cabrera, 'Draconian Law Punishes Gay Sex in Venezuelan Military', *Human Rights Watch*, February 3, 2022, https://www.hrw.org/news/2022/02/03/draconian-law-punishes-gay-sex-venezuelan-military# (accessed April 10, 2022).
126. Ana Vannesa Herrero and Samantha Schmidt, 'In Venezuela, a Soldier Can be Sent to Prison for Being Gay', *The Washington Post*, January 21, 2022, https://www.washingtonpost.com/world/2022/01/21/venezuela-gay-military/ (accessed April 10, 2022).
127. María Candelaria Domínguez Guillén, 'Algunas sentencias que declaran el cambio de sexo', *Revista de la Facultad de Ciencias Jurídicas y Políticas de la UCV* 130 (2007): 80–1.
128. Domínguez Guillén, 'Algunas sentencias que declaran el cambio de sexo', 99.
129. Human Rights Council, *Report of the Independent International Fact-Finding Mission on the Bolivarian Republic of Venezuela*, 4.
130. *Ley Orgánica de Registro Civil*, G.O. 39264 Asamblea Nacional de Venezuela, 2009, 1674.
131. DIVERLEX Diversidad e Igualdad, *Informe sobre la República Bolivariana de Venezuela Examen Periódico Universal* (Caracas: DIVERLEX, 2011), 4.
132. Esther V. Figueredo, 'El novel registro del estado civil de las personas en Venezuela: preeminencia de los derechos de la personalidad en la reforma del sistema de registro civil', *Revista de la Facultad de Ciencias Jurídicas y Políticas de la UCV* 6 (2010): 183.
133. Jesús Puerta, *Los rasgos de la cultura política chavista*, 95.
134. Nicolás Maduro, 'La llamativa "FE en DIOS" del Presidente Nicolás Maduro (entrevista en Venezuela) ¿Es Cristiano?', *YouTube*, August 11, 2021, https://youtu.be/Pv03MYZcGBA (accessed April 10, 2022).
135. BBC Mundo, 'Maduro y su campaña cuasi religiosa', *BBC*, March 19, 2013, https://www.bbc.com/mundo/noticias/2013/03/130319_venezuela_muerte_hugo_chavez_nicolas_maduro_deificacion_az (accessed April 10, 2022).
136. Carlos Ayala Corao, 'Inconstitucionalidad de la denuncia de la Convención Americana sobre Derechos Humanos por Venezuela', *Estudios constitucionales* 10, no. 2 (2012): 44.
137. United Nations, 'General Assembly Establishes New Human Rights Council by Vote of 170 in Favour to 4 Against, with 3 Abstentions', *United Nations*, March 15, 2006, https://www.un.org/press/en/2006/ga10449.doc.htm (accessed April 10, 2022).
138. Amnesty International, *Hambre de justicia: Crímenes de lesa humanidad en Venezuela* (Mexico City: Amnesty International, 2019).
139. International Criminal Court, 'Trying Individuals for Genocide, War Crimes, Crimes Against Humanity, and Aggression. Venezuela I', *International Criminal Court*, https://www.icc-cpi.int/venezuela (accessed April 10, 2022).
140. Quiteria Franco, '¿Qué sucede con la Marcha del Orgullo LGBTI 2017?', *Red LGBTI Venezuela*, May 27, 2017, http://www.redlgbtidevenezuela.org/noticias/que-sucede-con-la-marcha-del-orgullo-lgbti-2017 (accessed April 10, 2022).

141. The International Lesbian, Gay, Bisexual, Trans and Intersex Association, *Trans Legal Mapping Report*, 176.

Acknowledgements

This research is the fruit of my Master's in Human Rights joint degree with the University of Minnesota's Humphrey School of Public Affairs and the College of Liberal Arts studies. I am thankful to my supervisor, Professor Barbara Frey, Director of the Human Rights Program, who carefully guided me through the process of writing the thesis and editing this paper. Additionally, I am grateful to Professor Amanda Lyons, Executive Director of the Human Rights Center at Law School, for her advice and support. Their comments and edits helped me sharpen my arguments. More importantly, they helped me overcome obstacles and encouraged my efforts.

Disclosure statement

No potential conflict of interest was reported by the author(s).

Appendix

Questionary guide

Basic questions to establish familiarity and convey essential information

(1) Please describe your work aiming to advance in (a) abortion liberalisation, (b) gender identity for trans people and equal marriage.

More detailed questions about international human rights community networking

(1) How does your work or organisation connect with other human rights defenders at the regional/international and national levels?
(2) What are the advantages for you or your organisation to be in a network or work in a coalition to advance (a) abortion liberalisation, (b) gender identity for trans people and equal marriage?
(3) How important is the international support to advance (a) abortion liberalisation, (b) gender identity for trans people and equal marriage?

Bringing in Venezuela and social justice

(1) How are the national authorities of Venezuela complying with the minimum standards regarding (a) abortion liberalisation, (b) gender identity for trans people and equal marriage?
(2) What is the level of political will on the part of the national authorities of your country in (a) abortion liberalisation, (b) gender identity for trans people and equal marriage?

Index

abortion 2, 32, 56, 155–8, 161–2, 165, 167; criminalisation 159; decriminalisation 156–9, 161–5, 167–8; policy 32, 56
abusive constitutional borrowing 24
access to justice 139, 140
activism 10, 16, 51, 97–9, 116
activist court 16, 98–101
Amici 144–5
Arato, Andrew 36
Austria 5, 8, 10
authoritarian populism 4, 43, 47, 69, 71, 79, 82
authoritarian populists 8, 47, 57, 61, 70, 72, 74–5, 81–3; abuse 75–6

Baroš, Jiří 51
Bencze, Mátyás 35
business-as-usual-model 10, 12, 17

Central and Eastern Europe (CEE) 23, 28, 43–4, 47, 51
charade triadic structure 45, 58, 60–1
chavismo 162–3, 165–8
civilised society 141
coalition for reform and democracy (CORD) 2, 114–30
Cohen, Jean L. 36
constitutional amendments 22, 27, 46, 49, 52, 54, 78, 81, 99–101
constitutional courts 4–5, 8–17, 22–3, 25–31, 33–7, 43–6, 48, 51–5, 57–8, 60–1, 82–3, 93–5, 97–100, 104, 106–7; instrumental abuse of 22–37; resilient 94–6
constitutional democracy 47, 59
constitutional frameworks 7, 13, 17, 23–4, 37, 95
constitutional identity 9, 12–15, 57
constitutional interpretation 3–7, 9–10, 12–17, 24–5, 27, 29, 36, 49, 53, 71, 74, 118, 124
constitutionalism 4, 7–9, 15, 23–4, 36, 61, 70, 137
constitutionality 9, 11, 17, 28–30, 35, 46, 49, 56, 99, 103, 122–4
constitutional judges 57, 82, 93, 95, 98, 105–6
constitutional majority 25, 27, 36, 48–51, 54, 56, 75

constitutional system 15, 78, 82–3, 101
counter-opposition technique 29, 33, 36
counterterrorism 114, 117–18
counterterrorism legislation 2, 114–30
court-curbing strategies 26–7, 44–5, 51–2, 55, 57–61, 95, 101, 107
court-packing methods 26, 28, 35, 48, 54, 59, 61, 95
COVID-19 135, 137, 140, 142–3, 147–8
Cross, Frank 115
Czech Constitutional Court 36, 93, 96–9, 101, 106–8; interventions 2, 92–108; resilience 96–7
Czechia 92–3, 97–8, 104, 107–8
Czech Republic 5, 8, 11, 99

Dave, Dushyant 135, 150
de-judicialization techniques 44–5, 51–3, 58
delegation technique 29, 31, 33, 36
deliberative democracy 72–3
democracy 2, 9, 32, 34–6, 47, 59, 61, 69–83, 93, 95–7, 114–19, 121, 126
democratic backsliding 93–4, 107
democratic institutional system 76
democratic parlance 44, 59–60
direct democracy 9, 72, 76–82
disruption 25, 121
Dixon, Rosalind 24
doctrine of avoidance 118, 123–4
doctrines on ripeness 123–4
Duda, Andrzej 28
Dufek, Pavel 51

Ely, John Hart 108
extra-legal technique 29, 31, 34, 36
extreme politicisation 44, 51–3, 55–7, 61

functional democracy 76

gender 157–8, 166; changes 160, 166; identity 2, 155–60, 162–8
governance 44–5, 53, 57, 61–2, 135, 139–40
governmental power 13, 35, 150

176 INDEX

Havel Court 102, 105
hegemony preservation 57
human rights 32, 70, 82, 119, 126, 134–5, 141,
    158–60, 163, 165, 167–8; law 157–8
Hungarian Constitutional Court (HCC) 12,
    14, 48–9, 51–2, 57, 60, 69–71, 75–83, 95, 98;
    choice of democracy conceptions 81–2
Hungary 5, 7–9, 15–16, 23, 25, 27, 48–9, 52, 57,
    60, 70–1, 82–3, 92–3, 104, 107–8

illiberal constitutionalism 23–4, 95
Inter-American Court of Human Rights 158, 160
interpretative practice 5–6, 10
interpretive institutionalist framework 73–5
interpretive practice 9, 11–12, 17; changing
    12–14
Italian Constitutional Court 11

Jubilee 114, 119–20, 122–5, 127–9
judicial independence 31, 44, 52, 56, 58–61,
    99–101, 104, 115–16, 130, 163, 165
judicialization 43–9, 52–3, 55, 59–60, 114
judicial power 43–4, 46, 52, 61, 78
judicial review 5–6, 43–6, 49, 95, 99, 115–16, 122,
    129, 138, 143, 147, 149
justiciability doctrines 118, 123, 129

Kenya 2, 114–15, 118–21, 126, 128–30
Kenyatta, Uhuru 120–2
Klaus, Václav 100, 102
Klaus Court 102–4
Koncewicz, Tomasz Tadeusz 56
Kosař, David 51

Landau, David 24
Latin America 2, 57, 155–63, 165–6, 168
legal constitutionalism 24, 26, 28–9, 35–6
legitimacy 9, 30, 105, 126, 147, 165
legitimation technique 31, 34, 36
liberal constitutionalism 8–9, 30
liberal democracy 4, 8, 15, 93–5, 102, 108
limitation period 137, 139–41, 147
Lindquist, Stefanie 115
litigation 94, 114–15, 117–18, 137, 141
long-term peril 58

Macejková, Ivetta 105
Mečiar 105
migrant workers 135, 139, 145–6
migration 13, 78, 145
modern populism 3–4, 8, 15–16
Morawiecki 32
Mudde, Cas 24
Müller, Jan-Werner 47
Mwangi, Oscar G. 2

National Council of the Judiciary (NCJ) 56
national security 118–19, 121–2, 125–6, 147
national varieties of populism 7–8
new interpretative doctrines 9–10

Odinga, Raila 121
opportunistic instrumentalism 26, 95

Paczolay 77
pandemic management 139, 142
parliamentary democracy 23, 76, 78–9, 102
participatory democracy 72, 77, 79, 163, 168
penal populism 117–18, 122
personalist leadership 163
Pink Tide 2, 155–63, 165–8
Poland 5, 7–8, 13, 15–16, 23, 27, 29–35, 37, 44–5,
    47–9, 56–7, 59–61, 92–4, 97–8, 107–8
Polish Constitutional Tribunal (PCT) 50–1, 53,
    56–7, 60
political actors 27, 36, 46, 53, 60, 82, 105, 117
political fragmentation 93, 96–7, 104, 107
political liberalism 24
political participation 69–74, 79, 81–3, 158, 168
political power 24–6, 31, 44, 52, 60–1, 93, 99, 107
political-strategic approach 116–17, 122
politics: dejudicialization of 43–62; judicialization
    of 43–8, 51–2, 54, 61, 117
popular sovereignty 9, 59, 116
populism, national varieties 7–8
populist aspirations 6, 9, 12, 14–15
populist constitutionalism 3–4, 8–9, 17, 22–5, 27,
    29, 35–6, 57
populist court-curbing 44–5, 51–2, 59–60
populist irritation 45, 47
populist politics 3–4, 47
populist tendencies 13, 101
Populus 28–31, 33–4
powers 4–5, 8–9, 11–13, 23–31, 33–7, 47–8, 56–7,
    59, 93–5, 99–102, 104–5, 115, 117–18, 123,
    125, 136, 138, 141–3, 147–51, 165
prison administration 139, 142
procedural justice 138–40
public participation 118–20, 125, 128–9

representative democracy 9, 72, 76–80, 82–3
resilience 2, 92–108, 134

same-sex couples 158, 161, 165
same-sex marriage 2, 155–9, 161–2, 164–8
Security Laws (Amendment) Act (SLAA) 115,
    118–30
selective activism 2, 92–108
separate opinions 74, 76, 79–81, 105
separation of powers 25
sexual orientation and gender identity (SOGI) 157

INDEX

state power 24, 27
strategic defection 57
Stumpf, István 79
substantive justice 138–9, 141
suo motu 2, 134–51
Supreme Court of India (SCI) 135–43, 145–51

trans people 157–60, 164, 166
triadic structure 44–5, 57–8, 61
trusteeship model 76

unconstitutionality 29, 35, 46, 48, 57, 79

vaccine distribution 144–5
Venezuela 2, 8–9, 155–9, 162–8

women 2, 32, 156–9, 161–2, 167–8

Zeman, Miloš 100, 103
Zeman Court 102, 104